Andy Rowell is a journalist and author. His previous books include *Don't Worry (It's safe to Eat)* and *Green Backlash*. Artist **James Marriott** and activist **Lorne Stockman** are part of the award-winning environmental social justice group PLATFORM (www.platformlondon.org).

D0189306

Chevron armed security guard at
Escravos, Delta State, November 2002

THE NEXT GULF

*London, Washington and
Oil Conflict in Nigeria*

Andy Rowell, James Marriott
and
Lorne Stockman

CONSTABLE • LONDON

Constable & Robinson Ltd
3 The Lanchesters
162 Fulham Palace Road
London W6 9ER
www.constablerobinson.com

First published in the UK by Constable,
an imprint of Constable & Robinson Ltd, 2005

A copy of the British Library Cataloguing in Publication Data
is available from the British Library.

ISBN 1–84529–259–6

Printed and bound in the EU

1 3 5 7 9 10 8 6 4 2

Contents

Acknowledgements

The authors would like to thank the following people for their help and assistance with the book. Jane Trowell, Ben Diss, Greg Muttitt, Dan Gretton, Tim Sowula and Nick McCarthy at PLATFORM all offered invaluable advice, assistance and comment. Irene Gerlach, Nick Robins, and Steve Kretzmann all read sections of the text.

The graphics and diagrams were provided by John Jackson. Dr Sue Hawley from The Cornerhouse, Tim Concannon, Chris Newsome and Joseph Hurst Croft from the Stakeholder Democracy Network all provided crucial insight and information.

There are certain documents referred to in chapter 3 that are from the UK National Archives. Documents from there are referenced in the text according to their file number. We thank the staff for their time and help.

We would also like to thank our editor, Dan Hind and Claudia Dyer for seeing the book through to its conclusion.

Some of PLATFORM's time was funded by the Arts and Humanities Research Council and the Sigrid Rausing Trust.

Finally we would like to thank the anonymous people who were interviewed, who for various reasons could not be named individually.

We dedicate this book to the people of Niger Delta, who for 49 years have paid all the costs and received little of the benefits of oil extraction in Nigeria.

Preface

'The struggle of humanity against power is the struggle of memory against forgetting', wrote the dissident Czech novelist Milan Kundera. Much of our intent in writing this book is to remember Ken Saro-Wiwa and the Ogoni struggle. The 10th November 2005 is the tenth anniversary of the execution of Ken Saro-Wiwa, the writer and activist, and his eight Ogoni compatriots, Dr. Barinem Kiobel; John Kpuinen; Baribor Bera; Saturday Doobee; Nordu Eawo; Paul Levura; Daniel Gbokoo and Felix Nuate.

All the authors have been involved with the issues surrounding the Ogoni, the Niger Delta, Shell and the ecological and human rights impacts of oil, since the 1990s. James Marriott and Lorne Stockman of PLATFORM[1] have worked on the ecological and human impacts of oil for a decade. They were inspired by the Ogoni struggle and the tragedy of Saro-Wiwa's death. Andy Rowell worked directly with Saro-Wiwa and assisted him in his campaign.

In the decade since those executions, we have all witnessed the tragedy of 9/11 and watched in horror at the conflicts in Afghanistan and Iraq, and at the wider war on terror. The pattern of global politics has radically altered, however in the Niger Delta it seems that the picture has remained the same. The villages and towns in the region are still locked into a cycle of extreme poverty, widespread unemployment, environmental pollution, and social injustice. The issues that Saro-Wiwa and others fought for are as relevant today as they were when they died.

Moreover, the situation for many communities of the Delta has got worse since 1995. Ogoniland may not be under total military siege as it was then, but the military are still active. Ten years ago the principle behind the Ogoni struggle was non-violence. In the ten years since there has been an increase in armed resistance. Today the Delta is awash with arms, and hostage taking has become a regular occurrence. The profits from the theft of oil, which is called bunkering, fund conflict. The future has the potential to be far more violent. We examine the development of these shifts in Chapter One.

The most significant events in relation to the future of the Delta have not taken place within Nigeria. They have occurred in Washington where, following the events of 9/11, the Gulf of Guinea is seen as strategically important for the US's security of oil and gas supply. In Chapter Seven we examine how the Gulf of Guinea – which as a region encompasses not only Nigeria, but also other oil-producing states of Equatorial Guinea, Cameroon, and Gabon – is set to become a key source of American oil and gas. To become the replacement of, or counterbalance to, the Persian Gulf. To become the Next Gulf.

Nigeria is by far the biggest oil and gas producer in the Gulf, and we have focussed upon it and to a lesser extent São Tomé. The situation in Equatorial Guinea is a major story, but one which is beyond the scope of this book.

This shift in US foreign policy represents an acceleration of a longer-term trend. The transition of Nigeria from the British sphere of influence to the American sphere, that has been taking place since the decline of the British Empire in the 1940s. A new axis of power has evolved. But in order to understand the current conflict in the Niger Delta it has to be seen in the light of its British colonial past. Chapter Two looks at the colonial exploitation of Nigeria and the Delta.

Chapter Three starts with the year that Shell-BP found oil in the Delta and examines some of the crises the company has faced including the Biafran War, nationalization of its BP share, community protests and the militarization of its operations. Chapter Four explains the way Shell and the oil industry has changed in the country over the last thirty years, and examines the inter-linked nature of the Nigerian state and the oil companies. Whilst Chapter Six examines how, despite Nigeria being renowned as a corrupt place to do business, much of the corruption is actually based in other countries.

Two themes underlie the entire book. The first is that Shell and the other oil corporations do not work alone. They are assisted by governments and a whole web of other companies, institutions and political groupings. Shell's interaction with these constituencies following crises in Nigeria is explored in Chapter Five.

The second is that the current pattern of oil and gas exploitation in the Delta carries a clear echo of the oldest relationship between America, West Africa and Europe: the Atlantic Triangle. From the seventeenth to the nineteenth century, that triangular economy existed between these three regions based upon slavery and the production of tropical goods such as sugar and rum. In the past four decades a new relationship between America, Europe and the Delta has emerged based upon oil and gas – a New Atlantic Triangle.

The first Atlantic Triangle impoverished West Africa, and enriched Europe and the cities of the American East Coast. We fear that the New Atlantic Triangle is reviving this pattern at a scale – in speed and capital – that dwarfs the hopes of those working for a new start for Africa, those working to Make Poverty History, and to reinvent popular conceptions of the continent through the year-long cultural festival, Africa 05. In Chapter Eight, we explore the possible futures of this triangle and the Delta in particular.

In Chapter 9 we give a series of recommendations, based on voices from the Delta. For we realize the limitations of a book on Nigeria written by three white, Northern-based authors. However we believe that what some will see as the book's limitation may also be its greatest strength. Our geographical, cultural and political location leads us to deliberately look at the relationships between London, Washington and Nigeria. It is easy for the governments of the North to dismiss the problems of Nigeria as home grown, but the majority of the companies and institutions benefiting from the exploitation in the country are based in Britain and the US.

We hope that the insight in this book will help people understand the truly inter-related nature of the oil business in Nigeria and enable them to assist the people of the Niger Delta in achieving what they want. All too often it is their voice that is silent in the debate. We hope we are helping their voices be heard.

The first Atlantic Triangle was dismantled by resistance in the villages of West Africa, by slave rebellions in the American plantations, and by the anti-slavery movement born in Britain. It may be that the New Atlantic Triangle will be similarly transformed by the actions of citizens in all three regions

We see this book as part of such a transformation, and we have created it together with a sister project 'Remember Saro-

Wiwa'.[2] Coordinated by PLATFORM, this brings together a coalition of groups including African Writers Abroad, Amnesty International, Greenpeace, Friends of the Earth, PEN and Index on Censorship, to establish a permanent memorial to Saro-Wiwa and the issues he died for. A Living Memorial that remembers the past and shapes the future.

Whilst we have tried to be fair and objective in the book, we end each chapter with a small reflective piece that is more subjective, based upon the authors' personal experience. We see these as exploring the 'location' from which we write, and in doing so we draw strength from the words of Jon Snow, from Channel Four News, who has said: 'There's no such thing as a neutral human being. You've got to tell it as you see it, to take the side of justice and truth.'[3]

CHAPTER ONE
A Span of Ten Years

'I'll tell you this, I may be dead but my ideas will not die.'

Ken Saro-Wiwa[1]

Port Harcourt Prison, 10 November 1995

Bariture Lebe and his fellow inmates knew something was horribly wrong. Armed soldiers had arrived early and sealed off the bleak courtyard in the prison that had been their home for the past eighteen months.

Looking out over the black imposing concrete walls, they could see wardens had started cutting down the few straggling sugar-cane plants that the prisoners had been growing near the gallows. The sound of the wardens singing began to fill their squalid cells. When nine o'clock came and the inmates were not allowed out for their usual exercise, their fears mounted.

Two days earlier Nigeria's Provisional Ruling Council had confirmed the death sentences on nine Ogoni, including their leader, Ken Saro-Wiwa. Other Ogoni in prison, such as Bariture Lebe, still awaited their fate.

Ogoniland is an area of some 400 square miles in the eastern part of the Niger Delta. It is small relative to the Delta as a whole, but densely populated. Shell-BP found oil there in the late 1950s and while the oil company has extracted vast profits from

Nigerian crude, the Ogoni live in abject poverty, with many villages lacking clean water, electricity or basic health care.

For the last five years Saro-Wiwa had been leading the Ogoni's non-violent struggle to stop the ecological destruction that Shell and the Nigerian government had permitted in his homeland and to secure a greater share of the oil wealth that had been drilled from under their land. This homeland bore the marks of decades of oil extraction. Rows of rusting pipes snaked over farmland, and spillages of toxic oil were common. Children played in the tropical sun a stone's throw from gas flares.

Much has been written about Saro-Wiwa, who at different periods of his life was a businessman, author and activist. He had been born Kenule Beeson Saro-Wiwa on 10 October 1941. After a stint as a teacher, he became Administrator of Rivers State following the Biafran War, Nigeria's civil war in the late 1960s, during which he had supported the Federal Government. By now he had started writing *Basi & Co.*, his soap opera about scheming Lagos lads that became a hit television series from 1985 to 1990.

In the early 1970s he set up Saros International, a publishing company, through which he published his many poems and novels, including his most famous *Sozaboy*, written in pidgin English. The novelist and Saro-Wiwa's friend, William Boyd, considers the novel one of the best anti-war novels of the twentieth century. Saro-Wiwa published what he considered his most important book, about his time during the Biafran War: *On a Darkling Plain*.

Saro-Wiwa was also a columnist for several Nigerian newspapers. In the last column he wrote before being sacked, 'The Coming War in the Delta', he said that the people of the Delta were 'faced by a Company – Shell – whose management policies are racist and cruelly stupid, and which is out to exploit and encourage Nigerian ethnocentrism'. It was pulled from the second edition. Shell has repeatedly denied such allegations.

Coupled with his writing, Saro-Wiwa was instrumental in mobilizing the Ogoni in their non-violent struggle. He was one of the main leaders behind the Ogoni Bill of Rights, which called for 'political control of Ogoni affairs by Ogoni people' and the 'right to protect the Ogoni environment and ecology from further degradation'. Signed on 26 August 1990, it set the Ogoni on a collision course with the Nigerian military regime and with Shell. Saro-Wiwa became the spokesperson for MOSOP – the Movement for the Survival of Ogoni People – which forced Shell to leave Ogoni in 1993. The company has never re-started production there.

As the Ogoni struggle against the oil companies became more radical, there were traditional leaders in Ogoni with whom Saro-Wiwa and MOSOP clashed. Like all good campaigners Saro-Wiwa was driven by an unnatural energy. But he was not a saint and it would be wrong to depict him as one. He had many enemies, both inside and outside Ogoni. To his detractors, Saro-Wiwa was 'the archetypal demagogue who exploited the real pain of his fellow Ogonis to feed an ego as big and complex as Nigeria itself'.[2]

Saro-Wiwa's increasingly vocal stance against the oil companies brought him into direct conflict with the Nigerian authorities. He was routinely imprisoned and tortured. The internal Ogoni conflict between conservative and more radical elements finally ended in tragic circumstances on 21 May 1994, when four Ogoni elders were attacked by a mob and killed. It was for these murders that Saro-Wiwa was later tried and judicially murdered. He was nowhere near the killings when they happened. He always maintained his innocence, that he had neither sanctioned the murders nor ordered them.

But in February 1995, Saro-Wiwa, Ledum Mitee (who was arrested with Saro-Wiwa but later released) and Dr Barinem Kiobel, the Commissioner of the Ministry of Commerce and Tourism and member of the Rivers State Executive Council, were alleged by the prosecution to have 'counselled and procured' the murders. John Kpuinen, the Deputy President of MOSOP's youth wing (NYCOP) and Baribor Bera, a farmer, were also charged with having been instructed to 'inflict grievous harm' on the four Ogoni chiefs.

The other Ogoni who would later be executed – Saturday Doobee, Nordu Eawo, Paul Levura, Daniel Gbokoo and Felix Nuate – were formally charged in April 1995.[3] All nine were convicted in a trial described by Michael Birnbaum QC as 'fundamentally flawed', and that represented a 'gross injustice and abuse of human rights'.[4]

Michael Birnbaum's report into the trial noted that the two chief prosecution witnesses later testified that they had been bribed to give evidence against Saro-Wiwa.[5] One, Charles Danwi, maintains that he was promised a house and a contract with Shell in exchange for his testimony. Shell vehemently denies the allegations, and says it has nothing to do with Saro-Wiwa's death. The company argues that it 'spoke out against the use of violence, and appealed for clemency for Saro-Wiwa and his fellow Ogonis'.[6]

Shell also maintains that Saro-Wiwa's trial was nothing to do with them. At the time people wondered why they had a lawyer present with a 'watching brief' (a QC hired by Shell only to observe the proceedings). Recently released 'restricted' documents obtained from the Foreign Office note that the lawyer's presence 'sits unhelpfully with Shell's insistence that the trial does not directly concern them'.[7]

But this flawed trial ended with tragic consequences. On that fateful Friday morning, the Ogoni leader and the others had been woken at five in the morning to be moved from their cells to the Port Harcourt Prison. The day before, special executioners had been flown in from the North to carry out the gruesome act. They would wear robes of red.

Lebe and the other inmates crammed against their prison window. They could hear a siren. The dark green doors of the prison opened, and they watched horrified when a van carrying empty coffins arrived. It was quickly followed by a Black Maria that sped to a halt. 'We saw them coming out of the vehicle and listened in absolute horror as they were screaming, crying and shouting,' recalls Lebe.

Saro-Wiwa was not crying but in obvious pain, with his hands chained behind his back, shuffling in leg-irons. His small frame – he was only five foot two inches – looked thinner. He had been considerably aged by his long incarceration, the effects of which were made all the worse as a result of his being starved for the last three days. He was wearing a white brocade gown. His request to see his wife for a final time had been refused. So was a request for his beloved pipe and a notebook to be given to his father.

Saro-Wiwa was still defiant. 'What have I done that I deserve death, other than that I spoke the truth, demanding justice for my poor people of Ogoniland?' he said. The first of the nine to be taken to the gallows, he began to shout, 'You can only kill the messengers, you cannot kill the message.' Saro-Wiwa's voice tailed off into a deadly silence.

Minutes passed slowly. But the gallows would not work for

Saro-Wiwa, as the trap door failed to open above the pit. The gallows failed for a second time. Saro-Wiwa was led away. 'We began to cry,' recalled Lebe, 'but there was no end in sight. Teh [Nigerian for 'Sir' – what the Ogoni called Saro-Wiwa] was taken back and hanged after the other eight.' Finally on the fifth attempt the gallows worked. Saro-Wiwa's final words were simple: 'Lord take my soul but the struggle continues.' It was 11.30 a.m.

'When the gallows worked and Ken died there was smoke everywhere. It was so quiet,' recalled Nyieda Nasikpo, another of the imprisoned Ogoni. 'We never thought they would do it.' But they had, and Saro-Wiwa and the others were dead.[8] His friend William Boyd wrote simply: 'Ken was fifty-four years old, and an innocent man . . . I am bitter and dreadfully sad . . . the bravest man I have known, is no more.'[9] He and the others were now officially classified as murderers.

Saro-Wiwa's death sent shock waves around the world. A UN Security Council debate on Liberia was interrupted; protests broke out in many European and American cities where Shell had a presence. Nigerian embassies were also targeted.[10]

Thousands of miles away, Saro-Wiwa's daughter Zina learned of her father's death whilst listening to a piano concert in Bath.[11] His younger brother, Owens, was hiding in Lagos. He too was being hunted by the military. 'I was devastated. Totally. I just asked where was God? How can you let an innocent man be killed in such a horrible manner?' he recalls.[12] Three days later Owens managed to cross the Nigerian border into Benin and then made his way to safety in Canada.

Saro-Wiwa's son, Ken Wiwa, was at the Commonwealth summit in New Zealand heading a desperate campaign to persuade Commonwealth leaders to do more to save his father's life – to do more to persuade Nigeria's detested military ruler, General Sani Abacha, to show a morsel of clemency. Restricted documents obtained by the authors show that British diplomats in Nigeria had warned the UK delegation in New Zealand that the executions were 'quite likely to be carried out in the near future'.[13] But the Commonwealth leaders appeared not to care. 'We would go into meetings and it was very clear that they weren't taking it seriously,' recalls Ken Wiwa. 'I didn't know why they seemed so relaxed about the whole thing.'[14]

The summit was thrown into turmoil by the news of the hangings, and the Commonwealth appeared impotent and futile at a crucial time. Instead of heading off to play golf or jet ski, Commonwealth leaders had to deal with an unfolding international crisis. 'I guess we thought Abacha was bluffing,' conceded one contrite New Zealand official.[15]

The hanging was filmed for the pleasure of the Nigerian military and officials. A woman went up to one of the bodies: 'Why can't the international community come and help you now?' she said as she put her foot triumphantly on top of the corpses, like a mountaineer on a conquered summit. Drinks were then served for the waiting dignitaries, whilst acid was poured on the bodies.

'When it happened it didn't sink in,' recalls Ken Wiwa ten years later. 'It was funny hearing about someone you know die in the news without actually seeing the body. Even now it seems like a bubble, like a dream.'[16]

Oil and Water

The Niger Delta is a land of water and the remains of what was once a tropical rainforest. It is a vast alluvial fan created by two great rivers, the Niger and the Benue, that join far inland to form the Niger, which spills into the Atlantic Ocean. This fan is divided into four distinct ecological zones. Furthest from the sea are the lowlands, where the forest has been cleared for farming. Then comes the area dominated by fresh water, regularly flooded by the Niger and lush with vegetation – the heart of the former rainforest. Next are the myriad brackish creeks and mangrove swamps. Finally, bordering the ocean, the Delta is fringed by sand barrier islands. The Delta has one of the highest levels of biodiversity on Earth and is a vital organ in the planet's ecosystem (see Map 2). The fertility of the soil means that this region is often referred to as the bread basket of Nigeria.

Estimates of the size of the Delta vary, depending on whether geographical features or political boundaries are used to define the area. The World Bank has estimated it as 20,000 square kilometres, but defines this as river and coastal areas only. A recent study based on the political boundaries of the region expands the Delta to 112,000 square kilometres. Depending on which boundary is used, the population of the Delta varies between 12 and 27 million.

The Delta is also rich in cultural diversity. The area is densely populated with a dozen different ethnic groups across the region and some 50 languages. Along with the Ogoni, there are the Ijaw and Ilaje, Ibibio and Andoni, Itsekiri and Uruhobo, all communities that have faced the wrath of the oil industry (see Map 3). One reason for this conflict between oil industry and community is the fight over land, for the Delta is densely populated. In Ogoni, for example, population density is 1,250 per kilometre compared to a Nigerian average of 300.[17]

Beneath this rich and densely populated land of culture and diversity are billions of barrels of oil. Nigeria's current 'proven' oil reserves stand at 35 billion barrels, which the Federal government plans to expand to 40 billion barrels by 2010. As its stands Nigeria currently accounts for over 50 per cent of the Gulf of Guinea's oil production and 70 per cent of its reserves. This equates to about a third of Africa's total reserves.[18] Nigeria is around the tenth largest producer in the world.[19]

'Whichever way you look at West Africa, you always come back to Nigeria,' argues Jonathan Bearman, from Clearwater Research Services, an oil industry consultancy. 'There will be growth in Equatorial Guinea, some growth in Cameroon, there will be some growth in São Tomé possibly but no one really knows, but it always comes back to Nigeria. It is the giant.'[20]

This giant produces desirable oil. First, it is light (in terms of gravity), which means less refining. Secondly, it is known within the industry as 'sweet' – its low sulphur content means it is highly desired by Western refineries. Thirdly, it is closer than the Middle East to the hungry markets of Western Europe and America, and close to easy shipping lanes. A tanker takes three weeks to reach the US from Nigeria, rather than the eight weeks it takes from Saudi Arabia. It is therefore not surprising that Nigeria is a major oil supplier to both Western Europe and the United States.[21]

This oil keeps Nigeria alive, accounting for more than 80 per cent of government revenues, 90 per cent of foreign exchange and 40 per cent of Gross Domestic Product. That is why oil is so important to the government, and why the fight to control the revenue from oil is so bitter.

One company is synonymous with oil in Nigeria: Shell. The Shell Petroleum Development Company of Nigeria Ltd (SPDC) produces nearly half of Nigeria's crude oil, with average daily production of approximately 1.1 million barrels per day (bbl/d) in 2004. Shell is the operator of SPDC, a joint venture agreement involving the Nigerian National Petroleum Corporation (NNPC), Shell, Total and Agip.[22] But Shell is, and has always been, the powerhouse behind the consortium. Because of this, it has been the company that has had most conflict with the communities of the Delta, although there has also been a history of struggle with Chevron and Agip.

Even on a map the potential for conflict between Shell and the communities of the Delta is clear. The oil map of Nigeria (See Map 5) shows the natural curves of both coast and sea in the Gulf of Guinea segmented with square and rigid rectangular blocks. These are concession blocks, and each concession is a designated area where a company – or a consortium of companies – has been given the right to explore for oil and gas. The right to extract oil is owned, but not by the people who live there. Shell owns concession areas of around 31,000 square kilometres, including both onshore land and the shallow offshore waters of the Delta.[23]

The same map on which oil and gas fields are marked shows the whole of the Delta and its offshore waters covered with blobs. In those blobs are wells – thousands of them, producing oil. Shell itself has over 1,000.[24] The company has 6,000 kilometres of pipelines and flowlines taking this oil to market from the oil fields to the coast.[25] All this impacts on the people of the Delta. Along its journey the oil criss-crosses people's farmlands. The communities live with the underbelly of oil development: the gas flaring and routine spillage. In return they have received almost nothing. It is not surprising therefore that they blame the oil companies for their ills.

After the Hanging

Following Saro-Wiwa's murder Shell was under intense pressure to pull out of Nigeria, but within days of the Ogoni leader going to the gallows the company signalled its intention of staying by signing a $4 billion deal for a new natural gas plant at Bonny, around which a major corruption scandal has since developed.[26] Its press release dated 15 November 1995 said that the LNG plant was 'On Course', and argued that the 'people of the Niger Delta would certainly suffer' if the plan collapsed. The company was on the point of investing in the largest industrial development in Africa. Irrespective of the pressure placed on them, they were unlikely to pull out.[27]

Although the then British Prime Minister John Major called Saro-Wiwa's execution 'judicial murder', one civil servant from the Foreign Office said simply: 'Whatever we think of the military regime – choke, spit – trade goes on.'[28] And so it did. That year Britain was the largest seller of industrial exports to Nigeria. The week after the hangings, there was a two-day trade conference in the Nigerian capital Abuja at which American, British, French, German and Japanese businessmen were all present.[29]

The Nigerian military may have killed Saro-Wiwa, but they had not killed the spirit of the Ogoni or the other communities in the Delta, who have continued to protest against the industry to this day. In January the following year, thousands of Ogoni celebrated Ogoni Day, 4 January. The numbers were smaller in 1996 than in the previous two years, but the intimidation was greater. Nigerian soldiers and Mobile Police (known locally as the 'Kill and Go') fired tear gas and live ammunition, killing four youths and wounding eighteen.[30]

Protests were held in London too, against Shell and the Nigerian High Commission. Ken Wiwa, wrapped up warmly against the January cold, addressed the crowd outside Shell's headquarters: 'I urge all of you here to keep the pressure on Shell to accept responsibility for what happened in Ogoni, and for what is still happening.'[31] Shell refused point-blank to accept responsibility. The intimidation by the military continued. Two months later, in March 1996, the UN High Commissioner for Refugees (UNHCR) reported that 1,000 Ogonis had fled to Benin since Ogoni Day. The UNHCR called the rate of increase 'worrisome'.[32] That month, the US State Department declared that Nigeria constituted a 'classic picture of human rights abuse',[33] but the US failed to act.

In March and April 1996 there was a UN fact-finding mission to the country, led by John Pace of the UNHCR. In Ogoni, hundreds defied the military to complain about their plight, but the UN too failed to act.[34] The European Parliament also condemned Nigeria's 'appalling human rights record' and called for an oil embargo, but that also failed to materialize.[35] In total, apart from the suspension of Nigeria from the Commonwealth for a short period, the most the international community could muster was a few visa restrictions and token sanctions – an oil embargo was deemed unacceptable to the United States.

The same month, Saro-Wiwa was posthumously elected to the United Nations Environment Programme's (UNEP) Global 500 Roll of Honour for advancing the cause of environmental protection. 'At all stages of his campaign, Saro-Wiwa advocated peaceful resistance to the forces that would deprive the Ogoni people of a say in the development of their region,' UNEP said in a statement.[36]

In May 1996, Shell offered a 'Plan of Action for Ogoni', in

which the company offered a range of measures to facilitate its return to Ogoni.[37] To effect this, Shell would need the support of at least some of the Ogoni traditional rulers, the chiefs. There then emerged a claim that the military were trying to force communities to accept Shell's return.

MOSOP, the organization at which Saro-Wiwa had been first spokesperson and then President, reported a dangerous turn of events. Major Obi, the head of the task force overseeing security in the State – the 'Rivers State Internal Security Task Force' – had held two secret meetings. MOSOP alleged that the chiefs in the villages of Kpor and Bori were forced to sign documents calling for Shell's return to Ogoni.[38] Two months later, Lieutenant Colonel Komo, the Military Administrator of Rivers State, was said to be in consultation with Shell over the company's return to Ogoni. Komo 'expressed pleasure that his talks with Shell have been positive, as the company will soon return to Ogoniland'.[39]

The recurring allegations of military and oil industry collusion and possible corruption resurfaced later in the year. Shell held a meeting with the Rivers State Internal Security Task Force and certain groups in Ogoni, but not MOSOP. The latter accused Shell of employing 'divide-and-rule tactics',[40] and argued that Shell was paying Naira 50,000 for the signatures of village chiefs and community development committees on a Memorandum inviting the company back into Ogoni. In response Shell has stated that the company was 'not aware of any payment being made'.[41]

The First Anniversary, 1996–7: A Great Man of Africa

Everyone knew that the first anniversary of Saro-Wiwa's death would make global headlines. Shell was desperate that the almost universal condemnation it had received the year before should not be repeated, so it reverted to a public relations technique – get a 'third party' to be your voice. One of the issues Shell wanted to lay to rest was that the company was operating to double standards – one set for Nigeria and a higher set for its operations in the UK. The company was particularly sensitive to the accusation of 'environmental devastation' in the Delta, caused by spills and gas flaring. It flew numerous journalists over the Delta in helicopters.

It was not long before articles started to appear in the international press that dismissed the claims of the Ogoni and various human rights and environmental organizations.

As these articles appeared in the West, soldiers and the Mobile Police raided Ogoni communities and detained activists. The government had ordered them to arrest church ministers who mentioned Saro-Wiwa's name. Despite this, thousands of Ogoni defied a heavy military presence to hold memorial church services at designated locations. But some were shot, and women were raped in Saro-Wiwa's home town.[42]

Nine days before the first Anniversary, on 1 November 1996, Claude Ake, the Director of the Centre for Advanced Social Science in Port Harcourt and a UN advisor passed through London on his way back home to Nigeria. Ake was a man of great bravery and integrity, who has been described as 'one of the great African thinkers of the twentieth century'.[43]

It was Ake who had been asked by the government to chair a commission on the violence that had erupted between Ogoni and its neighbours in 1993. He had concluded that there was evidence to suggest that 'broader forces' such as the Nigerian military were involved 'to derail the Ogoni agenda'. It was Ake who had been asked by Saro-Wiwa to serve on the Shell-sponsored Niger Delta Environment Survey, although he re-signed after Saro-Wiwa's execution.[44]

Ake had been an outspoken critic of the close link between the oil companies and the military. He had called Shell's use of the military, the 'militarization of commerce' and 'privatization of the state'.[45] In an interview, Ake was asked about new revela-tions that Shell had finally admitted that on two occasions it had paid the field allowances of the military. It was a significant admission because for 18 months the company had been denying it.

It was also significant because one of the payments had been to the notorious Lieutenant Colonel Okuntimo, who had headed the Rivers State Internal Security Task Force and who was personally responsible for the campaign of terror the military had inflicted on Ogoni in 1994 and 1995. In many ways Okuntimo was Ake's total opposite. Ake was an academic: a man of peace. Okuntimo was a soldier with a brutal reputation.

It was Okuntimo who had written a memo just nine days before the murder of the four Ogoni in May 1994 that said: 'Shell operations still impossible unless ruthless military opera-tions are undertaken for smooth economic activities to com-mence'. To counter this, Okuntimo had recommended 'Wasting operations during MOSOP and other gatherings making con-stant military presence justifiable'.[46]

Okuntimo had undue influence at Saro-Wiwa's trial. He had attended conferences for the defence lawyers, been close to the prosecution and probably had access to members of the Tri-bunal.[47]

Ake said the new 'findings about the support of Shell to the Security Force confirms what we have been saying all along, that essentially Shell has been driving the violence by creating excessive concern about security in the mineral producing areas'. He called the payment to Okuntimo 'a clear act of hostility against the people of the Niger Delta.'[48]

At the end of the interview on that cold November evening, Ake let slip he was going to make a significant new announcement on the anniversary, but refused to be drawn on what exactly it was. He hinted heavily it was going to be dramatic. But he never made it. Ake's plane crashed on 8 November, just a few days later, en route from Part Harcourt to Lagos. It disappeared into a swamp that was then cordoned off by the military.

There was immediate speculation that Ake had been assassinated by the Nigerian military, which had a habit of murdering its critics. 'We believe it was sabotage,' said a prominent Delta activist. What happened to Ake will probably never be known, but another great man of Africa was dead.

The Second Anniversary, 1997–8: A Pan-Delta Resistance Movement

In January 1997 some 80,000 Ogonis (over 15 per cent of the population) celebrated Ogoni Day in spite of ongoing repression by the military. Four people suffered gunshot wounds whilst twenty were arrested, tortured and detained.[49] MOSOP said this 'frightening wave of state terrorism' meant that 'Ogoni stands in the threshold of complete extinction'.[50] The World Council of Churches issued a report confirming the dire situation in the Delta: 'A quiet state of siege prevails even today in Ogoniland. Intimidation, rape, arrests, torture, shooting and looting by the soldiers continue to occur.'[51]

It is worth comparing the despair of the Ogoni to the hope of Shell. An inter-office memorandum from Shell written three days after Ogoni Day was circulated from SPDC in Port Harcourt. In the memo, entitled 'The Journey Towards Reconciliation in Ogoni', Egbert Imomoh, the General Manager of Shell Eastern Division, noted that 'Shell has held a series of discussions and meetings with many different communities and opinion leaders in Ogoniland . . . our discussions with the various groups have assured us that the time is now ripe to commence the implementation of our proposal.'[52]

Despite Shell's attempts to persuade a select group of Ogoni elders to invite the company back, the grass-roots remained hostile. Just as Ogoni men had become active in the struggle against Shell, so too had the women. The Federation of Ogoni Women's Associations (FOWA), with some 57,000 registered members, set up in 1993 and affiliated to MOSOP, resolved in April 1997 that 'Shell cannot and must not be allowed in Ogoni . . . we say no to Shell as it remains *persona non grata* in Ogoni.'[53] FOWA's international representative was Diana Wiwa, the wife of Owens Wiwa, Ken Saro-Wiwa's brother. Diana had acted as a courier to get letters to and from Saro-Wiwa in prison; she and Owens were now living in exile in Canada, unable to return home.

Diana met some of the FOWA representatives later: 'The women were very concerned about the continuing military presence in Ogoni, particularly the rapes, beatings and murders, and disruption of markets, and the extortion of money by soldiers. They called on governments worldwide to help stop this reign of terror,' she recalls.[54] The gulf between the community and Shell was as great as ever. The company seemed oblivious to the plight of the people.

But by now protests were beginning to spread across the Delta, and not just against Shell but against other oil companies too. It was what the oilmen and generals had feared all along: that other communities, inspired by Ken Saro-Wiwa and the Ogoni struggle, would rise up against the devastation of their environment.

In August 1997 over 1,000 people from across the Delta attended a rally at the remote Ijaw village of Aleibiri in Bayelsa State. The rally gave birth to the 'Chicoco movement', named after the organic soil found in the Niger Delta, on which mangroves grow. The Chicoco demands included, amongst others, an 'end to the ecological devastation of the Niger Delta by transnational oil companies and the Federal government; reparation and compensation to the peoples of the Niger Delta; and an immediate demilitarisation of the Niger Delta communities.' The main driving force behind Chicoco was an Ijaw, the environmental lawyer Oronto Douglas, who called for the 'solidarity of all producing communities'.[55]

If Saro-Wiwa had been the elder statesman of the Delta protest movement, Douglas, who had been a junior counsel on Saro-Wiwa's defence team at his trial, was one of the leaders of the next generation. He was committed to non-violence, with a long-standing belief that social justice cannot be achieved without ecological justice too. Douglas was both a lawyer and an environmental activist and was one of the founders of Environmental Rights Action (ERA), the Nigerian affiliate of Friends of the Earth. He comes from a village near Oloibiri, where Shell first found oil in the late 1950s.

'The Chicoco movement is a pan-Niger Delta resistance movement committed to reclaiming our humanity,' explained Douglas. 'Over the years we have been dehumanized, our environment has been plundered, our people raped, some jailed, others hanged, and we feel that the time has come that we should put our hands together to struggle so that we can achieve justice together.'[56]

A month after the Chicoco movement had been formed, Douglas was as frank as ever. 'To us the last forty years have been forty years of sorrow, forty years of blood, forty of desecration of our customs and traditions, forty years of the total elimination of our livelihoods that we hold so dear – I mean our land, our air, and our water. Our fight today is a fight for survival,' he continued. 'We are being systematically wiped out by the multi-national corporations in Nigeria, principally Shell. The issues we are raising are environmental. The issues we are raising are human rights. It does not matter where you are, whether London, Lagos, Amsterdam or Port Harcourt, we want Shell to direct its efforts not through public relations campaigns, not through propaganda, but directly to redress the ecological war they have waged on our land for forty years.'[57]

The Third Anniversary, 1998–9: Killings and Kaiama

Like the Ogoni before them, the Ilaje community in Ondo State were fed up with living under the shadow of an oil giant, but in this instance it was the American company Chevron, not Shell. 'Over the years Chevron has consistently waged a war on our land, forests and water,' recalled one Ilaje, Bola Oyinbo, who later led a non-violent protest against the company. 'Everything there is dead: mangroves, tropical forests, fish, the freshwater, wildlife, etcetera. All killed by Chevron.'[58]

Oyinbo argues that the community repeatedly tried to in-stigate a dialogue with the company, but it would not listen to their concerns. So in May 1998, 121 youths from the 42 communities of Ilajeland got into boats and canoes and set off to occupy Chevron's Parabe platform, miles off-shore. Their demands, argues Oronto Douglas, were modest: 'Don't pollute our water, don't destroy our mangrove forest, don't devastate our ecology. Come and listen to us, come and talk to our elders.'[59] Chevron Nigeria's acting Head of Security, who accompanied the security forces, stated that the young men were unarmed.

What happened next, depends on who you talk to. According to George Kirkland, Chairman of Chevron Nigeria, the oil platform was attacked by 'belligerent youths' who 'forcibly occupied' the barge. When negotiations failed, the company called in 'federal law enforcement agencies'. 'The officers arrived at the platform announcing that they had not come to effect any arrests, but to evacuate the platform peacefully,' argued Kirkland. However, 'some of the youths attacked the officers and attempted to disarm one of them. In the ensuing scuffle, two of the youths, regrettably, died, while another was injured.'[60]

Douglas's group, Environmental Rights Action collected a testimony from Oyinbo, who said that for four days they had occupied a barge tied to Chevron's rig. They were still awaiting a response from Chevron when early one morning, flying low in the African sky, three helicopters arrived. All were being flown by foreign Chevron pilots, but they were full of Nigerian military and navy and the Mobile Police Force. 'They came like eagles, swooping on chickens,' recalled Oyinbo.[61]

'We never expected what followed,' he adds. 'As the choppers landed, one after the other discharging soldiers, what we heard were gunshots and fire. They started shooting commando-style at us even before they landed. They shot everywhere.' Two youths were killed, thirty more youths were wounded, most with gunshot. Those who went to help the dying were shot too.

'We were defenceless, harmless,' argues Oyinbo. Eleven protestors, including Oyinbo, were arrested and held for twenty-two days before being released. On one occasion Oyinbo's hands were cuffed behind his back and he was hung from a hook on the ceiling. His feet could not touch the floor, so he spun around and around.[62]

It later transpired that Chevron had specifically called for the Mobile Police. In response to questioning from Human Rights Watch, Chevron did not indicate that any attempt had been made 'to prevent abusive actions by the security forces in advance of the confrontation. Nor did it state that concern had been expressed to the authorities over the incident or that any steps would be taken to avoid similar incidents in future.' One of the helicopters had a Chevron security person on board who 'apparently did nothing' to stop the shooting.[63] In the eyes of the communities, another company now had blood on its hands.

Another Delta youth group – the Ijaw – were also about to mobilize. While Ogoni is small in size, Ijaw is 56,000 square kilometres. If Ogoni signalled trouble for the oil companies, the Ijaw were potentially disasterous.

In December 1998, Ijaw youths from over five hundred communities in Ijawland met in Kaiama to 'deliberate on the best way to ensure the continous survival of the indigenous peoples of the Ijaw ethnic nationality'. The meeting place was symbolic: it was the home village of Isaac Boro, the Ijaw revolutionary who had tried unsuccessfully to declare an independent Delta State in the mid 1960s.[64]

The delegates adopted the 'Kaiama Declaration', which demanded an end to oil production and to military operations in Ijawland. It also gave the companies a deadline by which to pull out of Ijawland.[65] The Declaration started with an attack on colonialism: 'It was through British colonization that the Ijaw Nation was forcibly put under the Nigerian State.' It continued: 'We are tired of gas flaring, oil spillages, blowouts and being labelled saboteurs and terrorists. It is a case of preparing the noose for our hanging. We reject this labelling.' The deadline set by the Declaration was 30 December 1998. All oil company staff and contractors were to withdraw from Ijawland by this date, 'pending the resolution of the issue of resource ownership and control in the Ijaw area'.[66]

Douglas was one of the organizers. By signing Kaiama he knew he might have been signing his death warrant. 'I and a few others who organized the all-Ijaw youth conference which resulted in the Kaiama Declaration are now marked persons,' he wrote in an email. 'We may or may not be arrested or eliminated as the 30-day deadline issued for the oil corporations to withdraw from Ijawland approaches.'[67] Where Saro-Wiwa and the Ogoni had dared to lead, Douglas and the Ijaw were now following.

As the deadline approached in the region around Warri, SPDC evacuated its staff from front-line positions. Warri is the second most important oil town in the Delta after Port Harcourt and home to three ethnic groups: the Itsekiri, the Urhobo, and the Ijaw. The violence that Douglas had feared started. The Ijaw Youths managed to stop the flow of oil in ten places – but at a cost. The Military Administrator, Lieutenant Colonel Obi, declared a state of emergency. Some ten to fifteen thousand troops moved into the region.[68] On the bright morning of 30 December thousands of youths protested, wearing black and carrying candles. Their message was peace and justice. But soldiers were waiting for them, and opened fire.[69]

According to the Ijaw Youth Council, 'Several people were shot dead or wounded . . . This was followed by widespread looting, senseless raping, and extra-judicial executions. Even men of God were not spared. Reverend Atari Ado was beaten, chained and prevented from taking water for three days. Chief Torumoye Ajako had his ears chopped off with a dagger. He was given his own ears to eat.'[70] Some 200 Ijaw men had limbs amputated, including hands and arms.[71]

The Nigerian military rulers may have been talking about holding democratic elections but their soldiers were still acting with the brutality of a despot. In the days after the Kaiama deadline expired, there occurred the deaths of 'possibly over 200 people; the torture and inhuman treatment of others; and the arbitrary detention of many more', as Human Rights Watch recorded. Girls as young as twelve were raped or tortured.[72]

ERA reported that on 4 January 1999, soldiers arrived on speedboats owned by the oil companies to attack the villages of Opia and Ikenyan. The soldiers were ordered to 'shoot on sight'.[73] Four people were killed and 67 were subsequently found to be missing when Nigerian forces, paid by Chevron, attacked two small villages.[74]

The Fourth Anniversary, 1999–2000: From Dictatorship to Democracy?

Over a decade of brutal military dictatorship came to an end as civilian rule was restored in May 1999 when former head of state and Nigerian war hero General Olusegun Obasanjo was elected civilian president. The task facing him was daunting. The military ruled during all but ten of the thirty-nine years since Independence in 1960. This meant Obasanjo 'assumed the helm of an ailing ship of state almost lacking in morality or legitimacy', wrote Karl Maier in his book on Nigeria, *This House Has Fallen.*

As he was sworn in, looking splendid in flowing white Nigerian robes, Obasanjo promised to wipe out the cancer of corruption. 'After 15 years of military rule, today is a day of promise for a great future,' he told such visiting dignitaries as Nelson Mandela, Prince Charles and Jesse Jackson, who had come to witness the ceremony in the purpose-built Eagle Square Stadium. There was a festive mood.[75] Nigeria had reason to celebrate. Its people had supposedly been freed from military oppression.

For the people of the Delta, Obasanjo's promises were as depressingly hollow as the reality of the election. In Bayelsa State, as elsewhere, there was widespread ballot-rigging. In November 1999, as the fourth anniversary of Saro-Wiwa's death approached, the Nigerian military destroyed Odi, a town of 15,000 in Ijawland, demolishing every building except the bank, the church and the health centre. It was the largest deployment of troops since the Biafran war. As many as 2,000 people were killed.[76] 'I was in the house with my 90-year-old husband when the soldiers came,' recalled one terrified villager. 'They had already set fire around the house before I noticed their presence. As we came out, I was pushed aside and thereafter they shot my husband.'[77]

A week after the massacre, Nigerian Senate President Chuba Okadigbo visited the town. 'The facts speak for themselves,' he said, visibly shocked. 'There is no need for speech because there is nobody to speak with.'[78] A town had been vaporized into submission. When Saro-Wiwa's brother Owens visited the scene where the Nigerian military had wreaked havoc, he was stunned. 'It is the same story, just what happened in Ogoni.'[79]

The Fifth Anniversary, 2000–1: Some Things Never Change

In April 2000 Ken Saro-Wiwa was symbolically buried. The authorities had blocked the release of his remains on the grounds that his body still belonged to the state since he was seen as a murderer. Placed in his coffin were two of his favourite novels and his pipe, requests that he had made in his will. The day dawned bright as Ogoniland awoke to the sounds of drums, whistles and dancing. Saro-Wiwa's symbolic coffin was buried under the Ogoni flag, flapping defiantly in the breeze.

The Ogoni still hold Shell responsible. The main sign of the funeral had a picture of Shell's famous logo followed by 'killed Saro-Wiwa'. It then read: 'Shell is forever *persona non grata* in Ogoni.' The 'S' of 'Shell' had been crossed out, leaving 'Hell'. Over 100,000 Ogonis attended ceremonies during the week of events held to mark the occasion.[80] It was another four years before Saro-Wiwa's bones were finally returned to the family after a fight led by his brother Owens and son Ken.[81]

The symbolic burial was one of a number of issues covered in an article entitled, 'Some things never change' published in the *Guardian* newspaper in the run-up to the fifth anniversary of Saro-Wiwa's death. Its aim was to highlight the continuing plight of the Ogoni people, and the fact that so little had changed in the last five years. It noted that 'For millions of people, there is a daily struggle to gain access to basic necessities such as clean water, health care and education.' It quoted MOSOP's claim that 'Ogoni people still languish in poverty, deprivation, marginalization and environmental devastation.'[82]

In a letter to the *Guardian*'s Readers' Editor, the Vice President of External Affairs for Exploration and Production in

Shell International, Alan Detheridge, complained that the company had not been asked to respond to the allegation that 'Shell's activities have led to "devastation of the environment"'.[83] Detheridge then quoted from 'a number of independent respected journalists' who had 'visited the region'. He referred to six press reports. The majority mentioned 'flying in helicopters' or 'flying over the delta'. Shell was quoting journalists from the public relations campaign running up to the first anniversary, four years before.

But the public relations campaign backfired. Academic Jedrzej George Frynas found that 'on their return from Nigeria, many journalists presented Shell in a more favourable light than before and downplayed the environmental and social impact of oil operations on the ground.' Frynas notes that 'Shell's attempts to influence media coverage were exposed by Media Watch, a German non-governmental organization which monitors journalistic reporting from developing countries.' One journalist from Media Watch was sued for defamation after accusing one of the Shell-sponsored journalists of undertaking 'journalistic prostitution for Shell'. However, 'the German court dismissed the defamation suit and confirmed the fact that Shell undertook expenses for the journalist.'[84]

The company was still quoting these same 'independent' journalists in its defence five years later, in 2005, as part of its new public relations campaign 'Tell Shell' (see Chapter 5). One of the commentators wrote: 'Would it be too cynical to infer that the flight plans of the "Shell helicopter" might have deliberately avoided the less salubrious parts of the producing operations?'

The Sixth Anniversary, 2001–2: Towards Reconciliation?

While the Nigerian military carried on a murderous reign of terror, the politicians talked of peace and reconciliation. The new government set up a panel to examine human rights abuses under the military. Officially the 'Human Rights Violations Investigation Commission', it was known simply as the 'Oputa Panel' after its chairman Judge Chukwudifu Oputa. The panel also included the Reverend Kukah, named as the facilitator of the Ogoni reconciliation process when it was launched years later, in 2005. MOSOP submitted a fat file documenting 8,000 cases of human rights abuses.[85]

When the Oputa Panel sat in January 2001, Saro-Wiwa's father, Jim Beeson Wiwa, known as Pa and aged 96, refused to testify. 'My mind is not peaceful. I will not appear before the Oputa Panel because that will not bring back my son for me,' he said. It is Ogoni tradition that the eldest son looks after his parents in their old age, so Saro-Wiwa's death had robbed them of their primary carer. The fact that his body had not been released meant that the long process of healing and of coming to terms with his death could not even begin.[86]

In February 2001 Egbert Imomoh, who is referred to further in chapter 3 in connection with the military assistance that he requested for Shell's operations in Ogoni in 1993, was now Deputy Managing Director of SPDC. He told the Panel that Shell 'completely rejects all accusations of the abuse of human rights'.[87]

Imomoh had replaced Godwin Omene, the previous Deputy Managing Director of SPDC who had just been nominated by President Obasanjo to head the new 'Niger Delta Development Commission' that began sitting in 2001. Obasanjo had set up the commission in response to community demands for greater ownership of oil resources, but its formation did not stop either the violence or the resentment felt by the communities.[88] Omene's appointment was a severe blow to the communities, who had thought an independent development organization might assist their plight,[89] and it illustrated the crossover between the company and the Nigerian state.

In May 2002 the Oputa Panel published its report: a 'lament' about the state of Nigeria. 'Oil, one of the greatest blessings God has showered on our nation, has turned out to be a curse,' the Panel concluded. It had become an instrument 'sounding the death-knell of such key principles of good governance as democracy, federalism, transparency, accountability and national growth'.[90] The curse of the Delta was the curse of oil. And oil was the curse of Nigeria.

Nothing seemed to change, as the conflict between communities and companies spiralled into a permanent vortex of despair and death. Five months later, in October 2002, the Commissioner for the Environment in Bayelsa State told Human Rights Watch that: 'The situation of Shell is abysmal. It has not changed and we do not believe there is a possibility of change . . . As far as relations with communities are concerned we have not seen any changes at all. The flow stations are protected by armed soldiers, they don't give any employment to the youth. As commissioner of the environment I have not seen any changes in corporate philosophy.' Some 23 Shell facilities had an armed security presence.[91]

The Seventh Anniversary, 2002–3: Rig Invasions

Rig invasions by communities and oil workers had now become common in the Delta and the international community was becoming increasingly concerned about the protests. Four months after the seventh anniversary of Saro-Wiwa's death, a 'Restricted' briefing note was written for Baroness Amos, then Under-Secretary of State at the Foreign and Commonwealth Office. Now released under the British Freedom of Information Act, it concerns the take-over by oil workers of a rig owned by the American company Transocean.

The official who wrote the document took the side of the oil industry. It notes that the Delta 'has a history of inter-ethnic clashes, hostage-taking of oil employees for money and of antipathy to the oil companies, regarded (not entirely justifiably) as exploiters and polluters'. It went on to say that Alan Detheridge from Shell International had told the government that the situation could continue for 'some time'. Though not overtly concerned about the British situation, as 'Britain is not especially affected by the Nigerian closures', the UK was still worried about 'supply disruptions and rises in oil prices'. The country primarily affected was the 'US, which receives one-third of Nigerian production, some 6 per cent of US oil imports'.

An interesting paragraph indicates that the international community was relying on Iraq to take up any deficit caused by the Nigerian action: 'Were the disruption to be prolonged over several months, the impact on the oil market would partly depend on how production developed in Iraq.'[92]

An even more interesting document than this briefing note is one that concerns hostage-taking; names have been blanked out to protect the people concerned. The list of recipients is also revealing: the document was sent from Lagos to the Foreign and Commonwealth Office, the Cabinet Office, the Ministry of Defence – and to 'Snuffbox in Washington' (Sic). The message reads:

BLANK has thanked us for our role in helping to secure the agreement on down manning of the rigs. Transocean managers in Port Harcourt quizzed BLANK about the report that mercenaries were flying in at the request of a 'government involved in the dispute'. If they had arrived while negotiations were still in progress, the effect would have been disastrous. We were, of course, vigorously denying that the mercenaries were engaged by the British government.

The last sentence can be read as a candid admission that mercenaries had been employed. If so, it was not the first time the British sent in soldiers to assist their Nigerian operations, as we shall see.

The note ended: 'One of the positive elements resulting from this incident is that there are moves to draw up a code of conduct for Nigerian oil industry workers. It will include disciplinary measures to deal with the occupations of rigs. Transocean floated the idea with the American Embassy, who have agreed to become involved in the talks with the Nigerian Ministry of Labour. We propose supporting this initiative.' Once again America and Britain were meddling in the affairs of the Nigerian oil industry.

The Eighth Anniversary, 2003–4: An Integral Part of the Conflict

By 2003 another lethal ingredient was being added to the tinderbox of the Delta. 'Oil bunkering' involved groups (normally armed) in siphoning off oil from the myriad of pipes, then selling this crude on the black market. Some 10 per cent of Nigeria's oil production was now thought to be going into illegal bunkering, in an extremely lucrative trade controlled by local politicians who hired armed militias to look after their interests. 'Bunkering is not a business for poor people,' argues Patrick Naagbanton, an Ogoni and Director of the Niger Delta Project for Environment, Human Rights and Development. 'It is rich people that are involved.'[93]

Naagbanton's concerns have been backed up by a report from the UK Department for International Development into the bunkering which concluded that the illegal trade 'would not be possible without the complicity of some senior government personnel for whom this is evidently profitable'. The report noted that, in part because of the bunkering, Warri was now a major focal port for arms imports into the country.[94]

Warring factions fighting for control of the bunkering trade had now become a major problem in the Delta that was sending worrying signals around the world. Rampant government corruption and fighting between ethnic groups engaged in lethal arguments over the control of money and resources once again ignited the Delta in bloody conflict. In April 2003, Human Rights Watch wrote to Shell and other oil companies expressing their 'concern regarding recent violent clashes in Nigeria's Niger Delta'. They called on the Nigerian government and the oil companies to take immediate measures to prevent further violence.[95] However, over the next couple of months hundreds were killed, hundreds of homes destroyed and thousands displaced as rival factions fought around the oil town of Warri. At the height of the violence, 40 per cent of Nigeria's oil production was closed down.[96]

If the closure of many of its wells was giving Shell the jitters, it was also having to deal will another equally explosive issue. In response to the violence and 'increased risk of resource extraction', Shell had 'initiated the development of a Peace and Security Strategy, an integrated and comprehensive approach to establishing security through peace rather than through purely fiscal means'.

In December 2003 a key part of this strategy – a report by the consultants WAC, hired by Shell – was leaked. Rather than indicating how the company could be a solution to the problem of the Niger Delta, WAC identified Shell as part of the problem. The report concluded that the way Shell operated 'creates, feeds into, or exacerbates conflict' and that 'after over 50 years in Nigeria' Shell had become 'an integral part of the Niger Delta conflict system'.[97]

Its conclusions were alarming: first, that the company's 'social license to operate is fast eroding'; secondly, that 'If current conflict trends continue uninterrupted, it would be surprising if SCIN [Shell Companies in Nigeria] is able to continue on-shore resource extraction in the Niger Delta beyond 2008, whilst complying with Shell Business Principles.'[98]

Here were Shell's own consultants saying that a business-as-usual scenario was no longer possible for Shell. If things did not rapidly change, the company might have to give up its on-shore oil production – the majority of its oil and gas reserves being on-shore. The report sent shock waves to London, The Hague and Washington, at about the same time that the reserves crisis was hitting Shell (see Chapter 5). It also sent shockwaves to the City brokers, who worried that the 10 per cent of Shell's oil originating in Nigeria could be under threat. Shell disputed that it would have to leave onshore oil extraction in Nigeria.

Whilst Shell's consultants were saying that the company was on the verge of failing to comply with its business principles, the company's website was declaring: 'In general, we would withdraw from Nigeria (and indeed any country) when we found that we could not operate there in a manner which was consistent with our business principles.'[99]

The Ninth Anniversary, 2004–5: Niger Delta People's Volunteer Force

By 2004 oil bunkering was escalating out of control. The WAC report had concluded that between 275,000 and 685,000 barrels of oil were being stolen on average every day, generating a staggering $1.5 to $4 billion a year for those involved. Shell has tried to play down these figures, saying 40,000 to 100,000 barrels per day are more likely.[100]

The bunkering and the violence were alarming the Americans as well as the British. Two weeks before the ninth anniversary of Saro-Wiwa's death, a delegation of American businessmen, the 'Business Executives for National Security', had drinks with the US Ambassador to Nigeria, John Campbell.

Trip notes from the delegation show just how important the region had by now become to the US (see Chapter 7): 'The Gulf of Guinea already provides 10% of US oil needs, a number that could easily increase to 25% by 2015.' The Ambassador told the delegation that although the Delta was strategically important, there was only one problem – 'It's wild there.'[101]

The delegation also noted ominously that 'As this region finally begins to leverage its natural resources, it will undoubtedly attract increasingly negative influences and attention, making the need to focus on security issues of growing importance.' For the US, security of oil supply means militerization.

The 'security issue' was reinforced when a conflict erupted between two rival groups for control of the lucrative bunkering trade. When Alhaji Dokubo Asari, the Ijaw leader of one of the groups, the Niger Delta People's Volunteer Force, threatened to launch an all-out war in the Delta, it sent shock waves through the oil industry. The name of Asari's force was symbolic – it had been inspired by the Ijaw revolutionary Isaac Boro, who had been the first Delta leader to attack the oil companies. Asari was threatening to launch 'Operation Locust Feast', to reclaim the oil that he said was rightly that of the Ijaws. The announcement helped send the international price of oil through the $50 a barrel mark for the first time.

A peace deal, reportedly brokered by the Americans, was hastily arranged by President Obasanjo, calling for the 'disbandment of all militias and militant groups'. Although over a thousand weapons were collected, the Delta remains awash with arms and is still ready to ignite at any moment.[102] Many observers believe that the flashpoint will be the federal and state elections in 2007. The process starts with primaries in early 2006 and the risk of armed confrontation seems inevitable.

Towards The Tenth Anniversary, 2005

In March 2005 six people were feared dead after an anti-Shell demonstration in the Ahoada area of Rivers State descended into inter-community violence. One of the communities told the Nigerian press that they 'wanted to engage Shell and the government in discussion as to how certain issues concerning environmental devastation, the loss of their means of livelihood, could be solved.[103]

On 1 April 2005 Ken Saro-Wiwa's father, Pa Wiwa, finally passed away, aged 101. A long-term colleague of Oronto Douglas, activist Ike Okonta, recalls meeting Pa Wiwa before he died.

'He told me of the morning, now so long ago, when Ken came to him and sought his permission to lead the Ogoni to freedom from the tyranny of Shell and the Nigerian state. "It was a difficult decision for me to make," Pa Wiwa told me. "I asked my son, who will bury me after they have killed you? I asked him this question three times. But he was still determined to do something to save our people. In the end, I gave him my blessing." '[104]

Owens Wiwa travelled back to Nigeria to bury his father. An estimated 200,000 to 250,000 took part in the celebration of Pa Wiwa's life. The ten years since his brother's death have not eased Owens's anger or pain. He still blames Shell for Saro-Wiwa's death. 'Ken told me in 1993 that Shell would like to see him dead, and not only dead but disgraced. That Shell would like to have him in for murder. He told me that in 1993. I thought it was a joke.'

He believes that Brian Anderson, the Chairman of Shell Nigeria, who met secretly with Owens before his brother's death, 'had the power to stop that trial, but he refused when he didn't get what he wanted from me'. Anderson had wanted Owens to call the international protests off. 'Shell made it possible for the government' to kill Ken, he said.[105]

The increase in violence in the Niger Delta is directly attributable to what people saw as the injustice of Ken's murder, argues Owens. He says that when people saw what had happened to Saro-Wiwa's peaceful struggle, they took up arms. 'Unfortunately we now have this combination of violence, greed, in terms of illegal oil bunkering taking over from the empowering, non-violent struggle for the environment and for resource control.'

He adds that 'The oil companies do not really appear to have learnt any lessons. Their response has been, in my view, "get more oil as fast as possible".' But in Ogoni, he adds, 'there is strength among the women and men to prevent the return of Shell. There is a restoration of dignity.'[106] A dignity the Ogoni had been denied by years of colonial, military and oil company rule.

Saro-Wiwa's son, Ken Wiwa also blames the oil company for his father's death. 'Shell could have stopped it at any time they wanted to,' he says. 'They have that kind of power in Nigeria. Shell basically encouraged state violence against the Ogoni people, and eventually against my father. OK, they didn't tie the noose around my father's neck, but without Shell's intervention and encouraging of the military government it would never have happened.'

Wiwa continues: 'As far as I am concerned they encouraged the military Internal Security Task Force that violated the human rights of the people. All that was done to enable oil production to resume. Whether they like it or not, they are involved in the murder of my father, they are a co-conspirator in the murder of my father. All the blood on Abacha's hands is also on Shell's logo.'[107]

Remembering Saro-Wiwa

ANDY ROWELL

I remember the day Ken died. I was one of the 'international community' that had been helping the Ogoni with their plight. I had first met Saro-Wiwa over three years before, when I was writing a report for Greenpeace on the social and environmental impacts of the seven largest oil companies.

Saro-Wiwa was drumming up support for the Ogoni, a people no one had ever heard of from a far-away Delta that Ken would bring a little closer on every visit. This awoke the consciousness of many environmental NGOs in London and Washington, for whom Africa was off the radar. But more importantly, it dismayed Shell officials in London, who thought that a little local difficulty in Nigeria would never reach the international stage.

They underestimated Saro-Wiwa and his unnerving commitment to gaining justice for his people. But he could not do it alone. He needed to bring the fight back to London, The Hague and Washington – Shell's power centres, where it would have to sit up and listen. 'It's just going to get worse, unless the international community intervenes,' he told me. On his visits we would talk, share information, and sometimes go for a drink.

During the research for this book, I found a long-forgotten interview that I never used. I switch the tape on. It is December 1992, just weeks before the Ogoni Day March of 1993. I listen to the voice of a younger me. I listen to the voice of a dead man. It is strange to hear Ken's gravelly voice again, but it is strong and alive. He laughs a lot. We talk about the Niger Delta and Shell.

'You have two problems, the human rights problem and the environmental problem. You cannot talk about the environment without human rights,' he says. Shell must bear 'responsibility' for the pipelines, the gas flaring, and environmental devastation. He talks about Nigeria's 'bandit government' that 'subordinates all other tiers of government to its own wishes. Those that are running the government are just anxious to transfer the money from the Delta to the North of the country. They are happy collaborators with Shell. So the people at the local level are suffering both at the hands of Shell but also the ethnic majority who run the country.'

We talk about Shell's response so far. 'Shell employees have also told me that they are stepping up their community development efforts. But so long as Shell is doing this over and above the heads of the local people it has no meaning whatsoever. They come around with their concrete classroom blocks, but what is that? It is a joke.' Ken offers a long, room-filling laugh. I remember his laughter being infectious. 'They can only do that to people who do not know how much money they are taking away.'

We talk about what will happen. 'The awareness about the environment now is very high. When I did a tour of Ogoni recently for two weeks, many people said they were willing to die. They were ready to march. We have planned that on the fourth of January there will be a massive demonstration by all Ogoni people, men, women and children. The march is against the devastation of the environment. It is against the non-payment of royalties. It is anti-Shell. It is anti-Federal Government, because as far as we are concerned the two are in league to destroy the Ogoni people.'

We then move on to the authorities' response to Ken. 'There is a lot of concern now in the local areas because they think I am at risk.'

'Have you had any threats?' I ask.

'No, they are not going to send warning letters,' Ken laughs. 'They couldn't really arrest me now, but they could organize an accidental death or something of that sort. But I am not too worried about it.'

I was worried about it, even if Ken wasn't. Between his visits, I had wondered how anyone could take on the might of a corrupt military regime and the might of the oil industry and win. Each time we met, I wondered if it would be the last. But Ken was never frightened. Or if he was, he did not show it. In many ways he knew what his destiny was, as if the dice had already been rolled.

On 10 November 1995 I remember sitting at my desk, still holding on to a shred of hope that he would be pardoned – that he and the others would be set free, because the international pressure would finally buckle the military's resolve. I don't think he thought they would kill him. How wrong he was. How wrong we were.

I remember the phone ringing continually, puncturing the quiet of my office. Would it be good news or bad? First we got unconfirmed reports that Saro-Wiwa and the others were dead. Then it was confirmed: Ken had been hung, along with the other eight.

It is said that those who are old enough knew where they were when Armstrong landed on the moon, when Kennedy was shot, when Lennon was murdered, and we all remember where we were on September 11th 2001. I and others will never forget 10 November 1995, and the dreadful feeling that the international community had let Ken down. I still believe that we failed him in his darkest hour.

CHAPTER TWO

The Colonial Company

'To take away the resources of a people, and to refuse to give them anything in return is to subject them to slavery.'

Ken Saro-Wiwa[1]

The Company of Kings

In 1664 the crew of the Royal Navy vessel *Jersey*, commanded by Major Robert Holmes, looked across the brown sea at the dark line of mangrove swamps. After several weeks sailing from England, they could feel the steamy heat rising from Africa. The air was filled with the strange smell of tropical vegetation.

Holmes's force, financed partly by King Charles II, was charged with destroying the shipping and forts of the Dutch West India Company in the Gulf of Guinea. The English, having taken the Dutch settlement at Cape Coast Castle (now in Ghana), had sailed east. They were unaware that they looked upon the creeks that formed the Delta of the river Niger.[2]

The task of Holmes's squadron was to prise the Guinea coast away from the Dutch Empire, just as the Dutch had taken it from the Portuguese Empire. The Portuguese had been drawn to this coast in the 1490s by gold, and their first militarized trading port was called El Mina – 'The Mine'. The English were drawn by the commodity of slaves, and the coast was soon known across the European world as the Slave Coast.

King Charles II himself was one of the shareholders of the English slaving company, the Royal Adventurers into Africa. Its founding charter in 1662 declared: 'How necessary it is that the English Plantations in America should have a competent [i.e. sufficient] and constant supply of Negro-servants for their use in planting, and that at a moderate rate.' Other shareholders included Queen Catherine, Queen Luisa of Portugal, a prince, three dukes, seven earls, and six other lords. A quarter of the stock was held by aristocrats, the remaining three-quarters by the merchants and bankers of the City of London.

The company had a monopoly on the slave trade with West Africa, a status it enforced with the assistance of the Royal Navy. It was contracted to supply 3,000 slaves per year to the planta-tions, acquiring them through the barter of copper bracelets, cloth and guns.[3] The concept of an imperial navy protecting the commercial interests of its companies off the shores of Africa was well under way.

In 1672 the Royal Adventurers into Africa Company was superseded by the Royal African Company. Its founding charter also gave it a monopoly over the West African trade, again enforced with the assistance of the Royal Navy.

These European merchants rarely went ashore, kept at bay by the strength of the Delta communities, and by disease. The Ijaw restricted them to the very fringes of the land, in order to maintain their control of the ancient trade routes and the new trade in Igbo slaves from inland. In trading-canoes with up to 40 rowers apiece, slaves were brought through the channels of the Niger from as far north as Aboh or Onitsha in Igboland.[4] These canoes brought out slaves to the ships waiting off-shore: what lay beyond the mangrove shoreline remained *terra incognita* in the European imagination.[5]

The Black Holocaust

The slave trade had a devastating impact on West Africa. An estimated 12 million African slaves were transported to the English, French, Dutch and Portuguese plantations in the Americas between the early 1500s and the late 1860s – a constant export of human raw material, draining places such as the Delta of women, children and the fittest men. Perhaps 38 million Africans were killed in the process of enslavement and transport. Increasingly, this history is referred to as the Black Holocaust.

The ships were like transports to the underworld, in which millions left never to return. The Delta became a thoroughfare for the slave trade and inland kingdoms and Delta 'city states' – such as Brass and Bonny – arose on the back of the trade in captured peoples. In the late seventeenth century, the Niger Delta was seen as a strategic piece in the Europeans' 'global economy' because of slavery.

The parallels do not end there. Just as oil has increased conflict in the Delta, so too did the slave trade. It was a trade that needed conflict to survive. There was almost constant inter-ethnic warfare, raiding and kidnap. Just as oil has helped militarize the Delta, so did the slave trade. European arms were exchanged for slaves: a slave was worth 16 guns. By the 1750s, Europeans were exporting between 283,000 and 399,000 guns each year into West Africa.[6]

Olaudah Equiano was one such slave. Eventually he won his freedom and came to live in London, where he wrote his autobiography. In it he related how at the age of eleven he was kidnapped from his Igbo village near the northern edge of the Delta, together with his sister. They were bound and gagged and driven through the forest, separated, reunited, and separated again. After several months he arrived at the coast, where a slave ship was waiting. Carried onboard, chained to prevent suicide, flogged to force him to eat, he crossed the Atlantic.[7]

Slaves like Equiano became the property of the Royal Adventurers into Africa, or the Royal African Company, or, later, other independent companies. They became ciphers in an accounting book, for they were seen as an investment, a unit of production. John Barbot, a London slaver, visited the Delta in 1699. He described how slaves were led down to the shore where the ships' surgeons examined 'every part of every one of them, to the smallest member, men and women being stark naked'. Those 'good and sound' were set on one side, 'marked on the breast with a red-hot iron, imprinting the mark of the French, English or Dutch companies' and told to await shipment.[8]

After the appalling journey across the Atlantic, captives from the Delta arrived in the Americas. Within twelve years of its foundation in 1607, the colony of Virginia in the USA was using African slaves. Other colonies followed the same 'development path'. Within the next fifty years, at St Kitts, Barbados, Nevis, Monserrat, Antigua, Maryland, Jamaica and Carolina, slaves from the Delta were sold to British plantation owners. Olaudah Equiano arrived in Virginia where he 'was constantly grieving and pining and wishing for death, rather than anything else'.[9]

After selling their cargos of slaves, the Royal African Company purchased sugar, tobacco, spices, molasses and rum. The slaving ships, thus laden, sailed back across the Atlantic to London, Liverpool and Bristol, where this tropical produce was sold on the British market or re-exported to such ports as Amsterdam or Hamburg. British traders controlled this sale of sugar and tobacco to the European merchants, and British manufacturers produced the fire-arms, textiles and other goods that were used to barter for slaves in West Africa.

These were the three corners of the Atlantic Triangle: West Africa – the place of extraction in the form of slave labour; the Caribbean and the American East Coast – the places of production in the form of sugar and tobacco, through the use of slaves; and Britain and Europe – the places of consumption and political control. Between the Delta, the colonies of Virginia, Maryland (and later the new city of Washington) and London a pattern had been set that would be repeated centuries later (see Map 8).

Slavery Begins at Home

With its headquarters in Leadenhall Street in the City of London, the Royal African Company swiftly established itself as an engine of wealth in the capital. By 1700 it had sent to the Gulf of Guinea some 500 ships carrying goods worth £500,000, transported 100,000 slaves to the plantations and imported 130,000 tons of sugar. The company and its trade were deeply embedded in London's ruling establishment – 15 lord mayors, 25 sheriffs and 38 of the City's aldermen were shareholders.[10]

The wealth from the slave trade helped fuel London's rapid growth and finance key cultural undertakings such as the building of St Paul's Cathedral or the compositions of Purcell. The products of this slave-fuelled company flowed through the bodies of London's citizens, as coffee and chocolate houses boomed and addictions to sugar and tobacco took hold. On the back of the trade grew financial systems that facilitated it and profited from it. A web of banks which evolved to form today's household names – such as Barclays, HSBC and the Royal Bank of Scotland – and ship insurers – such as Lloyd's – all profited extensively from the trade. Their role in the slave trade is part of the forgotten history of the very same banks that later profited from the oil industry in West Africa.[11]

By the mid eighteenth century Bonny, on the eastern side of the Delta in Andoniland, had grown to be a substantial 'city state'. It was the largest place of trade on the Slave Coast, and each year 50,000 slaves passed through it. Meanwhile the profits and products of the Atlantic Triangle helped make distant London the premier city in Europe. On the Thames lay the market place from which slave products found their way up the Elbe, the Seine and the Rhine, to the coffee houses frequented by Bach, Voltaire and Mozart. A classical European civilization was fuelled in part by the far-distant labour of those carried down the creeks of the Delta in canoes.

Slaves built America too. Across the Atlantic, African labour and voracious European consumption made the plantation owners of Georgia, the Carolinas, Virginia and Maryland fantastically wealthy. In the 1780s, James Madison explained that he could make $257 on every Negro in a year, while spending only $12 or $13 on his keep. With this wealth came a confidence expressed not only in the mansions built along the James, York, Rappahanock and Potomac rivers, but also in a desire for self-rule, for independence from the English Crown. The slave plantation owners – Madison and Jefferson among them – were a driving force in the War of Independence, the drawing up of the Constitution, and the founding of the new capital, Washington.[12]

In 1807 the British abolished the slave trade, making it an illegal business for its own subjects, and began to enforce this new understanding upon other European slavers. A naval squadron was stationed at the island of Fernando Po (now Malabo, in Equatorial Guinea) to suppress the trade. Over the next 50 years, the Royal Navy seized almost 1,600 ships and freed 150,000 slaves destined for the Atlantic crossing – spending approximately £40 million in the process. Sierra Leone was established by the Abolitionists as a colony for freed slaves, its capital named Freetown. The transatlantic trade had effectively ended by the 1860s.[13]

In April 1864 the Thirteenth Amendment to the US Constitution passed through the Senate in Washington outlawed slavery, thereby decisively marking the end of the first Atlantic Triangle.

The First Oil Exploitation

In 1886 the Royal Niger Company was established in London. Again, as with the Royal African Company, British commercial and political interests were intertwined. Lord Aberdare, who had been Home Secretary for four years, was appointed the new company's Governor.

The aim of the Royal Niger Company was to gain monopoly control over the export of palm-oil from the Delta and further inland, and the import of manufactured goods from Britain, including tobacco, gunpowder, 'trade muskets' and vast amounts of spirits. In order to establish this position, they had to break the hold of powerful Nigerian traders in the Delta.

One such trader was called Nana of Itsekiri, on the Warri and Benin Rivers, on the western side of the Delta. Nana believed the British were cheating him on the price of palm-oil, and in 1886 decided to boycott them. In retaliation, he faced the full force of the Royal Navy, with large numbers of troops and four gunships armed with the most technologically advanced military equipment of the day.

Major Mockler Ferryman describes what happened next. When the 'final' attack was made, 'one hundred Constabulary men and one hundred and thirty-six bluejackets proceeded by land, while the remainder of the force advanced up the creek in the ship's boats. The result was a complete success, and the enemy, finding their guns taken in front and flank, made but a feeble resistance before taking to flight. The town was in the possession of the British force by 8 a.m., and during the next two days it was destroyed.'[14]

Once captured, Nana was tried for armed resistance, found guilty, and exiled to the Gold Coast for ten years. The clear message was: do not disrupt British commercial interests, or hinder the operation of 'free trade', otherwise you face the wrath of British military might. A pattern of military attacks on Delta towns had been set that was to continue for more than a century.[15]

Other palm-oil traders soon suffered the same fate. In the east of the Delta, an Igbo named Jaja had risen from slavery to become an enterprising palm-oil trader in Bonny. By now Bonny and its hinterland was exporting over 25,000 tons of palm-oil a year, more than half the quantity exported from Africa. In 1869 Jaja founded a trading community called Opobo, 25 miles to the east of Bonny. He successfully exploited the fleet of coal-steamers owned by Macgregor Laird that had begun to operate between Liverpool and West Africa, exporting palm-oil directly to Europe . In this way he effectively cut out the British palm-oil traders working out of Bonny, resulting in a series of skirmishes, which led Jaja to sign a treaty of protection with the British Vice Consul.

Mockler Ferryman describes how Jaja had 'made himself generally objectionable to the British traders'. He was subsequently invited onto a British gunboat by the Vice Consul, Harry H. Johnston, with the false promise of protection, whereupon he was kidnapped and sent into exile in the West Indies. Eventually in 1891 he was allowed to return to Opobo, but died on his return, a broken man.[16]

Four years later, in 1895, a British naval force under the command of Admiral Sir Frederick Bedford laid siege to Brass, the chief city of the Ijaw people of Nembe in the Delta. The siege was the result of a power struggle between King Koko of Nembe and the Royal Niger Company. Once again the company was keen to destroy the local palm-oil traders and called in the Navy. Ike Okonta and Oronto Douglas in their book *Where Vultures Feast* recall how 'After severe fighting, the city was razed to the ground. Over two thousand people, mostly women and children, perished in that attack launched in the name of Queen Victoria.' Whereas London has long forgotten these incidents as minute events in a Victorian empire, their memory is still vivid in the Delta.[17]

The Royal Niger Company was chartered by the British government to administer its newly established Niger Coast Protectorate, and in order to do so, the company established its own army. Like the East India Company before it, it was a private profit-making venture with its own private army. It expanded its operations inland, participating in the destruction of Benin (now Benin City, 20 miles north-east of the Delta), and the attack on the Fulah Empire of Nupe in 1897. The treasures of Benin were stolen, becoming in time a centrepiece of the British Museum's collection. The plaque in the museum reads: 'In 1897, following an attack on a British consular mission, a British punative expedition took Benin City, and sent the king into exile. Many of the brass objects from Benin City fell to the troops, and others were sold abroad to defray the costs of the expedition and compensate the victims.' By these means, the majority of what is now Nigeria was brought under the company's command.

By the mid 1890s, the Royal Niger Company had monopoly control of the export of palm-oil from ports such as Bonny, Brass, Opobo and Lagos. About 65 per cent was shipped to Britain and 25 per cent to Germany, passing through ports such as London, Liverpool and Hamburg into the industrial heart of Europe. Here it was used to make soap, candles, glycerine (and thence nitro-glycerine) and principally as a lubricant for machines and wheel-grease. 'Lagos oil', as it was known, was particularly vital to the tin-plate manufacturers of South Wales. Here was an economic relationship of two locations – West Africa and Europe – a new configuration of trade that had arisen from the demise of the three-cornered economy of the Atlantic Triangle.[18]

Just as sugar and tobacco had flowed through the bloodstream of London from the 1660s, manufactured by slave labour extracted from the Delta, now palm-oil from the Delta lubricated the workings of coal-driven machines whose motive power supplanted slaves as the engine of industrial production. The vegetation of the Delta lubricated Europe's industrial machine.

The Royal Niger Company's charter was revoked by the British government in 1899. The territories it had conquered were gathered together as the Niger Coast Protectorate, the Protectorate of Northern Nigeria, and the Lagos Protectorate, coming under the control of the Foreign Office and the Colonial Office. During the parliamentary debates concerning this process, the Prime Minister Lord Salisbury spoke in the Lords: 'It is impossible to mention the names of the founders of the company – the late Lord Aberdare, and especially Sir George Goldie – without recognising . . . the great enterprise and resource which place them high on the list of pioneers of English civilization in the dark places of the earth.'[19]

Colonial Rule in the Delta

One of the new governors of the Protectorates was Sir Frederick Lugard, who later became the first Governor of Nigeria. A soldier and explorer, Lugard had worked for the Royal Niger Company. It was his mistress who first coined the name 'Nigeria'.

In the book *Ogoni's Agonies*, Kwame Appiah quotes a letter from Lugard to his wife that shows the contempt the British had for the Ogoni: 'This evening I hear the Ogonis are up,' wrote Lugard. 'Moorhouse came to tell me and read the telegram that they have eaten two persons. "What sort of person," I asked, "were they Government employees?" He said, "Oh no, they were no one in particular." "Then let them eat some more," I said. "If Ogoni eats Ogoni, my withers are unwrung." '[20]

It was not until 1901 that colonial forces claimed Ogoni as a British Protectorate. The brutality of British rule clearly infuriated Ken Saro-Wiwa. 'The Ogoni,' he wrote, 'refused to accept British overlordship. In 1903 and again in 1905, the records speak of patrols being sent "to enforce administrative control" and of a number of villages being "destroyed". Such wanton destruction of life and property was not acceptable to the Ogoni and they resisted it.'

In 1913 yet another attack was launched against the Ogoni. 'This finally broke the resistance,' recalls Saro-Wiwa, 'and when in 1914 the religious centre of the Ogoni at Ka-Gwara was razed to the ground by Major Webber and a large police escort under Major G.H. Walker DSO, the Ogoni were finally subjugated.'[21]

It was not just the Ogoni who suffered repeated attacks. So did the neighbouring Andoni people. A force led by Captain A. Whitehouse, acting commissioner of Eastern Division of Niger Coast Protectorate, destroyed what his report called 'The House of Skulls' in the town of Andoni. The artefacts in it, the Andoni Hoard, were taken to the British Museum, where they remain.[22]

Military action necessitated, and facilitated, the building of infrastructure in the Delta – roads, bridges, jetties, harbours, the telegraph, barracks, courts and prisons. Port Harcourt, for example, was founded in 1913 – named after Viscount Harcourt, Secretary of State for the Colonies – to assist in the export of palm-oil, the import of British and European goods, and the movement of troops.

It also made possible the export of the coal discovered at Enugu, north of the Delta, in 1909: a railway from Enugu to Port Harcourt was rapidly constructed. Completed by 1913, this proved a military asset for the British when conflict broke out with the German colony of Kameroon in August 1914. Military actions often provided a source of forced labour, and in its turn the enlistment of forced labour for construction projects by the Colonial authorities sparked conflict.[23]

Colonial law and order was administered through a system of district commissioners, assisted by armed police, troops and the courts, and it was designed to ensure the safety of European commercial companies and the large number of Christian missionaries operating in the region. The district commissioners ruled 'indirectly' – as it was known – through the naming of approved chiefs, or 'Warrant Chiefs': heads of communities chosen by the colonial power because they were supportive.

Such appointments, made by the overwhelmingly dominant force in the Delta rather than by the communities themselves, were in stark contrast to the long tradition of clans choosing their own elders. They represented a system of control very similar to the methods used by the Nigerian government and the oil companies in the Delta today. By choosing which chiefs to recognize and which communities to favour with development projects, the outside powers, like the colonial power before them, can maintain control with minimal outlay, albeit at the cost of exacerbating intra-community tensions.

The rapid building of infrastructure between 1900 and 1940 later facilitated the exploitation of oil and gas in the Delta. A scheme of 'development' undertaken by the Colonial Administration in Lagos and overseen by the Colonial Office in London, it was financed largely through taxes raised in Nigeria. It marked a radical shift from the previous 250 years of British trade in the Delta, when the footprint had been limited to coastal barracoons (temporary slaving posts) and trading stations. Now forests were cleared for palm-oil, rubber plantations, and timber such as mahogany, which was felled for export.

The colonial industrial economy, though it had broken free from the monopoly of the Royal Niger Company, continued to be controlled by a handful of British companies – Paterson, Zochonis & Co. Ltd (still operating as PZ Cussons), Lever Brothers (now Unilever), the Bank of British West Africa, Barclays Bank, the United Africa Company, and Guinness.

Six of these firms formed the Association of West African Merchants, an oligopoly which by 1949 handled 66 per cent of Nigeria's imports and nearly 70 per cent of its exports.[24] As the Nigerian historian Toyin Falola argues, this 'near total control of economic power exercised by a small group of European firms, together with government support, gave rise to hatred of the aliens, and hence [of] the colonial government.'[25]

These were the norms of the monopoly control within which the industrialization of the Delta started. The first exploration for oil in Nigeria began with the Nigerian Bitumen Company, a subsidiary of a German firm, prospecting for oil in the area north of Lagos between 1907 and 1914. By 1912 German industry and government had realized that oil was the fuel of its economic future, not only for land transport but also for naval vessels. Germany and Britain were engaged in a fearsome arms race, which centred around the design of the Dreadnought-class warships.

In 1913, under Winston Churchill as First Lord of the Admiralty, the British fleet switched to oil as the fuel for its battleships, and the struggle between the two European empires could be seen in the search for oil in West Africa. When Britain established Nigeria in January 1914, it was declared that only British companies might prospect for oil in the colony. The defeat of Germany in 1918 meant the end of its colonial expansion in Africa, and the end of its oil exploration industry.[26]

The vast majority of the population of the Delta continued to live in a peasant economy of yams and cassava, fishing and hunting, interacting with the colonial system as conscripted labour, consumers of manufactured goods, and producers of a palm-oil cash crop on smallholdings. The industrial companies, which the colonial forces inevitably protected, were seen as the source of many of their woes, and effectively as the face of the government. A pattern had been set for the future.

The Second Oil Exploitation

In extensive grounds near Ascot in Berkshire lies Buckhurst Park, an imposing mansion and once home of Sir Henri Deterding, Chairman of Royal Dutch Shell. Deterding, the colossus who had overshadowed the company as executive director of Shell Transport & Trading (T&T) for 29 years, was approaching retirement at the age of 70 in autumn 1936.

At Shell's head office in St Helen's Court, off Bishopsgate at the heart of the City of London, Deterding was a commanding personality, engaged in the detail of the company's management and renowned for his brilliant financial acumen. In the board room of St Helen's, Deterding, along with other directors of Shell agreed to sanction release of the capital needed to purchase the exploration concession for the entire territory of Nigeria.

The venture was undertaken in collaboration with the Anglo-Iranian Oil Company (the AIOC, now BP), based at Finsbury Circus off Moorgate, five minutes' walk away from St Helen's Court. The deal negotiated with the chairman of AIOC, Sir John Cadman, established a new joint venture company – Shell-D'Arcy Explorations Parties – to prospect for oil in Nigeria. Such collaboration between the companies was not uncommon, and included a joint company for the marketing of oil products in Britain, Shell-Mex and BP Ltd.[27]

After discussions with the Secretary of State for the Colonies, William Ormsby-Gore, at the Foreign and Colonial Office, and with Sir Bernard Bourdillon, Governor of Nigeria, in Lagos, a decision was made to purchase an oil exploration licence for 370,000 square miles. This licence gave the company the right to search and drill for oil, but not to produce it. Most importantly, it gave Shell and BP a monopoly over Nigerian oil, echoing the monopoly held by the Royal Niger Company, and that held by the Royal African Company. Nigeria belonged to Britain.

Shell and BP were looking to secure reserves of oil – to ensure their 'energy diversity', by which they meant their diversity of supply. At the time they were heavily dependent upon just seven sources of oil production – the Dutch East Indies, the USA, Romania, Venezuela, Iraq, Mexico and Iran. The last two of these looked worryingly insecure at this time. Reza Shah of Iran had unilaterally cancelled the AIOC's concession in November 1932, and the company had only rescued itself from destruction by six months of painstaking negotiation with the Shah, led by Sir John Cadman. The AIOC concession was reduced by 75 per cent, and the Iranians forced hard terms on the company – 'I felt we'd been pretty well plucked,' said Cadman.[28]

Similarly, in Mexico, when he came to power at the end of 1934, General Lazaro Cardenas had signalled that there would be a renegotiation between the state and the oil companies. Shell's subsidiary, Mexican Eagle, produced 65 per cent of Mexico's oil, so the company fought hard to resist Cardenas over the following three years. Deterding was determined not to bend to the government's demands, so much so that the resident Mexican Eagle manager in Mexico said the Chairman of Royal Dutch Shell 'was incapable of conceiving of Mexico as anything but a Colonial Government to which you simply dictated orders'. Eventually, on 18 March 1938, Cardenas nationalized the entire Mexican oil industry.[29]

Nigeria was one such colonial government. However unknown the value of the geological prospects might be, the political prospects were strong. Nigeria remained firmly a part of the British Empire and the possibility of Nigerian independence seemed remote. Elsewhere in the Empire the two companies purchased concessions in Uganda, Kenya, New Zealand, and Canada, through the Foreign and Colonial Office and the respective governors. At the same time they were conducting explorations in the Gulf states of Bahrain, Kuwait and Qatar – all of which were clearly within the British Imperial sphere of influence.[30]

A Colonial Sound

The sound of explosive charges across the Delta announced Shell's decision to explore for oil. Utilizing the infrastructure of roads, railways, ports and telegraphs created by the Colonial administration, geological teams of the Shell-D'Arcy company criss-crossed the Nigerian concession from 1937 onwards searching for oil. Events in Mexico and the rumblings of war in Europe only served to emphasize the importance of this search, to the company and to the British Government. But the Second World War brought a halt to exploration in 1941.

After the war, with Shell and BP's connections to the British State enhanced by their vital role in supplying fuel to the Allied forces, the company resumed its search. However, the renewal of licences in 1949 had the geologists concentrating their attentions on the Niger Delta, reducing the concession from 370,000 to 60,000 square miles of southern Nigeria. In 1948 the company had begun a five-year mapping process, using aerial surveys. After 400 years of European engagement, the Delta was finally being measured out by Western eyes – by an oil company. Even today no detailed maps of the Delta are publicly available: large-scale charts have to be obtained from the oil companies.[31]

In September 1951 the increasing determination with which the exploration was being conducted was reflected by the formation in London of a new joint company, Shell-D'Arcy Petroleum Development Company. Although it was owned equally by Shell and AIOC, the management and technical advice was provided by Shell. So low key was AIOC's involvement that their representative in Nigeria noted 'a general impression that it was an entirely Shell project . . . the name D'Arcy meant nothing to the Nigerian.'[32]

William Knox D'Arcy was the gold-mining millionaire who had founded the company that became AIOC – in effect, the grandfather of BP. In 1954 a new government in Iran nationalized the oil industry, a blow that nearly destroyed the company, and AIOC changed its name to BP. The new joint venture thus became the Shell-BP Petroleum Development Company.

A month later, in October 1954, the first deep test well was drilled at Ihuo in Igboland, 10 miles north-east of Owerri, at the northern edge of the Delta. But it was dry. Over the following four years about fifteen further exploration wells were drilled across the Delta. Oil was discovered at Akata east of Bonny in Andoniland in 1954 – but in quantities too small to be commercial. The search continued until 1956, when the company first found sizeable oil reserves at Oloibiri in Ijawland.[33]

The Colonial Legacy

The find at Olobiri would not have been possible without colonial help. To Shell-BP, the colonial government was more than just a favourable government: Shell-BP's interests in Nigeria and those of the British state were completely intertwined. The British state was central to facilitating the oil company in its development of the Delta.

Any oil development undergoes a series of stages, some of which overlap. New stages – such as environmental assessment – have been added since the 1970s, but an oil well in the Delta in the 1930s had to be built in politics, in law, in finance, in geological data, and in engineering design, before finally being built on the ground.

For all of these, Shell-BP's relationship with the colonial government meant that it enjoyed extremely favourable conditions as manifest in The Mineral Oil Ordinance No. 17. Instituted by the British administration on the founding of the colony of Nigeria in 1914, the Ordinance decreed that: 'No lease or licence shall be granted except to a British subject or to a British company with its principal place of business within Her Majesty's dominions; the chairman and managing director (if any) and a majority of the other directors of which are British subjects.' Ostensibly decreed in order to protect the Imperial economy from German or French companies, this ordinance ensured that Shell-BP held a monopoly over Nigerian oil from 1936.[34]

The political underpinning of the venture was negotiated with the colonial authorities, the legal framework was ensured by the colonial legal system, the finance was allocated to the project because of the security for investments that the Empire provided, the colonial infrastructure facilitated the geological search, and so on.

It is an imperative of any corporation to maximize its profitability by dominating both the sites of production and its share of any particular market. The two oil companies with their Shell-Mex & BP Ltd. oil retail joint venture dominated the petroleum market in Britain, and through the legal regime in colonial Nigeria they were able to dominate a potential place of production.

Shell's continuing dominance in the country is part of Britain's colonial legacy. Some ninety years after the Mineral Oil Ordinance Act of 1914, Shell still enjoys a privileged position in Nigeria that is based on its colonial past. While the company has lost its monopolistic control, it is still by far the largest producer of oil in Nigeria. It still holds vital concessions. It still has a distinct advantage over its competitors. In June 2005, the journal *African Energy* ran an article on the state of Nigeria's oil and gas industry and talked of the company's dominance in the country: 'Such is Shell's historic position and the extent of its operations in Nigeria that no other company can compete in terms of reserves.'[35]

Who Am I?

JAMES MARRIOTT

My family possess a set of photographs taken in Eastern Nigeria around about 1913. One of them shows a man with curling moustache, broad-brimmed hat and rifle. He is seated upon the vast carcass of a hippopotamus splayed on a riverbank. 'Who am I?' he would later ask, moving around on all fours in a Surrey nursery. 'Mr Hippopotami' his stepdaughters would answer.

Cyril Pyke, my step-great-grandfather, was in the Colonial Civil Service in Nigeria between the ages of 33 and 42, from 1905 to 1914. From March to August 1912 and again between October 1913 and January 1914 he was District Commissioner of the Owerri District of the Eastern Province of Southern Nigeria. Approximately 925 square miles in extent, Owerri District covered the north-eastern quarter of the Delta.

His job was to impose and maintain law and order, and ensure that taxes – in the form of labour and crops – were collected from the Igbo peoples in his District. His retinue included a detachment of armed police. He could call upon troops stationed in the district under the command of Captain Taylor and Lieutenants Daley and Tyndal. Those arrested were tried in the District Commissioner's court or in one of the five Native Courts in the district. Those convicted could be imprisoned in leg irons at the district prison in Owerri.

Cyril's diary records the conscription of labour to assist the movement of troops: '*April 26 1912*: Warned Oguta chiefs for 50 carriers to take soldiers loads to Owerri. Reply from chiefs cannot do it.' A day later: 'Crossed over [Lake] Oguta with Capt. Sewell and 15 soldiers and interviewed the chiefs and warned them that the carriers must be supplied and that I should suspend their warrants should they fail to do so and take more serious action. These people have defied every District Commissioner stationed at Owerri.'

Labour was also conscripted to build roads – 'Took three Oguta chiefs over some of their section of road and showed them what work I required done at once.' The Port Harcourt–Enugu railway – 'Held a meeting of chiefs re railway labour . . . Dispatched 536 labourers to Port Harcourt for railway . . . Sent 1,820 labourers for the railway to Port Harcourt.'

As he conducted his tours of duty, Cyril took photographs of shrines, markets and the peoples in the area. He amused himself by hunting and, during his short posting as District Commissioner of Afikpo, playing golf.

On 1 January 1914, on the parade ground at Owerri, Cyril inspected the Guard of Honour of the Southern Nigerian Regiment drawn up before the flagpole from which flew the Union Jack, and then read the Governor General's message announcing the foundation of Nigeria:

To all the people of the Owerri District . . . I am going to read you a Proclamation from the Governor of Nigeria to all the peoples of Nigeria. His Majesty the King of England has decided that from today all the country from the sea, and all the country from the Hausas shall be one single country under one big Governor, so that all may work together for peace and prosperity. His Majesty the King of England has been pleased to appoint Sir Frederick Lugard as the big Governor over all, and by the help of God, he hopes that he will obtain wisdom to do this big work properly. He will try to make peace and justice to all.

On the completion of the reading, his typed memo records that the Igbo children of the Owerri school sang the National Anthem (one verse) then a royal salute was taken, and finally three cheers were called for His Majesty the King and His Excellency the Governor General.

After what seems to have been a standard experience as District Commissioner, Cyril Pyke returned to London and retired from the Colonial Service to work in the War Office. Soon after he married my great-grandmother, and settled near Dorking in Surrey.

When the First World War ended Cyril took up pig-breeding, and had a garden shed built in which to house his collection of artefacts collected in Nigeria and Borneo. My mother says that as a child she was never allowed to go inside. On his death in 1951, Cyril's wife donated the collection to the British Museum. Among the items were:

Composite drum, of wood with skin membrane attached by iron nails, plaited fibre and wooden wedges. Tomtom, used for dances by Natives, Southern Nigeria.

Wooden carved and painted mask, with white face. 'Maiden spirit' mask, Ibo, South East Nigeria.

Wooden carved paddle with a crocodile at the end. Itsekiri, Niger Delta.

Antique muzzle-loading Snider rifle taken from a prisoner at Lake Oguta, Southern Nigeria.

They were the remnants of an empire, gathered together in a garden shed in Surrey, mementoes of a colossal imbalance of power.[36]

CHAPTER THREE

Crisis After Crisis

Ogoni protest song, 1970:
'The Flames of Shell are flames of hell
We bask below their light
Nought for us serve the blight
Of cursed neglect and cursed Shell'[1]

We've Got Oil

The children thought it was a giant bird flying in the sky, making a terrible noise. They had never seen anything like it before. The helicopter landed on the long green grass of the lawn of Oloibiri's St Michael's church, built by missionaries sixty years earlier. It bore a logo they did not understand: that of the Shell–BP Development Company. As the village children watched open-mouthed, two more helicopters appeared over the palm-oil trees and landed on the clean, blue-green river, named after the town of Oloibiri in Ijawland. The oilmen had arrived.

The local teacher at the time, Princess Joy Amangala, recalled that 'several days later, some of the white men came back screaming "We've got oil! We've got oil!"' No wonder they were happy. Having spent some £15 million and more than 14 years looking for oil, Shell-BP had finally struck lucky: they had found oil in commercially viable quantities. Nigeria's oil in-dustry was born. The year was 1956.

Over the next few months a parallel town was built close to Oloibiri. It was called 'Shell Oloibiri', and in came a new road, electricity, water, prefabricated houses, and everything the oil workers wanted. Well, not quite everything. 'One Shell worker, Mr Taytee, asked for some girls to be brought to his cabin,' recalls Joy Amangala, 'but my friends and I laughed at the idea. Mr Taytee's tummy was a bucket-size.'[2]

Two years later the first shipment of oil was ready. In February 1958 Eric Drake, Chairman of Supply and Development for BP, flew from Heathrow airport to Lagos, then travelled on by road to Port Harcourt for the ceremonial announcement of the first shipment of Nigerian crude – 'Bonny Light'. Standing alongside Drake were senior representatives from Shell and the Shell-BP Development Company of Nigeria. The crude tanker slipped down the Bonny River and began its journey to Shellhaven in Essex, Shell's refinery at the mouth of the river Thames.

The crude that was loaded onto that first ship had come from a number of wells in the oil fields at Oloibiri and Afam in Ogoniland. She was the first of a steady stream of ships that sailed to Shellhaven and at BP's complex on the southern shore of the Thames estuary, the Kent Refinery.

At Shellhaven over the following weeks the Nigerian crude was refined into petrol, aviation fuel and other products. The petrol was reloaded onto a Shell river tanker which transported the fuel 30 miles up the Thames to the Shell-Mex & BP terminal at Wandsworth, in south-west London. From this depot, road tankers distributed the petrol to service stations in south London, Middlesex, Surrey and Sussex – fuel for the cars that symbolized the booming British post-war economy. That same year, 1958, saw the opening of the first motorway in the UK, the M6 near Preston.

Meanwhile, the aviation fuel refined from Bonny Light at

Shellhaven was transported to Heathrow, energy for planes such as that which had taken Drake to Lagos. That same year of 1958 saw the first transatlantic passenger service from London to New York. Oil from the Niger Delta was fueling the engines of the South of England. The geology of Nigeria burnt in the streets of London and in the skies above it.

Two years later, at Nigerian Independence, Shell-BP's spider's web of operations had begun to spread out from Oloibiri and Afam into other areas of the Delta (see Map 4). The company had twenty-four oil fields with commercial potential, of which around eleven were already producing. Although the first oil had been found at Oloibiri in Ijawland, it was Ogoniland, with five of the first eleven fields, that bore the brunt of Shell-BP's oil development.

These first finds were all oil fields, although when oil comes out of the ground, it is very rarely extracted just as oil: normally it has some natural gas with it, called in the industry 'associated gas'. Under the high pressures underground, this gas is actually dissolved in the oil, but separates from it as the pressure on the liquid is reduced on its way to the surface. At the surface the gas can be captured, piped away, and used as fuel for domestic or industrial purposes.

But for nearly fifty years Nigeria's 'associated gas', has been burnt off in vast flames tens of feet in length that roar across the landscape, flaring day and night. Within four years of the first oil find at Oloibiri, there were a hundred gas flares in the Delta. These huge flames are today still visible from the satellites in space. From 1958 to 2003, according to the Organisation of Petroleum Exporting Countries (OPEC), Nigeria produced a total of 22.8 billion barrels of oil. According to Shell, on average, 1,000 cubic feet of gas is flared per barrel of oil. The total gas flared – roughly 22.8 trillion cubic feet – is slightly more than the UK's total natural gas reserves in the North Sea in 2004. 'Some children have never known a dark

night even though they have no electricity,' wrote British envir-
onmentalist Nick Ashton-Jones after one visit.[3] The flares created a
new sound that had never existed before, and a new smell that
burnt villagers' nostrils and throats. And the acid rain that it
created rotted the corrugated roofs of their homes.

For the villagers living next to such constant degrading noise,
air and heat pollution, flares cause a lethal cocktail of health
problems such as child respiratory illnesses, asthma and cancer,
all leading to premature deaths. A groundbreaking report by
Environmental Rights Action (ERA) and the Climate Justice
Programme (CJP) has tried to quantify the damage gas flaring
does. They have estimated that in Bayelsa State alone, it is
statistically likely to cause 49 premature deaths, 5,000 respiratory illnesses among children and some 120,000 asthma attacks
and 8 additional causes of cancer each year.[4]

In all, this 'toxic cocktail' violates the communities' rights
guaranteed under Nigerian law, such as to live in dignity, and 'to
enjoy health and a satisfactory environment', conclude ERA and
the CJP.[5] If systematic and chronic pollution of the local
population were not a serious enough crime, there is also
pollution of the planet, and climate change.

The flaring that started at Oloibiri has continued every day
since. ERA and CJP describe it as 'a story of appalling careless-
ness, greed, corruption, double standards and environmental
racism. Perhaps, above all, it is a story of serial, cumulative and
shameful failure, on the part of British colonialism, the oil
companies and the Nigerian ruling elite.'[6] Shell has not responded formally to the report but its Non-Executive Chairman,
Lord Oxburgh, has provided one possible explanation for its
policy on flaring. In a 2005 interview he insisted that 'the locals
appreciate the flares as a heat source to dry their fish.'[7]

In the 1970s each field in the Delta was operated by a team of Shell engineers manning the drilling rigs, all brought in from Europe, assisted by some locally employed labour. The split between local and European labour has always been a source of contention. 'It is interesting that Shell should be encountering this difficulty about employing expatriates,' one Foreign and Commonwealth Office document noted in 1970. 'It seems to me ridiculous to suggest that "there are plenty of Nigerians who could work computers".'[8]

With the Europeans came all the trappings of a Western lifestyle, alien and luxurious to the locals, like constant electricity and water, televisions and fridges. So too came the prostitutes, alcohol and all the other less salubrious by-products of the oil industry.

And in came the bulldozers. For each oil field, forest was felled or farmland cleared to create the new industrial landscape. The shiny steel structures of the drilling rigs rose high above the flat land, mangrove and palm-oil forests. They created a new horizon that had never existed before.

From each well-head where the gas was flared, pipelines carried the crude oil in 'flowlines' to a central gathering point, or 'flow station'. Each flowline meant a strip was cut through the forest, mangrove, or farmland that had to be kept clear of vegetation – lines of industrialization cutting across villages or fragile ecosystems. In contrast, companies undertaking on-shore oil production in England buried these flowlines in order to minimize their environmental and human impact. But in colonial and immediately post-Independence Nigeria, communities bore the burden – in terms of the impact on their villages, farmland, creeks and forests – of Shell-BP taking the cheaper option of laying pipes above ground as opposed to burying them.

The oil's journey continued from flowline to flowstations –

large installations, once again built on land cleared of forest and farming, where the oil from each oilfield was gathered together and pumped into a main oil pipeline. These main lines ran to the terminal at Port Harcourt, where Shell engineers had designed and built a terminal on the banks of the Bonny River. Here tankers would load up to transport the oil to Europe.

Slowly but surely a grid of industrial oil development began to spread across the Delta. Communities faced the loss of their farmland. The web of pipelines was an echo of the web of roads and railways constructed at the opening of the colonial period fifty years before. They woke to the belching and burning of flares. Resentment about flaring burnt deep in the communities of the Delta, and while it might have been the cheaper option for the companies not to bury their pipelines, this issue would come back to haunt them.

As the first petrol from Nigerian crude was transported up the Thames from Shellhaven to the Wandsworth Shell depot, the river-tanker passed another construction site, that of the new Shell Centre at Waterloo. Constructed in Portland stone, with 26 storeys and its own cinema, shooting range and swimming pool, the building was opened on 12 June 1963 and towered over the Houses of Parliament on the opposite bank of the Thames.

Shell had moved its headquarters from St Helen's Court in the City, the place of the market, to Westminster, the place of the state. It was a bold statement of Shell's position in the political life of Britain and her colonies, a statement of confidence built on the back of the prospects for and the profits from oil extraction in provinces such as Nigeria. The Shell Centre was a set of towers, and the chairman's office on the 26th floor commanded one of the best views in London. It was a fitting representation of the hierarchical nature of the company. Each floor contained a different department – accountants on one floor, the marketing department on another. It was a building that emphasized the hermetic nature of the company – with all but a handful of its global activities being carried out by Shell staff.

For forty years Nigeria has helped fuel Shell's global empire, run predominantly from the Shell Centre in London. During the decades, as military dictators came and went, Shell stayed put in Nigeria. The oil industry is all about risk – political and financial – and the rich financial rewards for the company far outweighed the risks. Nigeria might have been politically unstable, but it was still more stable than the Middle East.[9] In this country of change, Shell stayed solid as a rock. The more unstable the regime of the day, the more important it was for it to give incentives for the oil companies to stay, because they were now providing the financial life-blood that enabled the regime to stay in power. Shell and the Nigerian government became intertwined.

Nigeria has also been a root cause of a corporate crisis that has resulted in the the merger in 2005 of Shell's two parent companies, Royal Dutch Shell and the Shell Transport and Trading Company. But this is not the first crisis Shell and its close collaborator, the British government, have had to face in Nigeria.

Just Not Cricket

Oloibiri, the Nigerian town where oil was first produced, is also the birthplace of the Ijaw leader Isaac Boro, seen as one of the first people to stand up and fight for the rights of the minorities of the Niger Delta. In February 1966 Boro, equipped with £150 and a red flag, formed the Niger Delta Volunteer Service. 'If we do not move,' he said, 'we would throw ourselves into perpetual slavery.' His mission was to take up with the oil companies 'their continued atrocities to our people and their wicked reluctance to improve the lot of the people they were bound to be associated with for long'. He wanted to 'make out estimated bills for payment by the oil companies with respect to inadequate damages paid to natives for cash crops and economic trees destroyed during their operations.' He declared an independent state in the Niger Delta, and announced that all oil contracts were null and void. But the revolution was short-lived.

In a reflection of how the colonial authorities had dealt with 'subversion' that was also a precursor to later events, the Army was called in. Boro and his men watched the soldiers move into position using pontoon boats provided by Shell. The following month, Boro handed himself in. The first Ijaw revolution was over, though not forgotten. Boro was charged with treason, but his death sentence was commuted. He was killed during the Biafran War, fighting as a Federal soldier.[10]

The Biafran War that started in 1967 nearly ripped Nigeria apart. It also threatened the Shell-BP oil operations which had been growing in the region for the past decade. Political, ethnic and economic factors all played a part in the build-up to the war, but at its heart the conflict was about oil. It was 'not so much a war to maintain the unity and integrity of the country,' argue Ike Okonta and Oronto Douglas, 'as a desperate gambit by the Federal government to win back the oil fields of the Niger Delta from Biafra.'[11]

In January 1966 a military coup against the democratic government had resulted in the death of the then Federal Prime Minister, Sir Tafawa Balewa. It was followed by a counter-coup in July 1966 that landed a Christian northerner, General Jack Gowon, in power. The governor of the Eastern region, where the vast majority of Nigerian oil reserves are found, proclaimed independence, wanting to keep the precious oil revenues in the new state of Biafra. On 6 July 1967 the Federal government, led by General Gowon, declared war to prevent this secession.

An indication of how concerned the British were about the war is given in a document sent from Harold Wilson, the then Prime Minister, to the Foreign and Commonwealth Secretary. Dated some three weeks into the war, it states: 'It is of national importance that the Shell-BP investment in Nigeria, which is a major British interest, of crucial importance for our balance of payments position and for our economic recovery, should be protected. I therefore wish that everything should be done, as a matter of the greatest possible urgency, but for the present within the context of our existing policy on Nigeria, to help Shell-BP and the Federal Nigerian authorities to establish effective protection of our oil investments.'[12]

Although the British government saw Shell-BP's oil as 'our' oil, they had a problem: they could not be seen to become directly involved in the war. The Foreign Secretary Michael Stewart replied to the Prime Minister that the Foreign and Commonwealth Office (FCO) were in 'continuous touch with Shell' and David Barran over what to do. Barran, as Chairman of the Committee for Managing Directors, working out of the Shell Centre in London, was ultimately responsible for Shell-BP's operations in the country. In his book about the global oil industry, *Seven Sisters*, Anthony Sampson says Barran 'was a figure of stature in the oil world; he was precisely articulate, wore a monocle and had the style of a cultivated country squire.'[13]

After Shell-BP's installations came under attack by the Biafrans, the FCO arranged for 'some light guns for anti-aircraft defence to be made available to the Nigerians . . . whilst obviously we cannot attach strings to the supply, we will do our best to see that they play their proper part in the defence of the Shell-BP installations.' The government also gave Shell the 'names of five suitably qualified retired officers . . . to advise them on passive air defence measures (e.g. camouflage, decoy installations).' This man would be employed by Shell-BP on a temporary contract.

Stewart also offered General Gowon 'a visit by two Royal Air Force officers to see whether there is anything they can do to advise the Federal authorities on how they could better prosecute the air war'. However, 'the officers would be ostensibly on a visit to, and attached to, the High Commission and would be in plain clothes. We would hope that their presence would escape the attention of the press . . . we should certainly wish to avoid any impression that Her Majesty's Government were directly involved in the conduct of air operations in Nigeria.'[14]

The British government was walking a tightrope. On the one hand, they were helping the Federal government and Shell-BP in private; on the other, they wanted to be seen to be doing little in public. In October 1967 Michael Stewart met representatives of Shell and BP. A speaking note prepared for him said: 'We cannot allow Nigeria to become our Vietnam. It is a matter for the Nigerians but if, because of the urgency of the need, they wished to recruit white mercenary gunners and took the initiative in looking for them, we might be able to give them some covert help in recruitment. You might like to suggest to them they should do this. To save face the gunners could be described as technicians . . . the continuance of your operations is a matter of national importance to us.'[15]

South of the Nigerian coast in the middle of the Gulf of Guinea are the islands of São Tomé, which in the late sixties were still a Portuguese colony. Shell's operations on the islands were also causing the British government some concern. A letter from the High Commission in May 1969 outlined them: 'You will, I imagine, already be aware from your close relations with Shell in the context of the Nigerian war, that Shell are also fuelling the planes carrying the airlift into Biafra from São Tomé. This presents them with a minor conflict of interest.'[16]

The letter continued: 'Shell are the only company who have been supplying aviation fuel at São Tomé. When the war began they supplied the few planes staging there with fuel. This represented a small amount. As the war continued the amounts became larger, and in a modest way represented what appeared to be a money-spinner for Shell. One of their customers was the American gun-runner, Wharton, who a year or so ago was flying arms into Biafra via Portugal and São Tomé. Shell was apparently unwise enough to give him credit, and he has left them with the bad debt of 5 million escudos (say £75,000). According to the local and newly arrived Shell manager here, his head office told him in London that the less they knew about the Shell operations in São Tomé the better. They are evidently willing to do business there as long as this does not attract unfavourable publicity.'

The British wondered 'whether any interruption or reduction of the airlift from São Tomé into Biafra could help to bring about the end of the war? If so, then Shell could perhaps be prevailed upon to cut off their supplies of aviation fuel to São Tomé for a short period.'

One of the hand-written suggestions from the FCO in response was: 'If you felt that this might be put to Shell, it could perhaps be in the basis that gun-running to armed rebels against a regime with which we (and the Dutch) have close and cordial relations is naturally an activity on which HMG frowns and would hope that any partly British company would avoid entanglement in such activity.'[17]

The war ended when the commander of the 3rd Marine Commando Division, Olusegun Obasanjo, now President of Nigeria, accepted the surrender of Biafran forces in January 1970. The oil industry, having scaled back operations during the war, was keen for a full-scale expansion. It soon happened. By the early 1970s BP and Shell's combined investment in the country was some £100 million a year.[18]

There were setbacks, however. The British felt that their support for the Federal side in the war should have paid commercial dividends for Shell-BP. This was not to be. Hand-written notes on documents from the UK National Archives in London reveal that 'Shell-BP do not seem to expect to get further concessions in Nigeria' but just 'hoped the Nigerians will not try to change the terms of the existing concessions'.[19]

The British and Shell were also annoyed that their support for the Federal government had not stood them in greater stead than the Italians and French, who had supported the Biafrans. After Shell 'expressed surprise' to the FCO that nothing more had been made of the French and Italian involvement with the Biafrans, one FCO official wrote: 'We have allowed the French to get clean away with what they did in Nigeria and it is we, and not the French, who are now having a rough time with the Nigerians. I think myself this is deplorable, but results from our playing cricket while other people are playing karate.' [20]

A Forty-Year Fight

In 1965, two years after Shell moved into the Shell Centre and two years before the Biafran war started, an Ogoni school teacher from Taabaa, Sam Badilo Bako, sent a letter to Shell-

BP. 'Today, we need education, we need employment, we want to eat, we want to live,' said Bako. 'We do not want our children to remain out of school . . . we do not want to lack money because Shell has removed land, which used to be our main source of revenue. In short, we do not want to live in a vicious circle in which we shall see Shell-BP as the authors of our misfortune and our oppressors . . . Is it not an irony that those who live on top of wealth should be the poorest people in the nation?'[21]

At the height of the Biafran war, in April 1968, Ken Saro-Wiwa, then a member of the Rivers State Executive, penned a pamphlet that came straight from the heart. Titled *The Ogoni Nationality Today and Tomorrow*, it embodied his first published ideas on the Ogoni struggle. 'The Rivers State has been created, and a new Nigeria born. But we must remember that no matter the system of government, unless a people take a destiny into their own hands, no improvement will come to them.'[22] It was his first rallying call to his people.

Saro-Wiwa later wrote about how his 'pious' hopes failed to stir the Ogoni leadership at the time. But by 1970 certain Ogoni chiefs had had enough of living with Shell-BP as their neighbour and occupier. In his book *Genocide in Nigeria*, Saro-Wiwa recalls what happened: 'Matters came to a head in April 1970 when Ogoni leaders, unable to bear the chicanery and heartlessness of the Company, were forced to petition the Military Governor of Rivers State in a carefully considered memorandum.'

In a 'Humble Petition', Ogoni chiefs wrote that they were 'alerting the State Government to the fact that the Shell-BP operations in this Division are seriously threatening the well-being, and even the very lives, of the people of Ogoni Division.' They argued that Shell-BP 'destroys cash crops and economic trees without giving adequate compensation to their owners'. As the current Commissioner for Education in Rivers State, Saro-Wiwa also received a copy.[23]

Just under two months later, a Mr J. Spinks, the Manager for Eastern Division for Shell-BP, (see Chart 1) noted that this petition was 'one of a series which have originated' from Ogoni over the 'past few years'. 'Statements are made,' he argued in his reply to it, 'which, on examination, bear little relation to what is actually taking place. Regrettably this petition is no exception to the rule.' Spinks went on to argue that Shell-BP had 'been extremely careful to ensure that our operations cause minimal disturbance to the people in the areas in which we operate . . . There can be no doubt,' he concluded, that 'the incidental benefits accruing to Ogoni Division from Shell-BP's presence there greatly outweigh any disadvantages.'[24]

Saro-Wiwa met Spinks on a couple of occasions and characterized him as 'a genial and accommodating man', but decribed his letter as 'Shellspeak' that could easily be dismissed. Saro-Wiwa also argued that Shell-BP's assertion that it had a good record was publicly undermined when just over a month later there was a major installation blow-out at Bomu, in Ogoniland, that lasted three weeks. The blow-out caused outrage. 'Our rivers, rivulets, and creeks are all covered with crude oil,' the Dere Youths Association wrote. 'We no longer breath the natural oxygen, rather we inhale lethal and ghastly gases. Our water can no longer be drunk unless one wants to test the effect of crude oil on the body. We no longer use vegetables, they are all polluted.'[25] Saro-Wiwa wrote in 1992 that the area remained a wasteland for decades.[26]

Spinks's contention that the Ogoni complaints were at odds with the situation on the ground is contradicted by internal FCO correspondence. It was Mr Spinks whom an FCO official met that November as well as the then Colonel Obasanjo, among others. While the FCO official was quite overcome by Spinks's 'enthusiasm' for oil, he noted that Spinks 'clearly has little interest in anything outside oil. He had no views on the political scene, local, national or international. When we asked about conditions in Port Harcourt, no more than 2–3 miles from the Shell-BP work area, he said he had little idea since he had only been there about four times in six months. Others confirmed that the oil company personnel keep very much to themselves. This appears to cause some resentment amongst other members of the British community.'[27] But it is the resentment of the communities of the Delta that has come back to haunt Shell time and time again.

'White' versus 'black'

In the early 1970s other issues to do with Nigeria were beginning to occupy Shell-BP and the British government, fundamentally intertwined as they were. At the birth of the joint venture in 1936, Shell's partner BP was 51 per cent owned by the British state. From 1914, when Winston Churchill purchased shares in AIOC on behalf of the state, until the sale of these shares from 1976, the British government held the controlling stake in BP. The government operated an arm's-length policy in relation to the company's management, through the simple mechanism of appointing two members of BP's board. The Shell-BP Petroleum Development Company was, consequently, in part a British state-owned company.

Shell-BP and the government worried that Nigeria might follow Libya and nationalize its oil industry. General Gowon had also expressed 'admiration for Algeria', a fact that was 'not welcomed' by the British government, worried about the closeness of Iraq, Algeria and Libya.[28] If Shell-BP operations in the country were nationalized, it would be the British government and not just Shell-BP that would suffer.

But what was really worrying the British government and Shell-BP was the threat of some kind of retributive action by the Nigerians in the face of British government support for the white governments of Rhodesia (now Zimbabwe) and South Africa. In July 1970 an FCO note outlined how Ashley Raeburn, a Director on the Board of Shell (see Chart 1) had called 'this morning to put on record the interest of Shell in the possible repercussions of policies which might be adopted towards South Africa and Rhodesia'.[29]

Ashley Raeburn was an Oxford graduate with a love of walking, gardening and music. He had come to Shell from the Civil Service, where he had worked at the then Ministry of Food and HM Treasury. Having been Group Treasurer, he was now Director of Shell International Petroleum Company with responsibility for Africa, India and Pakistan. He was later appointed CBE (Commander of the Order of the British Empire).[30]

After the meeting at the FCO Raeburn left behind a 'strictly confidential' note outlining the 'Implications for the commercial interests of the Royal Dutch/Shell group' resulting from the 'British Policy in Africa'. Although Shell's investment in South Africa was considered 'significant, profitable and one which the Group is anxious to preserve and develop', it was not so 'critical to future Group profitability as the investment in exploration and oil production activity in Nigeria'. Investment in Nigeria was also likely 'to grow more rapidly than [that] in South Africa over the next decade'. Because of Shell-BP's investment in Nigeria, the leverage 'Black Africa' had on the company was 'very considerable'.[31]

The recently independent 'Black African' states were stalwart in their opposition to the white apartheid regime in South Africa, and Nigeria, as the most populous of these states, had assumed leadership of 'Black Africa'. Hence Shell's concern. Later that month the Chairman of Shell, David Barran, met Sir Alec Douglas-Home, former Conservative Prime Minister and now Foreign and Commonwealth Secretary in Edward Heath's government. Barran 'raised the question of arms for South Africa as it affected Nigeria. Shell was apprehensive of the reaction of the African states' and feared that General Gowon might place restrictions on Shell-BP's oil production in Nigeria. 'This would be a serious matter for the UK', creating a 'dangerous situation'. Barran pointed out that Nigerian oil was 'good quality' and 'the one major counter-weight to Arab oil'. Douglas-Home responded that 'the whole issue had been immensely exaggerated.'[32]

So the British government was not yet publicly worried about possible Nigerian action with regard to South Africa; but their concerns were heightened when in May 1971 the Nigerian National Oil Corporation was established. Two months later Nigeria joined OPEC. The first step in the 'indigenization' of Nigeria's oil had begun. Oil now accounted for 75 per cent of Nigeria's export revenues – up from 1 per cent in 1958.[33] This meant that Nigeria was increasingly dependent on the international oil market.

The South African problem continued to vex Shell-BP. In April 1972 David Barran, now Sir David, met Sir Alec Douglas-Home again at the FCO. Shell-BP was by now investing a million pounds a week in Nigeria.[34] Barran said Shell were worried by the 'unpleasant threats and innuendoes and suggestions that Nigeria might follow the Libyan president' and once again 'stressed the importance of Nigerian oil to the United Kingdom' and the fact that it provided a 'counter balance to Arab oil'. Sir Alec replied that 'he had these considerations very much in mind'.[35]

By the following month the FCO and the Department of Trade and Industry had investigated potential scenarios of Nigerian action against BP and Shell. The conclusion was that the probable higher limit of Nigerian action designed to 'spite HMG [Her Majesty's Government] would be expropriation of the BP share (50 per cent) of the joint Shell-BP company'. However, 'expropriation of the Shell share alone is unlikely as a means of getting at HMG because only 40 per cent of the shareholding is British and HMG has no direct stake.'[36]

This latter observation led Lord Rothschild, ex-MI5 agent and head of Prime Minister Edward Heath's Central Policy Review Staff, to write to Robert Armstrong, Heath's principal Private Secretary: 'BP's vulnerability in such circumstances would clearly be less if HMG's shareholding were reduced (or eliminated) and if the all-British character of the company were diluted.'[37]

A document in the UK National Archive bears Armstrong's neat handwriting, informing the Prime Minister of Rothschild's suggestion: 'I am not clear that we do want to respond to this. Admittedly we might be less exposed to Nigerian threats of expropriation. Against that, however, German or Japanese participation would not be any help in arguments with OPEC about participation for the exporting countries – indeed it might whet their appetites. And we should be in a less strong position to maximise the benefits for this country (as opposed to Europe) for the exploitation of North Sea Oil.'

Above this note, in the right-hand corner, is Ted Heath's

scribble: 'I do not wish to reopen this, largely because of X below', which corresponds to the section on the North Sea. 'The reason the Nigerians would not go for Shell surely is because of the 60% Dutch holding, not because there is no British Gov. interest.'[38]

The issue continued to worry both Shell and the British government, but the National Archive has yet to release more up-to-date documents. Nigeria's military government finally nationalized BP's share in 1979. The person who ordered it was none other than General Olusegun Obasanjo, the country's military ruler at the time.[39] With BP's share nationalized, Shell would have to endure any further crises on its own. It had not long to wait.

The Militarization of Commerce

The company was about to enter a new, much more controversial stage of its Nigerian history, one that continues to this day. Iko is a small fishing village on one of the many sand-barrier islands that extend along the Nigerian coast. On the one side is the Atlantic, on the other mangrove swamps and brackish creeks. Shell-BP had struck oil in 1973 in the village in Andoniland, which is next to Ogoni. According to Environmental Rights Action the company was gas-flaring twenty-fours hours a day.

In 1980, the year after BP's nationalization, the community sent a letter to SPDC and the Federal government demanding 'compensation and restitution of our rights to clean air, water, and a viable environment'. They received no reply. Two years later they peacefully demonstrated against Shell, asking them to be a 'good neighbour to us'. The police were called, and demonstrators were arrested and mistreated.

In 1987, the community once again held a peaceful demonstration. In response SPDC called in the Mobile Police Force (MPF), who were transported in three company speedboats. Two people were killed and nearly forty houses destroyed, making 350 people homeless. The troop's use of Shell-BP's transport was reminiscent of Boro's experience 21 years earlier.[40]

This murder of two civilians by the state forces of the military government of General Babaginda, marks a watershed in the history of the Delta. The increasing mobilization of the military by the oil companies in response to community protests is resented by many in the Delta.

The communities point out the oil companies would not act like that in Britain or America. From now on any community protesting ran the risk of military repercussions. Repercussions could mean death. The pattern had been set. Since then oil operations have become intertwined with the Nigerian military and MPF. Violence has become the norm.

The use of the military and MPF by the oil companies has created huge bitterness in the communities. Initially Shell defended its position by arguing that requests for mobile 'police assistance was in strict accordance with Federal government requirements when interruption to oil production may be caused.'

However the company later modified its position to: 'SPDC is not required to inform the military or any governing body of any demonstration. It has never claimed that this is the case. What SPDC has said is that it regards itself as being under a duty to alert the authorities if it thinks that actions [sic] is going to occur which will result in damage to oil installations and disruption to oil production'.[41]

This change in their approach reflects the dilemma oil companies find themselves in, working in a country like Nigeria where the use of force is much more routine than in the companies' host countries. So the likelihood is that if the oil companies do call for 'military assistance' there will be violence, regardless of the oil companies' wishes. The communities, for their part, blame the oil companies for this violence as much as they do the police or military. They see the violence as being the responsibility of the oil companies. The use of the military by the companies is now becoming routine to protect their installations. Indeed the WAC report (see Chapter One) even noted that when Shell staff 'and particularly senior staff, visits the community they are typically escorted by the Mobile Police.'

This sends various messages to the communities, including the sense of 'victimisation when the company tries to bully us' and reinforces the notion that Shell was 'stealing oil' because 'why would they otherwise come armed [with police and army]?'[42]

In 1990 the Etche people demonstrated against Shell at the village of Umuechem 'because they had seen Shell continually exploit their land without adequate compensation', according to one villager. Despite what had happened before, Shell specifically requested the MPF. A letter written by Joshua Udofia, Manager for the Eastern Division for SPDC, said: 'In anticipation of the above threat, we request that you urgently provide us with security protection (preferably Mobile Police Force) at this location.'[43]

The MPF subsequently massacred 80 people and destroyed 495 houses, as well as countless vehicles and motor-cycles. The MPF then killed and ate all the livestock of the village, including the goats and chickens. The subsequent Commission of Inquiry heard from the villagers that the demonstrations had been peaceful. The reason for their protest was that Shell's 'drilling operations have had serious adverse effects on the Umuechem people who are predominately farmers, in that their lands had been acquired and their crops damaged with little or no compensation, and [they] are thus left without farmlands or means of livelihood. Their farmlands are covered by oil spillage / blow-out and rendered unsuitable for farming.'[44]

The Inquiry blamed the police for the massacre, and did not attribute any blame to Shell. The company tried to distance itself from the killings, saying the problems of the community 'were not really of Shell's making at all'.[45] The company also maintained it was 'inconceivable that SPDC would have suggested the deployment of the Mobile Police if it had had an inkling of what might happen'. It added that the Iko incidents three years previously in which the MPF had killed several protesters 'did not stand out in the minds of SPDC people'.[46] Despite these events, Shell was to again request military assistance and protestors would again be shot.

Shell argues that it has not operated in Ogoni since January 1993. However, in late April 1993 the Shell contractor Willbros started bulldozing people's farmland in the Ogoni village of Biara for the construction of the Rumuekpe–Bomu pipeline. Shell and Willbros claim that the company had followed all legal land acquisition procedures. The construction work provoked mass demonstrations that according to Human Rights Watch were totally peaceful. When Karalolo Korgbara attempted to collect what was left of her crops, she was shot in the arm by soldiers, and the arm later had to be amputated.[47]

On 3 May thousands of protestors gathered to complain about this shooting. Another demonstrator, Agbarator Otu, was shot in the back and killed, and a further twenty people were injured.[48] That same day James Ken Tillery, the Willbros Divisional Manager, wrote to Joshua Udofia, Managing Director of Shell's Eastern Division, who had called in the MPF in Umuechem. Tillery complained about the security situation and urgently requested that SPDC take 'necessary action for a timely resolution to the problems in order to mitigate further cost and schedule implications'.[49]

On receipt of this letter, the following day, 4 May, Udofia sent a letter to Chief Rufus Ada George, the Governor of Rivers State, enclosing a copy of the Willbros letter. Rufus Ada George was an ex-Shell employee, and relations between MOSOP and George were poor.[50] 'As at now, work has been suspended in this area of the line which carries a significant portion of the crude oil production from Shell and Elf operations,' wrote Udofia. 'We humbly request the usual assistance of His Excellency to enable the project to proceed.'[51] 'Usual assistance' meant the military. Shell later admitted that Willbros had paid the 'field allowances and transportation' of the military, although it maintained that 'the Willbros army escort was not involved in any incident that caused injury to or the death of third parties'.[52]

Five months later Udofia was again embroiled in controversy in Ogoni. In October 1993 Shell, eager to re-enter Ogoni, visited the village of Korokoro accompanied by 'security personnel provided by the government'. The community protested against the visit. But later that month 24 armed personnel returned to 'dialogue' with the community. Under the command of Lieutenant Colonel Okuntimo, soldiers from the 2nd Amphibious Brigade accompanied Shell staff into Ogoni. These soldiers were being paid field allowances by Shell. Three people were shot, resulting in the death of one person, Uebari Nna. Shell doubted whether 'any member of the community was shot or wounded': Dr Owens Wiwa, a medical doctor, carried out the autopsy.[53] Saro-Wiwa called it 'unprovoked murder' and 'further confirmation of the collaboration of Shell and the Nigerian security forces in the genocide of the Ogoni people'.[54]

The Korokoro community was so outraged that two company fire-trucks were 'stolen'. In a letter dated 25 October, Egbert Imomoh, the new Manager for Shell's Eastern Division, wrote to Ada George to seek 'possible assistance in recovering the fire vehicle'.[55] The following day Imomoh and Udofia wrote again to Ada George, reiterating the 'need for adequate security for our operations in the Ogoni area'.[56] To the commission set up to examine these issues, known as the Oputa Panel (see Chapter 1), Imomoh later swore under oath that Shell had not been involved in any human rights abuses in the Delta.

Despite his involvement in these incidents today, fifteen years later, Joshua Udofia is employed by Shell as a 'senior corporate advisor' based in London. He was Shell's representative at the launch of the All-Party Parliamentary Group on the Niger Delta in June 2005 in London. Some in Ogoni regard as insensitive Udofia's presence at a meeting that is investigating the causes and solutions to the conflict of the Delta.

According to Shell these two incidents in 1993 were the only ones before 1996 in which the company paid the field allowances of the military. But they were also paying the police. Just two months later, in December 1993, Phil Watts, the Managing Director of Shell Companies in Nigeria, wrote to the Inspector General of Police in Lagos to 'reiterate our appreciation for the excellent co-operation we have received from the Nigerian Police Force in helping to preserve the security of our operations'.

Watts also confirmed that 300 police in Port Harcourt and 250 in Warri had been assigned to Shell. To facilitate this, Watts gave Shell's 'commitment to provide complete logistics, accoutrement and welfare support' to the police assigned them, and to 'fully support the cost of setting up and maintaining the contingents'. Watts also confirmed the number of Shell's 'Spy police' at 600.

In the letter, Watts asked for permission to upgrade its firearms, which included semi-automatic weapons and pump-action shotguns. Possibly to persuade the police to agree to his request, Watts emphasizes 'that SPDC produces more than 50 per cent of Nigeria's oil, which has a consequential major impact on the country's economy.'[57] It was these revelations that caused Claude Ake, Saro-Wiwa's old friend, to say that Shell had privatized Nigeria and that 'it is time to call Shell to order and account'.[58]

As the Ogoni campaign intensified through 1993 and 1994, the backlash wrought on them by the military was beyond the comprehension of most people. Their campaign led to some 2,000 Ogoni being killed, some 30,000 made homeless, countless others tortured and raped.[59] It led to the judicial murder of Saro-Wiwa and the eight others. Saro-Wiwa claimed that he and the others had been condemned to death as a result of their campaign against Shell.

Although there is no longer a military Federal government in Nigeria, there are still claims that Shell operates behind the shield of the military and that the militarization of commerce continues to this day. Ledum Mitee, the President of MOSOP, says that Shell is still paying people in the police armouries. 'I have it on good authority that for the last year Shell has given contributions to the security forces of some $2 million.' Mitee argues that Shell are also 'engaging' retired military personnel who used to be in the Abacha regime, 'some of whom have been cited for human rights abuses'.

'They use these people to bring in the military to provide a security shield,' he continues. 'I think we have gone beyond the point where they can deny they operate behind a security shield. Some of the people who work in armoury departments of the security forces have top-up fees from Shell, which is supposed to be an inducement for them when there is some Shell-related operation. Guns are released without any bottle-necks.'[60]

In response Shell says that 'Due to the security situation in the Niger Delta, the Nigerian government from time to time deploys teams of combined forces to patrol areas around our facilities. These forces are paid by the government and, when requested by the government, we provide logistics support.' However, the company maintains that 'It is illegal to hire private security in Nigeria. Many companies use supernumerary police officers, who are assigned to protect companies' facilities from crime. We do not pay "top up fees". We do pay field allowances as requested by the government as part of our logistics support.'[61]

But many people, including Ken Wiwa, believe it is time to hold Shell to account for its close association with the military. 'You can't just commit a crime against a people,' he says. 'You have to be held accountable. It is a basic principle of law. If you commit a crime you have to be held accountable for that crime.'[62]

Chart 1. Structure of Shell, BP and Shell-BP Nigeria, 1970

Companies are 100% owned by parent company unless otherwise stated

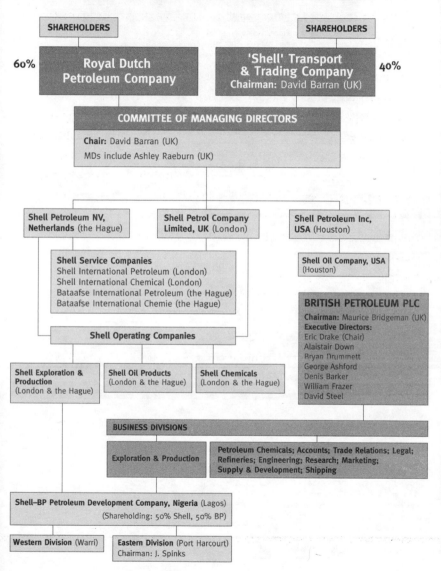

Chart 2. Structure of Shell and Shell Nigeria, 2005

Companies are 100% owned by parent company unless otherwise stated

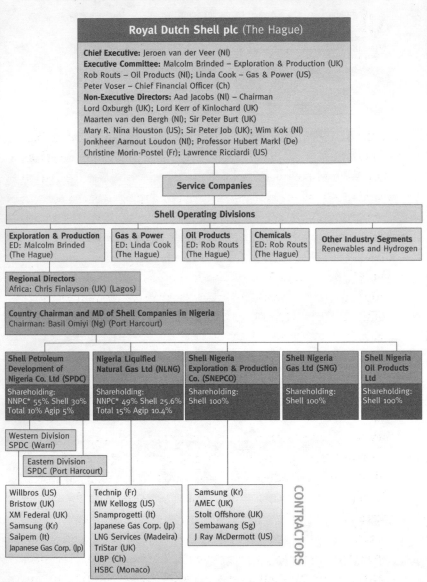

Royal Dutch Shell plc (The Hague)

Chief Executive: Jeroen van der Veer (Nl)
Executive Committee: Malcolm Brinded – Exploration & Production (UK)
Rob Routs – Oil Products (Nl); Linda Cook – Gas & Power (US)
Peter Voser – Chief Financial Officer (Ch)
Non-Executive Directors: Aad Jacobs (Nl) – Chairman
Lord Oxburgh (UK); Lord Kerr of Kinlochard (UK)
Maarten van den Bergh (Nl); Sir Peter Burt (UK)
Mary R. Nina Houston (US); Sir Peter Job (UK); Wim Kok (Nl)
Jonkheer Aarnout Loudon (Nl); Professor Hubert Markl (De)
Christine Morin-Postel (Fr); Lawrence Ricciardi (US)

Service Companies

Shell Operating Divisions

Exploration & Production
ED: Malcolm Brinded
(The Hague)

Gas & Power
ED: Linda Cook
(The Hague)

Oil Products
ED: Rob Routs
(The Hague)

Chemicals
ED: Rob Routs
(The Hague)

Other Industry Segments
Renewables and Hydrogen

Regional Directors
Africa: Chris Finlayson (UK) (Lagos)

Country Chairman and MD of Shell Companies in Nigeria
Chairman: Basil Omiyi (Ng) (Port Harcourt)

Shell Petroleum Development of Nigeria Co. Ltd (SPDC)
Shareholding:
NNPC* 55% Shell 30%
Total 10% Agip 5%

Nigeria Liquified Natural Gas Ltd (NLNG)
Shareholding:
NNPC* 49% Shell 25.6%
Total 15% Agip 10.4%

Shell Nigeria Exploration & Production Co. (SNEPCO)
Shareholding:
Shell 100%

Shell Nigeria Gas Ltd (SNG)
Shareholding:
Shell 100%

Shell Nigeria Oil Products Ltd
Shareholding:
Shell 100%

Western Division
SPDC (Warri)

Eastern Division
SPDC (Port Harcourt)

Willbros (US)
Bristow (UK)
XM Federal (UK)
Samsung (Kr)
Saipem (It)
Japanese Gas Corp. (Jp)

Technip (Fr)
MW Kellogg (US)
Snamprogetti (It)
Japanese Gas Corp. (Jp)
LNG Services (Madeira)
TriStar (UK)
UBP (Ch)
HSBC (Monaco)

Samsung (Kr)
AMEC (UK)
Stolt Offshore (UK)
Sembawang (Sg)
J Ray McDermott (US)

CONTRACTORS

* NNPC: National Nigerian Petroleum Company

All My Life

ANDY ROWELL

So the first recorded letter from Ogoni was sent in 1965, the year of my birth. That was forty years ago. The following year, Isaac Boro formed the Niger Delta Volunteer Service. For the last 40 years the Ogoni and Ijaw have fought for their rights to control their own resources and for a clean environment. For them, Shell has represented a forty-year fight for their right to control their resources and to a clean environment. Nothing has changed. For forty years. Just stop for a moment and think what has happened to the world in forty years: a generation of huge political, social, cultural and technological change. But in the Delta, it is as if time has stood still.

Yesterday a wire report from the Delta described how 'Hundreds of ethnic Ogoni youths attacked and burned a police station near the Nigerian oil city of Port Harcourt on Tuesday after officers shot dead one protester.' Riot police had been sent to the area.[63] Just as they were sent before. How many times will they be sent again?

All my life, people in the Delta have suffered because of the oil industry. It is an industry that has enriched my material world. My life has been shaped by oil. Since 1965, demand for oil has increased by 150 per cent worldwide.[64] I have grown up with the blessings of oil – the benefits of a consumer society based on oil. I have travelled to five continents. I drive a car. I expect electricity, twenty-four hours a day. I expect heating in my children's school. I expect to drink clean water.

My local Shell garage is open twenty-fours hours a day, for motorists expect to be able to fill up, even at three o'clock in the morning. Shell's global reach means that every four seconds a plane is re-fuelled by Shell. Every four seconds some 1,200 cars visit a Shell service station. Yet in Bayelsa State, the source of 40 per cent of Nigeria's crude exports, there is just one petrol station. In Nigeria you might have to wait for hours, days or even weeks to fill up, as routine petrol shortages cripple the country. Nigeria may have vast reserves of oil, but for much of its history it has had to import petrol to feed its motorists.

Over my life, Shell has grown rich too, partly from the profits taken from Nigeria. So why should Nigerians be poor? More than 70 per cent of the population live in poverty.[65] The United Nations Development Programme admits that living conditions and the overall quality of life of most Nigerians have deteriorated during the same period as Nigeria's oil exports have grown.

'It is sobering that the average Nigerian today is worse off than 25 years ago, despite $300 billion in oil revenues the country has generated since then,' says Malik Chaka, from the US House International Relations Subcommittee on Africa.[66] Oil provides each Nigerian with an average of about 53 cents or 30 pence a year.[67] The proportion of population with access to safe drinking water is 57 per cent and with adequate sanitation 55.5 per cent. Life expectancy is only 51.8 years, and one child in five dies before the age of five.[68]

Up to 3.8 million Nigerians have HIV/AIDS, and it is expected there will be nine million AIDS orphans by 2010. That is similar to the population of London. I try to imagine every commuter, shopper, office worker, every person on the tube and bus as an orphan. I try to picture everyone I see in that huge city as having no parents. I begin to understand the crisis of

Nigeria.[69] With its vast oil wealth, the country could have tackled the epidemic, but the cupboard is bare. All has been looted or wasted. Or it is in the bank accounts of City investors in London and Switzerland.

The vast majority of Nigeria's oil wealth has been exported to the benefit of Western oil companies and their shareholders. Those who have prospered in Nigeria have been the ruling elite. At the top of Nigeria, just as at the bottom, corruption is rife. Nigeria's Economic and Financial Crimes Commission has estimated that 45 per cent of the country's oil wealth has been wasted, stolen or siphoned off by corrupt officials.[70] That is nearly half. An estimated £220 billion was squandered, stolen or just wasted by Nigeria's rulers between Independence and 1999, when President Obasanjo came to power. And that is just a projected figure – the real figure may never be known.[71]

All my life they have had oil and I the blessing of a life driven by oil. But one person's blessing is another person's curse.

CHAPTER FOUR

An Intertwined Alliance

'If the Americans did not purchase Nigerian Oil, the Nigerian nation would not be.'

Ken Saro-Wiwa[1]

In League Together

On a cold dreary December day in 1992, Saro-Wiwa was in London on one of his many visits to the capital. Inside a nondescript office near Kings Cross he outlined the reasons for the planned Ogoni march early the following year. 'It is anti-Shell,' he said. 'It is anti-Federal government, because as far as we are concerned the two are in league to destroy the Ogoni people.' For many people in the Delta, like Saro-Wiwa, the government and the oil companies are effectively inseparable organizations. Many see the government and Shell as one.

It is first of all a financial relationship: oil is the life-blood of the Nigerian government, and Nigerian oil is vital to the oil companies, such as Shell. Oil now accounts for more than 80 per cent of the Federal government's revenues, 90 per cent of foreign exchange earnings, and 40 per cent of Gross Domestic Product.[2] Shell also operates joint-venture operations with the government, the most important being the Shell Petroleum Development Company, SPDC.

Oil and gas will continue to be the major source of revenue for the Nigerian government for decades to come. The future of Nigeria as a major player in the world oil market can be deduced from its reserves: just over 35 billion barrels, some 3 per cent of the world's total. Significantly, these reserves have more than doubled in the last decade, a reflection of the increase in exploration activity by multinationals and a reason for the growing geopolitical significance of Nigeria.[3]

Nigeria's future also lies in its vast gas reserves, twice as large as its oil reserves. After the annual audit of Nigeria's reserves, the journal *African Energy* stated in June 2005 that the latest audit 'reconfirms what industry experts have been saying for a long time – that Nigeria is really a gas province with some oil'. These reserves now stand at 188 trillion cubic feet, well exceeding Africa's other big producer, Algeria. Nigeria's gas reserves have the potential to power America's electricity generators and address the problem of declining North Sea reserves.[4]

Nigerian oil and gas are core assets in Shell, Chevron and ExxonMobil's global portfolios.[5] Nigeria is particularly important for Shell, as currently the Delta represents more than 10 per cent of Shell's global production. Shell has over 50 per cent of the oil and gas reserves in Nigeria – 18.17 billion barrels of oil out of a total of 35 billion, and 96.4 trillion out of 188 trillion cubic feet of gas.[6] Such is Nigeria's importance to Shell that despite all the crises the company has suffered because of its presence there, it stays put. As governments come and go, Shell persists.

While the Federal government and oil companies profit from the oil, the communities in the Delta receive little of the oil revenues (see Chapter 8). Currently the Federal government is supposed to return 13 per cent of oil revenues to the

Niger Delta states from which the oil is extracted. In reality, little money actually makes it back to the communities. As government fails to deliver basic services, communities often turn to the oil companies for financial assistance and help in development.

Shell maintains that since 1993, SPDC has spent some $500 million on community development programmes.[7] The oil companies also offer the local communities annual scholarships. Each year some 13,000 children in secondary school and 2,500 at university are sponsored by Shell.

While these could be seen as positive interactions between the oil companies and the communities, Michael Peel, the ex-*Financial Times* West Africa correspondent, writes that 'many villages in oil-producing areas echo the same complaint: companies have failed to execute the projects they promised.' On the matter of scholarships, Peel argues that 'these kinds of schemes raise important questions about whether companies use scholarships as a means of pacifying opposition or winning favours from community leaders.'[8]

The amount the oil companies themselves receive is also hotly disputed, and depends on the price of a barrel of oil. At $10 a barrel the companies get 9 per cent and at $50 it is only 4 per cent.[9] When asked the question 'Can Shell tell us how much profit the company has made from Nigeria since 1956?' the company's response was: 'We do not disclose our financial results by country.' Shell argues instead that it discloses 'the revenues accruing to the Nigerian government from our operations', which is known as the 'split of the barrel'. Shell maintains that 'we remain the only oil major in Nigeria making these disclosures. From this data, you can see that at $50 a barrel, 96 cents in every dollar of revenue goes to the government.'[10]

However, figures published by SPDC itself cast doubt on this, suggesting that at $50 a barrel, some $44.13 or 88 per cent goes to the government. Shell maintains that the remaining non-government partners of SPDC share out just $1.87 per barrel.[11] On paper this is a small amount; in practice, Shell's Nigerian operations are seen as its second most profitable in the world.

Secondly, there is a military relationship between the Nigerian government and the companies, by which the military or the navy protect oil company installations. In their turn, the oil companies occasionally provide logistical support and field allowances to the soldiers. The boundary between state and companies disappears, often with bloody consequences. This is what led Claude Ake to talk about the 'militarization of commerce' and 'privatization of the state'.[12]

Thirdly, there is the close personal relationship between senior Shell officials and Government. It happens at the state level: Chief Rufus Ada George, the former governor of Rivers State, was an ex-SPDC employee. It also occurs at regional level: Godwin Omene, a Deputy Managing Director of SPDC, was appointed head of the 'Niger Delta Development Commission'. It also happens at the Federal level: Ernest Shonekan, who briefly became President in 1993, was an SPDC director.

In July 2005 President Obasanjo undertook a major government reshuffle in which ten ministers were sacked. One of the people promoted was the former Presidential Adviser on Petroleum and Energy, Dr Edmund Daukoru, who became the new Minister of State for Petroleum Resources, although Obasanjo remained in overall control of the Oil Ministry. Daukoru too is ex-Shell. 'I have been an oilman right from the beginning,' says Daukoru. 'After acquiring primary and secondary education, I was picked by Shell to go abroad for my studies; I studied Geology at the Imperial College of London. On finishing my doctorate degree programme, I came back to join Shell. I have thus been a Shell-man right from the beginning: first as a scholar, then an employee.'[13]

This Shell-man 'went through the ranks and became the first indigenous chief geologist in the industry, then first indigenous general manager and director of exploration'. At the time this was the highest position a Nigerian could reach in Shell. Daukoru was then seconded by Shell to become the Managing Director of the NNPC (Nigerian National Petroleum Corporation) for eighteen months in 1992–3.[14]

However, in 1993, soon after Abacha came to power, Daukoru was sacked from his position at NNPC, promptly arrested, and charged along with five other senior officials with stealing $41 million. The deal allegedly involved payments made by the NNPC for the lease of two oil-storage supertankers at above-market rates. Daukoru always denied the charges, and was never convicted.[15] He retired, only to be asked by Obasanjo to be his Presidential Advisor. He is now the new Minister. 'We must take our destiny in our own hands,' he said on his appointment.[16] The reality is that the destinies of Nigeria and Shell will be intertwined for the foreseeable future.

A Changing Company

Before looking at the future it is worth examining how Shell has changed in Nigeria. In 1970, the year that Dr Daukoru received his PhD in Geology from Imperial College, Shell was a very different company from the one it is today. A snapshot reveals the shape of Shell-BP (see Chart 1). On the ground in the Delta,

Shell-BP had two Divisions: Eastern, based at Warri and Western, at Port Harcourt, the latter managed by J. Spinks (see Chapter 3). The two divisions were overseen by the Chairman of Shell-BP in Nigeria based in Lagos, who was answerable to the Chair of Shell Exploration & Production, in London and The Hague, and the Chair of BP Exploration & Production in London.

Beyond this, the structure of Shell itself was complex. The two distinct companies of Shell Transport & Trading, based in London, and Royal Dutch Shell, based in The Hague, were controlled together by the consensual decisions of a Committee of Managing Directors – the CMD. The most important voice on this board was that of the Chairman of the Committee, in 1970 David Barran.[17]

Shell Transport & Trading had responsibility for the day-to-day control of Shell-BP in Nigeria. Furthermore, Shell played a significant role in international negotiations concerning the Nigerian industry – indeed, arguably a more significant role than the Nigerian government itself. Consequently, it was from The Shell Centre in Waterloo that the likes of Barran and Ashley Raeburn journeyed the few hundred yards to visit the British Prime Minister or Foreign Secretary in Whitehall when the need arose to discuss matters relating to Nigeria – such as the Biafran Crisis.

Today, Shell's presence in Nigeria has changed significantly. There are currently five distinct Shell companies operating in the country, known collectively as Shell Companies in Nigeria (SCIN) (see Chart 2).

The lead company is the Shell Petroleum Development Company of Nigeria, SPDC. SPDC is the operator of a Joint Venture Agreement involving the Nigerian National Petroleum

Corporation. The NNPC holds 55 per cent, Shell 30 per cent, Total 10 per cent and Agip 5 per cent. Confusingly, the joint venture is generally referred to by the name of its operator, SPDC.[18] SPDC accounts for 43 per cent of Nigeria's production and holds 55 per cent of the country's reserves.[19]

In January 2005 SPDC's headquarters moved from Lagos to Port Harcourt while Shell's African regional headquarters for Exploration & Production also moved from The Hague to Lagos. Since 2004 SPDC has been headed by Basil Omiyi, the first Nigerian ever to become Managing Director. From 1 September 2005, Omiyi also became the chair of Shell Companies in Nigeria (SCIN).

The next company is the Nigeria Liquified Natural Gas Company Ltd (NLNG), established in 1989. It is owned by NNPC (49 per cent), Shell (25.6 per cent), Total (15 per cent) and Agip (10.4 per cent), and operates the Bonny LNG terminal. Shell is also the technical adviser to the project.

In 1993 the Shell Nigeria Exploration and Production Company (SNEPCO) was established. This wholly-owned subsidiary of Shell is focused particularly on offshore deep-water oil and gas fields, such as Bonga and Bonga South West, both of which it operates as part of a consortium with ExxonMobil.[20]

Shell Nigeria Gas (SNG), which is 100 per cent owned by Shell, was incorporated in 1998 with the aim of creating a gas grid in Nigeria to provide natural gas to industrial customers in Aba, on the eastern edge of the Delta.[21] Finally, in 2000, Shell Nigeria Oil Products (SNOP) was established to sell petrol at service stations, lubricants to suppliers, chemicals to industry, and aviation fuel at Nigeria's airports.

Three important trends have occurred. The first is a dramatic increase in Shell's engagement in Nigeria over the past 15 years, at the same time as the company has faced sustained criticism of its Nigerian operations.

The second notable trend is that following the decline of its stake in Nigerian oil production in the 1970s, the company's position since has actually strengthened. SNEPCO, SNG and SNOP are all 100 per cent owned by Shell. The stake held by the Nigerian state has decreased. For example, NLNG is 49 per cent Nigerian owned, compared to the 55 per cent share it controls in SPDC. Indeed, the Nigerian state has no formal stake in the deepwater field of Bonga lying some 120km southwest of the Niger Delta, the first deepwater project for SNEPCO, which is estimated to hold some 1.2 billion barrels of oil.

The third trend is that oil companies such as Shell have become increasingly dependent upon contractors and oil service companies. Shell employs approximately 5,000 staff in Nigeria, but as a rule of thumb twice this number are employed as contractors.[22] On average only 20 per cent of the staff on an SPDC oil well are actually direct Shell employees; the remaining 80 per cent are contracted firms.

Subcontracting has important implications as to who is ultimately responsibility for an oil operation. One of SPDC's largest contractors onshore is Willbros International, registered in Panama with its headquarters in Tulsa, Oklahoma and an office in Port Harcourt. Willbros is infamous in Ogoni for the fatal shooting incident in 1993 (see Chapter 3).[23]

Willbros was acting on behalf of SPDC, itself a partial subsidiary of Shell. Shell was however able to separate itself from the incident, in the minds both of the public and of its own staff. The Willbros staff on the ground are subject to two masters, the internal Willbros line of command leading to Tulsa, and the contractual line of command to Shell – a line that leads to The Hague and London.

So Shell's operations in Nigeria are only possible through the engagement of a web of other companies. Shell's activities are no longer just a British/Dutch operation but now a product of a network of companies in Italy, France, Japan, and South Korea and, increasingly, America. In parallel with the steady rise of America as Nigeria's chief export market and the increasing presence of the US major oil corporations in the Nigerian oil sector, there has been a steady Americanization of Shell's operations in Nigeria (See Chapter 7).

A Changing Industry

In 1960, when Edmund Daukoru was a teenager at school in Bayelsa State, Nigeria gained its independence. At the time, Nigeria was a minnow in the global oil scene, producing 20,000 barrels a day,[24] only 0.09 per cent of world production.[25] A comparison between Maps 4 and 5 shows the evolution of oil production in the Delta in the 45 years since Nigerian Independence. The map for 1960 shows a small web of pipelines leading from a scattering of oil fields to the single export terminal at Port Harcourt. The map today – onshore and offshore – is a mass of oil fields and pipelines leading to six terminals – at Escravos, Forcados, Pennington, Brass River, Bonny, and Qua Ibo. Bonny has both an oil terminal and the new Liquid Natural Gas (LNG) terminal. Two further LNG terminals are planned for Brass and Olokola.[26]

Since the finds in the mid-1960s more than a hundred further oil fields and gas fields have been discovered offshore. Compared to the 140 fields that have been found onshore since 1956, it becomes clear that after the first decade there was a significant re-orientation of the Nigerian oil industry – from being solely onshore, to being balanced between onshore and offshore.[27]

Like major producers in the Middle East, Nigeria's oil industry was structured from the start for export. As a result of this export focus, Nigeria has slowly become an important player in the global oil market.[28] By 1970 the country was producing 1,085,000 barrels a day, 2.25 per cent of world production.[29] A measure of this new role was marked by Nigeria joining the Organization of Oil Exporting Countries (OPEC) in 1971.

Today, 35 years later, Nigeria is an integral part of OPEC. The country produces some 2,508,000 barrels a day, or 3.2 per cent of global production. It is one of the top ten producers in the world.[30] Its production status is enhanced by the quality of its oil, Bonny Light, and its position close to the US market. It is also far from the insecurity and violence that afflicts some of the Middle Eastern OPEC members.

In June 2005, a month before being promoted to his new position, Dr Daukoru was in Vienna for a meeting of OPEC. Daukoru, currently OPEC's alternative president, will become its full president next January when Nigeria takes over the reins of the organization. So in 2006, Nigeria will be the central player in the oil industry's most powerful cartel. The ex-Shell man will be incredibly powerful in deciding the price of oil in today's volatile market.

On his trip to Europe, Dr Daukoru was also part of an OPEC delegation that had a meeting with EU officials, including Malcolm Wicks, British Minister for Energy, and Andris Pie-balgs, the European Commissioner for Energy. The meeting concerned an EU–OPEC Energy dialogue 'in the interests of producers and consumers'.

The rationale for the meeting was obvious. The EU currently imports around 40 per cent of its oil from OPEC countries, and officials have become extremely concerned about the spiralling crude oil price and the long-term security of supply. Having once been Nigeria's main export market, Britain only imported 130,000 barrels of Nigerian crude in 2003. As North Sea production falls, however, Britain's reliance on Nigerian crude is set to rise rapidly.

Countries in the EU, including Spain, Portugal, Italy, France, the Netherlands, Germany and Austria, all import large quantities of Nigerian crude, as do non-EU countries such as Brazil, Canada, South Africa, China, Japan and India (see Map 9). Like tropical goods and palm-oil before, the produce of the Niger Delta flows through the bloodstream of Europe. By 2030, up to 70 per cent of the European Union's energy requirements and 90 per cent of oil needs will have to be covered by imports. The EU countries were looking to OPEC for security of supply and a fixed price. The EU Council later stressed the 'key' contribution of the EU–OPEC Energy dialogue is 'security of supply and transparency and predictability of the market'.[31]

However, in its efforts to secure OPEC and Nigerian oil, the EU countries face stiff competition from the hungry markets of the US and also, increasingly, China and India. The US is currently the largest consumer of Nigerian oil, importing some 415,735,000 barrels in 2004,[32] over 40 per cent of the country's exports. Nigeria has become important to the US as a source of non-Middle Eastern oil. The US is also looking to Nigeria to supply its gas needs (see Chapter 7), and Europe too is set to import Nigerian gas.

A Changing Future

In March 2005, Dr Daukoru was in Port Harcourt with a roadshow to promote the Nigerian government's new licensing round for oil and gas concessions. On offer were some 60 blocks spread over Nigeria's part of the deep offshore in the Gulf of Guinea, the Niger Delta, as well as some inland basins.

'The Gulf of Guinea represents one of the most prolific deep-water oil and gas provinces in the world,' said Dr Daukoru, 'with Nigeria exercising jurisdiction over about one-fifth of the frontier play, and possibly more than half of the oil and gas resources located therein.'[33]

Daukoru told the assembled oilmen that deep-water reserves found so far accounted for some 25 per cent of the country's total reserves. The Nigerian government expected some 2 to 3 billion barrels per year to be found deep offshore up to 2010. The 'success rate and advances in technology have encouraged Government to open up new frontier acreage in water depths between 2000m and 3000m of which some 12 blocks are included in this bid round,' he said.

Two months later, at the OPEC conference in Vienna, Daukoru let slip that the Nigerian government was actually hoping for around 200 offers on the 60 blocks. All the majors such as Shell, Exxon, Chevron and Eni and Total were interested, he said. It is a measure of the increasing importance of the Gulf of Guinea in the international oil market that the Nigerian government received well over 350 applicants, including 120 from local companies.[34]

It is easy to understand why there is so much interest in the deep-water offshore. Constantly under pressure to find new sources of reserves, and unable to access resources locked away in the Middle East, the international oil companies have been looking for oil in deep-water regions in one of four global 'hot-spots' – Nigeria, Angola, Brazil and the Gulf of Mexico.[35]

The move offshore actually started in the early 1990s, after General Abacha came to power, when there was a series of licensing rounds for exploration blocks in the deep water of the continental shelf of Nigeria. Map 5 shows these blocks as rectangular or square units marked out across the Nigerian stretch of the Gulf of Guinea.

Here wells are drilled into the rocks below the sea bed from rigs that float in more than a thousand metres of water or deeper. Daukoru noted that 'Shell was very much in the vanguard of new companies in the deep water offshore from 200 metres to about 1500 metres of water depth.'[36]

The deep-water developments have given rise to some funda-mental shifts in the Nigerian oil industry. The first is the development of a gas export industry. When oil is discovered it is routinely found with gas. In many regions of the world gas is utilized through a national gas grid, such as that from the North Sea. However, in Nigeria the domestic gas market has never been developed by the companies, because they (and the government) have traditionally focused on the export of oil. The export of onshore associated gas has not until recently been developed, the gas merely being flared off, causing the environ-mental pollution that has led to the resentment in the Delta discussed earlier.

The distance between Nigeria and its primary markets has prohibited a gas export system based on pipelines, although there is now a plan to boost the regional gas market and supposedly reduce gas flaring. The $600 million West African

Gas Pipeline (WAGP) project will transport gas along the shoreline from the Niger Delta to Benin, Togo and Ghana, in an effort to build a regional gas market. It is being pioneered by Chevron, whose other partners include Shell, NNPC and Takoradi Power. The World Bank ($127.5 million guarantee) and African Development Bank ($460 million) are also backing the project.[37]

George Kirkland, the president of Chevron, argues that WAGP 'has long been a key component of our strategy to reduce flaring and commercialize gas resources in Africa'.[38] However, communities in the Delta and beyond disagree. They believe that the commitments to reduce flaring and pay fair compensation are inadequate. Environmental Rights Action argues that without an attempt to resolve these issues, 'there is the grave danger that WAGP will exacerbate the crisis in the area, which will lead to further disruptions in gas supply, while worsening the insecurity and impoverishment in the area.'

ERA also argues that 'WAGP has been falsely promoted as a gas flare reduction project even though its sponsors have not demonstrated commitment to addressing the problem in Nigeria.' Chevron has not 'given adequate guarantees that the WAGP would contribute to gas flare reduction', argues ERA.[39]

At the same time, the development of Liquified Natural Gas (LNG) technology has enabled Nigeria to develop its foreign gas markets, rather than confining itself to a regional market. LNG is essentially a process of super-cooling gas to the point where it becomes a liquid, transporting it in specially constructed LNG vessels, and then turning the liquid back into gas at the terminal in the market country.

In the wake of the offshore discoveries, LNG plants for transforming the gas into liquid are now being built along the Delta coast, the first at Bonny, with others following at Brass and Olokola.

The development of offshore fields and LNG plants impacts in other ways on Nigeria and the oil companies. Firstly, deep offshore oil is significantly more expensive to produce than onshore is. Whereas onshore and shallow-water offshore fields have been financed by the companies who have undertaken them, the new developments since the 1990s have required companies to draw in finance from other sources.

The LNG plants are also expensive. It is estimated that the Bonny LNG plant will cost around $10 billion. Finance for the Bonny plant comes from private banks such as BNP Paribas, Crédit Lyonnais, Citibank, Mediocredito and WestLB,[40] as well as export credit agencies. The UK's Export Credit Guarantee Department (ECGD) and the US's Export-Import Bank (EXIM) in Washington, are arms of national governments that provide guarantees to secure loans made by private banks in foreign projects. Thus, if there are problems with the loan repayments, ultimately the British or American tax-payer will pay the price to ensure that the loan is repaid.

Secondly, these massive infrastructure projects dramatically increase the importance of Nigeria in the strategic thinking of the US and Europe. The scale of the capital input draws more financial institutions into Nigeria. The importation of LNG means that countries such as the US, France, Italy and Spain are dependent not only on Nigeria's crude oil, but also on its gas to satisfy their domestic needs. This in turn drives a growing American military presence in the region (see Chapter 7).

The UK, which is currently a minor importer of Nigerian oil, is set to dramatically increase imports of both crude and LNG. Terminals to receive foreign LNG are already under construction at the Isle of Grain in Kent and at Milford Haven in Pembrokeshire in West Wales.

Finally, the deep-water developments may well shift the balance of power within Nigeria. The majority of Nigeria's oil production takes place onshore or in shallow offshore fields in Delta communities and within the fishing grounds of these communities. This fuels the tension between the communities and the Federal government, especially over issues of resource control and derivation. The deep-water fields, on the other hand, fall within Nigeria's national waters yet are far removed from the Delta. This may well weaken the claim the Delta communities have on the oil. That said, there is one significant exception to this rule. There have been persistent rumours that because of problems in the Delta, Shell was looking to move its operations offshore. But there is still too much oil and gas for Shell to exploit onshore for the company to move exclusively offshore. In 2003, Shell had proven reserves of 14 billion barrels onshore or in the shallow waters of the Gulf.[41]

The fact that the deep-water offshore fields are away from the communities is not lost on the oil industry. 'The development of the deep water – crucial to the government's plan to nearly double output – is enticing to international oil firms,' argues *Petroleum Economist*. 'As well as proved reserves, which have helped position West Africa as an exploration hotspot, the isolation factor, with fields located miles from the shore, suggests a more comfortable operating climate, free from vociferous communities and sabotage.'[42]

The Federal government and Dr Daukoru will hope that companies will be able to operate in splendid isolation without a protestor in sight.

A conflict closer than you think

ANDY ROWELL

July 2005. I have just come back from a week's holiday in Pembrokeshire. Pembrokeshire is a magical land dripping with ancient legends, Celtic saints and castles, and boasts Britain's smallest cathedral city, St David's. It has miles of spectacular coastal paths and famous sandy beaches. The area teems with wildlife, from birds such as kittiwakes, shearwaters, peregrines and lapwings to the largest concentration of Atlantic grey seals in southern Britain.

But it is also a land of contrast and conflict. The largest town in the county is Milford Haven, a busy oil port and terminal. Oil and tourism sit uncomfortably side by side. Just how uncomfortably was underlined in February 1996, when the *Sea Empress*, a 147,000-tonne supertanker, ran aground on rocks just a few miles from Milford Haven, spewing oil onto the tourist beaches, its black cargo choking the wildlife.

Sit on a beach in St Brides Bay now and you see oil tankers sitting peacefully out at sea waiting to offload their cargo. Go sailing near Milford Haven and the horizon is littered with the towers of the oil refineries that dominate the landscape. Go for a walk at night and the horizon is lit up like a Christmas tree.

Last week it was announced that Milford wants to become the energy hub of the UK, building its future not just on oil but on LNG. The construction of two LNG plants is already under way, to exploit gas from Qatar and Malaysia. The increase in traffic from LNG tankers could see Milford Haven become one of the UK's busiest ports, with nearly a third of the UK's gas imported in this way.

Not everyone is happy about this, and the battle-lines are being drawn. Friends of the Earth Cymru say that the LNG plants at Milford Haven would pose an 'unacceptable threat to the local population', that the LNG proposals would pose major public safety risks and raise issues of national security.

The week before my holiday, opponents of the scheme were in the High Court in Wales fighting to stop the development. The dispute made prime-time television with ITV Wales arguing that there were 'serious questions about what might happen in Milford Haven if there were an accident or in the event of a terrorist attack'.

It will be a couple of years before LNG tankers are seen docking at Pembroke. In the light of London's experience of Britain's first suicide bombing attacks, LNG raises a whole series of questions about security as well as about sustainability.

It also raises the possibility of gas from the Niger Delta being imported directly to Britain for the first time. Ledum Mitee, the head of MOSOP, said once: 'When I travel outside Nigeria people often ask me how far away Ogoni is. I tell them it's as far as the nearest Shell service station.'

Within two years, the gas from the Niger Delta could be burning in our kitchens, cooking our suppers or making our morning cups of tea. The Niger Delta is closer than we think. Soon it could be in our own homes.

CHAPTER FIVE

A Shock to the System

'It is well known that a boil on one's nose is more painful to the afflicted than an earthquake which happens thousands of miles away killing thousands of people. I am inclined to think that this is why the Ogoni environment must matter more to me than to Shell International ensconced in its ornate offices on the banks of the Thames in London. But I cannot allow the company its smugness because its London comfort spells death to my Ogoni chidren and compatriots.'

Ken Saro-Wiwa[1]

The First Shock

Shell had grown used to its troublesome but profitable Nigerian operations. The company had weathered the storm over Biafra and the nationalization of BP; it had weathered the storm over environmental pollution in the Delta and the original Ogoni protests. It had even weathered the outcry over the shooting of Ogoni protestors. But the hanging of Ken Saro-Wiwa and the Ogoni Eight had a dramatic, implosive impact on the company.

Coming hot on the heels of the Brent Spar fiasco in which the company was attacked by Greenpeace for dumping a redundant oil storage platform in the Atlantic, the public protests about the Saro-Wiwa murder and the consequent vilification of Shell in the media had two distinct effects.

First of all, it was externally damaging. It propelled Shell into a public relations crisis that severely affected the reputation of the Group. Saro-Wiwa's death made front-page headlines across the world, and so too did Shell's role in his death. On the front page of the *Guardian* their cartoonist, Steve Bell, drew Saro-Wiwa with the noose around his neck fed symbolically into a petrol pump; a row of petrol pumps with a Shell logo on them was depicted in the background. Other newspapers were equally blunt: 'Outrage in Nigeria: Did Shell Oil Help Execute Ken Saro-Wiwa?' ran *the Village Voice* newspaper in New York.[2]

Second was the impact internally. The morning after the executions every single staff member received a memo from Shell attempting to justify the company's position on Nigeria and exonerating itself from Saro-Wiwa's death. The whole episode nevertheless left many company staff deeply troubled, unsure of the nature of the institution they worked for and embarrassed to reveal the name of their employer to outsiders. 'Some years ago, I did not like to mention I was employed by Shell. I knew people would turn their noses up disapprovingly,' stated one employee in the late 1990s.[3]

The situation had to be addressed head-on. Shell embarked on 'a long-term campaign on the communications front',[4] pouring £20 million and extensive human resources into re-building the company's reputation.[5] In order to do this, the company had to alter the public peception of it from corporate villain to a caring company.

In 1996, within months of Saro-Wiwa's hanging, Shell hired Tom Henderson as manager of Shell Corporate Identity Communications, to pioneer a project entitled 'Society's Changing Expectations',[6] and a new 'Sustainable Development Team' was established under Tom Delfgaaw.[7]

The following year, 1997, a Social Responsibility Committee

was established on which were to sit six of the most senior Shell directors, including Mark Moody-Stuart, Phil Watts and Jeroen van der Veer, all of whom later became heads of the company. The committee's task was to review Shell's business principles, its health, safety and environment policy, and its commitment to sustainable development and human rights.[8]

A new Statement of General Business Principles was issued taking the line that Shell's core values were 'honesty, integrity and respect for people', and that these included an explicit support for the UN Declaration on Human Rights.[9] There was a clear commitment to a system of 'letters of representation' whereby each Country Chief Executive and Chief Financial Officer would annually sign a letter detailing performance in these fields. Shell declared: 'Managers who sign the letters are held personally responsible for their content.'[10]

As well as hiring new staff and establishing new internal teams and committees, Shell also engaged outside agencies to carry out this campaign on the communications front, outsourcing key activities to a web of companies (see Chart 3). Prior to the crisis, Shell had utilized 35 different advertising agencies in different markets and countries but essentially kept the reins of marketing very firmly in the hands of the centre. Now it chose to whittle these down to one advertising agency, J. Walter Thompson, and the same streamlining process took place in each sector of its communications work; for example, the media contract was given to Mediacom.

Tellingly, the overall coordination of the communications campaign was given to a public relations company, Fishburn Hedges, rather than an advertising company. Based in Holborn in London, Fishburn Hedges was engaged to run Shell's first global campaign, and handed an unprecedented level of control.[11] It was experienced public relations people who would design this attempt to completely redefine the company in the eye of its key public.

The 'Political Publics'

The news from Port Harcourt had an impact not only on Shell staff but also on other key constituencies for the company. Shell depends on the constructive engagement of a number of constituencies beyond its own staff – the financial institutions, the government, the public, and its customer base. The support of these sectors constitutes what the oil industry calls 'the social license to operate'.

Consider the concept of 'the social license to operate' in the context of an oil-producing region such as the Niger Delta. Without the support, or acquiescence, of communities around the oil fields, it is difficult to carry on production. In Ogoni, for example, Shell has lost its 'social license to operate' and has had to withdraw from the oil fields. The WAC Report, commissioned by Shell, into violence in the Delta (see Chapter 1) stated that the company was in danger of losing its social licence in the entire region in the next few years. Shell has rejected this aspect of the report. Without the support of the national government, a corporation can have its legal licence revoked – as the example of the nationalization of BP in Nigeria showed.

However, it is just as vital that the company should retain its 'social license' at the centre of its global operations, in the zone of political control as in the zones of extraction, such as Nigeria. Indeed, a close relationship between a corporation and the government at a political centre such as London is fundamental to the success of that corporation's global activities. Both the

Royal African Company and the Royal Niger Company ceased to exist, not because of opposition in West Africa, but because they lost the support of the political classes in London.

Although since the semi-privatization of BP in 1976 and the dissolution of the Shell-BP partnership in 1979 there is no longer direct British government involvement in Shell's Nigerian operations, the connections remain very strong.

In June 2005 Lord Kerr of Kinlochard, was appointed deputy chairman of the newly formed Royal Dutch Shell, bringing with him a wealth of government connections. He was UK Ambassador to the US from 1995 to 1997, while the storms raged over Shell's position in Nigeria. Upon the election of Labour in 1997, Kerr was brought back from the US and made head of the Diplomatic Service, and Permanent Under-Secretary of State at the Foreign & Commonwealth Office – the most senior civil service position in the FCO.[12]

In 2002 Kerr, aged 60, retired and became a non-executive director of Shell Transport & Trading. His role as a non-executive director is by no means ceremonial. For example, it was Kerr who headed the team that co-ordinated the restructuring of Royal Dutch/Shell in 2004. 'We non-execs perhaps took a little time to get our act together, to decide how to go about it,' he told the *Financial Times*, '[but] I gave up my summer last year [2004] and it wasn't for a PR bang. I mean, come on, it was not to achieve positive PR that we worked our butts off.'[13]

John Kerr's case is by no means exceptional. Sir Anthony Acland was Permanent Under-Secretary – the same job that Kerr later held – at the FCO from 1982 to 1985. Six years later he was a non-executive director of Shell Transport & Trading (1991–9), again during the height of the crisis centred on Ogoni.

Then there is Lord Oxburgh. During his nine-year tenure as a non-executive director of Shell, he was a life peer and chairman of the House of Lords Committee on Science and Technology – a pivotal position in the parliamentary debates concerning climate change. He was also Chief Scientific Advisor to the Ministry of Defence. Furthermore, he was Chair of Trustees of the Natural History Museum and Rector of the Imperial College of Science Technology and Medicine, part of London University.[14]

In March 2004, following the resignation of Phil Watts, Chairman of Shell Transport & Trading, Oxburgh was appointed non-executive Chairman until June 2005. According to the *Guardian*, 'He claims that he only agreed to the job because Shell HQ is close enough to Parliament to allow him to yo-yo between the two.'[15]

While it remains vital that Shell has close connections with the British government, Shell also needs to maintain a close link to the US government. The growing importance of this can be illustrated by the slow Americanization of the company board. After a century in which it has been almost entirely made up of British and Dutch men, the company's six-person board in June 2005 included two American women.[16]

Profits and Principles

Britain and, increasingly, America matter to Shell not just at the governmental level, but in the street. Shell depends upon its customer base, the wider public, both to purchase its products on the forecourts, and to provide the reservoir of support – or at least lack of opposition – that lies at the heart of 'the social license to operate'. This wider support is itself partially created by NGOs, the media and academics. Thus when, after the executions in Port Harcourt, voices in these sectors called for a boycott of Shell, or vilified it in public, the social licence was being undermined.

In response to this, Fishburn Hedges' first action, in 1996–7, was to conduct an extensive 'stakeholder survey'. They identified what were called 'special publics' – not the general public, but the sectors of the population that were important to Shell: opinion formers from the media, NGOs, financial analysts, academics, and government officials. They held interviews with individuals from such groups in 25 countries, in order to gauge their opinion of the company's reputation, policies and values. About 9,400 people in total were interviewed.[17]

The results showed that 50 per cent thought Shell was a good company, 40 per cent were undecided, and a vocal and influential 10 per cent were highly critical. As the magazine *Brand Strategy* later reported, Shell decided to focus on converting the undecided to favourable, and to isolate the minority who, they believed, would always be anti-big business. Tom Henderson, head of Shell's Corporate Identity Communications, claimed: 'The undecided only had one side of the story, because the critics were better at PR than us. We were too quiet for too long about the values of the organization. We needed to close the knowledge gap.'[18]

'Closing the knowledge gap' with the 'special publics' was overseen by Fishburn Hedges. The first step was the publication in April 1998 of *Profits and Principles – Does There Have to be a Choice? The Shell Report 1998*. A glossy, full-colour, 56-page booklet, it explored the new Statement of General Business Principles in detail, from objectives and responsibilities down to communications. And it went further, delving into six 'Issues and Dilemmas', including human rights, climate change and 'operating in politically sensitive regions' – trying to represent Shell's understanding and intentions with regard to these matters.

The inside cover of *Profits and Principles* reflected the two key messages constructed by the PR company: openness, and dialogue. In a friendly handwriting font the message read: 'We care about what you think of us. We want you to know more about how we strive to live up to our principles. This report is part of a dialogue, and we will continue to seek your views.'[19] Here was Shell saying that it was a caring company that listened to your views. The handwriting reminded you of your grandmother – it was comforting.

The production of the report was outsourced to a company named Associates in Advertising, with the text written by the former *Financial Times* journalist Peter Knight.[20] The report and the process behind it were endorsed by John Elkington, chairman of SustainAbility, who wrote a statement entitled 'Why we decided to work with Shell'.[21]

Given that SustainAbility, which had a strong profile in the UK environmental sector and – as the statement made clear – had been critical of Shell, their engagement in this process was clearly an important achievement in the process of 'converting the undecided'. It was a battle won 'on the communications front'.

The whole publication was intended to address directly the storm raised by the executions in Port Harcourt. 'We were all shaken by the tragic execution of Ken Saro-Wiwa and eight Ogonis by the Nigerian Authorities' said the Introduction.[22]

Later, in a section on 'responsibilities to society', the report stated: 'Before Mr Saro-Wiwa's arrest we said that while we did not necessarily agree with all of his views, he had the right to voice his opinions. After his arrest we said he should be treated fairly in prison and should be given the necessary medical attention. We did not seek to influence his trial, but after the verdict the Chairman of the Group's Committee of Managing Directors sent a letter to the Nigerian head of state urging him to grant clemency for all those sentenced.' This Chairman was Cor Herkstroter.[23]

Profits and Principles was a bold piece of PR work centred on the idea of an interactive process – a dialogue – and the engagement of the 'special publics', and here the report was putting the advice of its PR consultants into practice: use dialogue to co-opt your critics and win round your special publics. It is a tactic long used by PR gurus – such as E. Bruce Harrison, who co-ordinated the chemical industry's attack against Rachel Carson's *Silent Spring*. Harrison says that green companies need to be the model of openness. He calls 'openness and dialogue' magic keys for companies.[24]

Profits and Principles contained magic keys. Its most novel element was nine tear-out postcards for the reader to send back to Shell with texts such as 'Go in or stay out? Multinational companies may have to decide whether or not to do business with a developing country where bribery and corruption are commonplace and there is little regard for environmental issues: should you go in and expose yourself to possible criticism that you are willing to engage in business with such a government?'[25]

The company extended the process of interactivity with the creation of a new element of its website, www.Shell.com, which encouraged visitors to the site to e-mail the company – 'Tell-Shell' what you think. The aim was to engender responses, and these came in thick and fast, comments such as: 'I am Fortune Adogbeji Fashe, currently a permanent resident in the US. Last year I got a message from home about the death of my father,

Chief James Fashe. He was on retirement in Ewreni in Delta State, where you have one of your flowstations. He was killed and his house razed, I learnt as a result of Shell's activities in the community. I have read Shell's cheap denial and lame excuses for the atrocities the[y] carry out in Nigeria. But I did not expect it would come to this. I just want to know, what is Shell's side of the story on this, and what is Shell doing about it?'[26] Or: 'Rather than spend vast sums on a fake forum, why not have some real f***ing action?' Whilst Shell failed to reply to Fortune Fashe, it generally responded to e-mails, attempting to portray itself as listening and caring.[27]

Soon after the website came an 'interactive advertising campaign', undertaken by the advertising company J. Walter Thompson in London, under the guidance of Fishburn Hedges.[28] A series of five advertisements was run over an 18-month period from March 1999, built around questions as slogans: 'Wish upon a star or make a dream come true?', 'Cloud the issue or clear the air?', 'None of our business or at the heart of our business?', 'Cover up or clean up?' and 'Commodity or community?'[29]

Each addressed one of the 'Issues and Dilemmas' identified in the *Profits and Principles* report and encouraged the reader to get in contact via www.Shell.com or to write to Shell at 'The Profits and Principles Debate'. By appearing to be seeking to include the public in the decision-making process of the company, Shell was taking a radical step.

For the first time in Shell's history this was a global campaign, running in *Time* magazine, the *Economist*, *Newsweek*, the *Financial Times* and *National Geographic*.[30] Shell also used the internet, targeting sites frequented by environmentalists and scientists, contributing to online message boards and posting ads devised to improve its corporate identity.[31] The persuasive power of these advertisements was supplemented by 'relationship marketing, direct marketing and stakeholder forums'.[32]

These stakeholder forums were conducted in a number of selected countries and enabled critics of Shell to voice their concerns and put questions to Shell representatives. As *Brand Strategy* wrote: '[Tom] Henderson explains that the forums are an effective means of presenting another side of the story. In a Dublin forum [in February 2001], there were two church representatives who'd previously been missionaries in Nigeria and were critical of Shell in that market. They'd heard stories second or third hand, so we made sure we had Nigerian Shell employees there who could set the record straight.'[33]

These forums continued over the next few years. In 2002, a 24-hour stakeholder forum was held by Shell in Brussels, led by the political writer Will Hutton,[34] and following *Profits and Principles*, further Shell Reports were produced. Those of subsequent years had titles such as *People, Planet & Profits – an Act of Commitment* (1999), *How do we Stand? People, Planet and Profits* (2000), *People, Planet and Profits* (2001 and 2002), *Meeting the Energy Challenge* (2003), and then simply *The Shell Report* (2004).

Alongside this, J. Walter Thompson ran another series of five interactive advertisements between March 2001 and January 2003 with slogans such as: 'Not all the experts we listen to are employed by Shell', 'If our work affects others, we listen with particular care' and 'Five years ago we set off down a different road. Judge for yourself how far we've come – The 2001 Shell Report available now'.[35]

To answer the question whether this was just PR or a complete overhaul of Shell's business ethics, it is worth looking at the primary focus of the campaign. *Profits and Principles*, the key publication in this 'global' campaign, was available in only English and Dutch. Shell's overriding concern seems to have been to reach its three main financial and consumer markets, its special publics in Holland, Britain and the US.[36]

This fact was not lost on Oronto Douglas. When he was being interviewed on Australian radio, it was suggested to him 'that he might have noticed their report at least on the Internet, there is a space for people who are reading it to type in their responses to Shell, even about issues like Nigeria'.

'Nobody in Ogoni has access to Internet, nobody in Ijawland has access to Internet,' replied Douglas. 'So there will be no response from the Niger Delta, none at all. If that is the position, it is still being made to convince the international people, Europeans, people in the North, about how we [Shell] are changed, because they know that their bread will be buttered when Europeans begin to think positively on them.'[37]

The global campaign might not have been targeted at the communities of the Delta, but those communities were certainly utilized in the campaigns addressed to the world. In May 1997, almost a year before the publication of *Profits and Principles*, SPDC in Nigeria produced a *People and the Environment Annual Report 1996*. It was the company's first such report, and was clearly addressed to the concerned readership in cities such as London.

The report was keen to explain to this audience SPDC's positive record on both environmental management and community development. It announced: 'We spent over $36 million on community programmes in 1996, more than any other Shell operating company anywhere in the world.'[38] It talked of SPDC's support for vocational training, education, social amenities and agriculture, but top of the list was the work in health care – six SPDC hospitals started in 1996, six finished.[39]

It talked, for example, of Gokana General Hospital at Terabor, in Ogoniland. The previous October it had issued a press release about this hospital: 'This week [SPDC] takes over responsibility for the maintenance and supply of drugs for Gokana general hospital.'[40]

However, three years later, in September 1999, a mission made up of journalists and senior figures from The Body Shop International, including Gordon and Anita Roddick, visited this community development project: 'Gokana hospital has fewer drugs than most people in Britain keep in their bathrooms,' wrote the Roddicks. 'It has no electricity and no running or hot water. The beds have no mattresses, there are holes in the roof, the medical records are kept on the floor.'[41]

In order to create these projects, and to maximize their chances of 'converting the undecided', SPDC engaged development NGOs such as Living Earth Foundation, Pro-Natura International and the Conservation Foundation. These were organizations whose engagement, like that of SustainAbility, would provide the crucial endorsement Shell required. The issue of Shell's sustainable development has become a battleground between the NGOs. A recent salvo is a damning report published by Christian Aid in 2004 entitled *Behind the Mask: The real face of corporate social responsibility*. 'Shell claims that it has turned over a new leaf in Nigeria and strives to be a "good neighbour",' Christian Aid concluded. 'Yet it still fails to quickly clean up oil spills that ruin villages and runs "community development" projects that are frequently ineffective and which sometimes divide communities living around oilfields.'[42]

Despite this struggle over the interpretation of developments in the Delta since the death of Saro-Wiwa, the 'long term campaign on the communications front' was clearly successful. By 2000, 65 per cent of interviewees in a stakeholder survey were found to be in favour of Shell, 25 per cent were undecided and 10 per cent remained anti.[43] For the company this was a marked improvement on the survey conducted in 1996/7.

In July 2003 James Wilsdon, Head of Strategy at the think-tank Demos, could say: 'I'm impressed by the openness and honesty Shell has demonstrated in its approach to sustainability and social responsibility. I hope more companies will follow their example.'[44] Shell had become the darling of the social and ethical investment movement in the UK too.[45] Its rehabilitation was complete. The company had gone from corporate pariah to green leader, from being vilified to being praised.

The campaign was also successful with the key constituency of Shell staff. In contrast to the constant flow of information about Nigeria being put out to the public by the company, inside the company there seems to have been an averting of eyes. One retired senior manager who had never been to Nigeria explained that he had noticed how others who had been there talked about it.[46] On returning from the Niger Delta, Gordon Roddick went to meet the Chairman of Shell, Mark Moody-Stuart, and tried to persuade him to accompany him on a trip to the Delta. During the meeting Moody-Stuart showed signs of considering this idea, but Alan Detheridge, Vice-President of External Affairs, was also in the room and was clearly unhappy with the proposal. It came as no surprise to Roddick when he was phoned by Shell next day and told that Moody-Stuart would not make the trip.[47]

Speaking in June 2005 about Ken Saro-Wiwa, a senior Shell manager explained: 'We were right on Nigeria . . . they're sabotaging the pipes for their own gain . . . it's just inter-tribal conflict. I don't want to work in Africa, they'll kill you for no reason.' His confident response demonstrates that whatever the rights or wrongs of Shell's actions in Nigeria, perhaps the majority of the staff see the company's intentions in the Delta as having integrity.[48]

However, not all who were actually involved in the rebranding effort feel the same. One former Shell Environmental and Sustainable Development advisor, speaking on condition that his anonymity be maintained, said that although they saw 'some concrete progress . . . it was always felt that environmental and social issues were considered peripheral to the core business. At the end of the day, the priority is finding oil and getting it out of the ground. One time when I challenged a director about slow progress on sustainability issues I was told that first we need to focus on "strategic cost leadership" [i.e. cost-cutting], and then we can consider sustainable development. That just about summed up the attitude of many senior managers for me. They saw environmental and social sustainability as a cost, a "nice-to-have" rather than essential and potentially beneficial.'[49]

The Real Shock to the System

By early 2004, it appeared that the PR men had won. Shell had been reborn. The perception in the City and on the part of the special publics and many of the staff was that Shell was now fundamentally different from the company of nine years earlier.

All that changed on 9 January 2004 when the company issued a statement in which it came clean on something it had been trying to hide for too long: Shell announced that it had overstated its oil reserves by 3.9 billion barrels. It claimed that they had been falsely booked according to the US Securities and Exchange Commission rules, and that they would need to be re-booked. Essentially, they had to cut by a fifth their most important assets – the oil and gas in the ground over which they had rights – a loss of at least \$70 billion worth of value.[50]

Four countries were identified at the centre of the crisis – Australia, Oman, Brunei and Nigeria. Nearly ten years after Saro-Wiwa's execution, Nigeria had come back to haunt Shell.

The financial press was aflame with incredulity. The company's share price plunged 8 per cent, wiping £3 billion off Shell's value within an hour of trading on the London Stock Exchange.[51] The oil analysts in the financial institutions were further outraged that such an important statement should have been issued without the Chairman, Watts, even being present – only PR people were put up to stage a teleconference.[52]

Philip Watts, known always as Phil Watts, was a Shell 'lifer', a man who had spent almost his entire career at Shell, working his way steadily up the ranks. Born in Leicestershire in the English Midlands in 1945, he studied physics at Leeds University before doing a Masters in geophysics. Already a committed Christian, Watts spent a year teaching at the Methodist Boys High School in Freetown, Sierra Leone, before joining Shell.[53]

As it transpired his career in the company was to take him back to West Africa, and become intertwined with the fate of Shell in Nigeria. Watts was head of Shell Nigeria from 1991 to 1994, and so resident in Lagos during the waves of disturbances in Ogoni that led up to the final arrest of Saro-Wiwa and others. He was Director of Planning, Environment & External Affairs based in London between early 1996 and July 1997. Therefore he was directly responsible for the architecture of the 'campaign on the communications front' by means of which the company responsed to the Port Harcourt executions. From 1997 to 2001 he was Chairman of Exploration & Production, based in The Hague but directly responsible for Shell Nigeria during a period of rapid development in the deep-water offshore fields.

From 2001 he was Chairman of Shell Transport & Trading and at the same time the Chairman of the Committee of the Managing Directors, in command of the entire company. On that fateful morning of 9 January, Watts was nowhere to be found. A report from BBC TV claimed that he was at his home at Binfield in Berkshire, tending to his Japanese garden.[54]

Within 24 hours analysts were calling for his removal and the restructuring of the company. At Shell's 'Quarterly and End of Year Results' presentation in London on 5 February, Watts came before the analysts in a suitably contrite manner and tried to salvage both his and the company's reputations.[55]

That day, 9 January 2004, was arguably one of the worst in Shell's history: if the company's PR men had felt that the Brent Spar incident and Saro-Wiwa's execution were bad, this was infinitely more damaging to Shell's corporate reputation. This was not about environmental or cultural responsibility; this was the result of financial impropriety. Those who called for the chairman's resignation were not environmentalists or human rights activists, but financial analysts. In contrast to the 8 per cent drop on 9 January, the share price had barely registered Saro-Wiwa's death since all the 'fundamentals' of the company remained unchanged. In the case of the crisis over reserves, however, these very 'fundamentals' came into question.

Watts had had a difficult 33 months at the helm of Shell. He presented ten sets of Quarterly Results, and got poor reviews from the analysts for all but two of them. But the crisis that eventually destroyed Watts had been building for years, since at least 1998, when Watts was head of Exploration and Production and Mark Moody-Stuart was head of the company.

In 1998, Shell was undergoing an extremely difficult financial patch; indeed, for some years afterwards the financial press referred to it as an 'annus horribilis'. A collapsing oil price had meant that Moody-Stuart had to write off $5 billion of bad investments. At the same time, he made a pronouncement to senior staff that they should emphasize 'creating value through entrepreneurial management of hydrocarbon reserves'.[56]

'Entrepreneurial management' was particularly acute in Nigeria. Nigerian government officials later conceded that the country accounted for a third of the reserves falsely booked by the company.[57] The scandal was all about tax concessions – the more reserves Shell declared, the less tax it paid. 'Shell failed to inform shareholders and US regulators that it was receiving incentive payments from the Nigerian government for booking oil and gas reserves,' one oil industry publication noted.

It continued: 'Under Nigeria's reserves addition bonus scheme, Shell and other oil majors received tax credits for each barrel of oil booked. Nigeria benefited from the arrangement by being able to demand a bigger output quota from OPEC and higher prices from international oil companies when it auctioned off acreage. The bonus scheme ran for nine years from 1991.'

Watts had had direct involvement with Nigeria during the period of the bonus scheme. A report into the crisis undertaken for Shell by a firm of American lawyers laid the blame for the crisis firmly on Watts. Only the executive summary has ever been published, but it concluded that 'SPDC accumulated over the 1990s and, particularly, in the late 1990s very large volumes of proved oil reserves.'

The lawyers found that 'No later than early 2000, however, it became clear to EP [exploration and production] management that SPDC's substantial proved reserves could not be produced as originally projected or within its current license periods. Rather than de-book reserves, an effort was undertaken to manage the problem through a moratorium on new oil and gas additions, in the hope that SPDC's production levels would increase dramatically to support its reported reserves.

'This solution remained in place for the next several years, until January, 2004,' found the lawyers, 'notwithstanding the knowledge of EP management that, in fact, production was not increasing to a level which could support the booked proved reserves.'[58]

The company's practices in Nigeria in the 1990s were a key part of its difficulties in 2004. After the interim report by the lawyers, both Sir Phil Watts and Walter van der Vijver, then head of Exploration & Production, offered their resignations. The board accepted them, and in its century-long history Watts became the only head of Shell required to retire prematurely.

Following Watts's departure came further revelations. In 2002 the disparity between the actual reserves and the booked reserves had been apparent at least to Walter van der Vijver, who explained his concerns to a member of the board of Royal Dutch, Aad Jacobs.[59] However, Watts did not face up to this problem, hoping it could be ridden out.

But by November 2003 the strain was there to see in the e-mail that Van der Vijver sent to Watts saying he was 'sick and tired of lying about the extent of our reserves issue'. Van der Vijver continued to collude in the deception, however. On 2 December he received a memo from his own staff warning that the company must disclose to the market its need to reduce its reserves, or be in breach of SEC (Securities and Exchange Commission, New York) rules. He responded: 'This is absolute dynamite, not at all what I expected, and needs to be destroyed.'[60]

In the aftermath of the revelation of 9 January 2004, Shell ultimately had to cut 4.8 billion barrels of oil from its reserves in five separate announcements. By the end of 2004 Shell held less than half the reserves of ExxonMobil or BP, and lagged far behind Chevron and Total.[61] Worse still, its 'Reserves Replacement Ratio', or RRR, had plummeted.

RRR defines the rate at which an oil company replaces the amount of oil that it has in its oil fields – its reserves – in relation to the speed at which it is taking oil out of the ground. An oil company must replace what it is extracting by discovering – or gaining through acquisitions or mergers – more oil reserves. If the replacement rate is zero the company will, at some point in the future run out of oil. All major oil companies like to have an RRR of at least 100 per cent – that is, to be replacing as much as they are extracting year by year. Over the period 2001–4, Shell had an average Reserves Replacement Ratio of 70 per cent, whereas that of BP was 178 per cent, ExxonMobil's and Total's were 120 per cent, and Chevron's was 100 per cent.[62] The future of Shell in relation to its competitors looked bleak indeed.

Furthermore, Shell was found by the two premier financial regulatory bodies – the Financial Services Authority in London and the Securities and Exchange Commission in New York – to have misled its shareholders; essentially, to have manipulated the market with false information. Both the FSA and the SEC fined Shell, the former £17 million and the latter $120 million (£67 million).[63]

Finally, at least two US pension funds opened court cases against Shell for deception, citing ten senior directors and the two firms of Shell's accountants, PWC and KPMG.[64] Among the ten directors were Watts, Moody-Stuart, and the then Chairman of Shell, Van der Veer. About the court case, the latter said 'I am not concerned about that at all.'[65] Whereas Moody-Stuart said '[I feel] a sense of responsibility for what happened.'[66] In April 2005 it became clear from Shell's accounts that the company had advanced £6.4 million to help the directors pay their legal costs in these cases.[67]

By September 2004 Shell had announced that it was to engage in a serious restructuring. This whole episode reveals that the core task of the company is to maintain the value of its core assets – its future oil reserves. Everything is subservient to this, from the communities who live where it extracts oil to the 'special publics' in the metropolis. Shell had been turned upside-down, not by customers who scrutinized its forecourt prices, nor by the governments who watched the legality of its practices, nor by NGOs who judged its environmental record, but by those in the City who analysed its financial heart. It reveals the power of one of the company's key constituencies in the political centre – the investment managers of the predominantly American banks in London.

'I know that those deeply regrettable events mean that we have much to do to restore our reputation with stakeholders, and accept the urgent need to learn the lesson and ensure that such events cannot and do not happen again,' wrote the Chairman of the CMD, Jeroen van der Veer, in the *Shell Report* published in May 2004.[68] The reserves crisis of 2004 destroyed much of the work of the 'long term campaign on the communications front', symbolized by that *Shell Report*'s predecessor,

Profits and Principles. If Shell could be so duplicitous right at its financial heart, what hope was there for an honest deal in the company's commitment to sustainable development in Nigeria?

Patrick Smith from *Africa Confidential* has watched the whole drama unfold: 'On the reserves issue they were caught with their pants down and various individuals have taken a fall, but it seems to me, having talked to people who know a lot more than I do, there has been no real root and branch reform of the way Shell does business in Nigeria. At the end of the day, they feel they were right; there have been a few public relations errors, but broadly, life is going to go on as normal.'[69]

So what is normal in the eyes of Shell? The leader column about the reserves crisis in the *Financial Times* put it simply: 'The other lesson is the importance of high standards of corporate behaviour in an industry that operates in some of the most corrupt and poorest parts of the world. Oil companies are already very suspect to many local populations and non-governmental organizations which might well wonder, with Shell in mind, whether a management that lied to its biggest shareholders would have any compunction doing the same to Nigerian villagers.'[70]

At the heart of the Shell reserves fiasco were the issues of transparency and corruption. In this respect, Shell is not the only company to have been caught out in Nigeria.

Chart 3. The Niger Delta in London – the web of institutions and companies related to Shell's operations in Nigeria, 2005

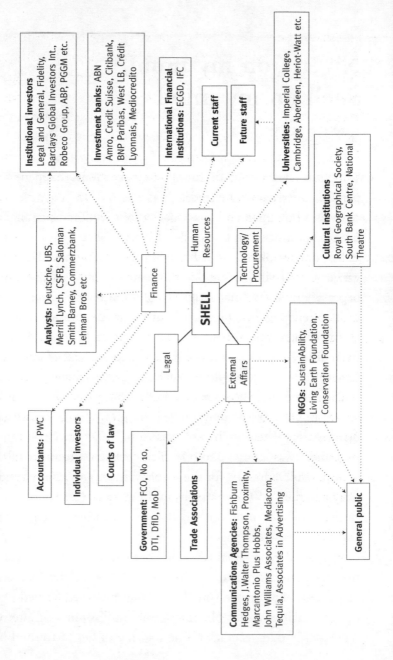

Nigeria on my mind, Shell on my mind

JAMES MARRIOTT

Sometime at the end of the 1960s two events happened in parallel, utterly unconnected.

I was a boy then, and passionate about wildlife, spending all my pocket money on books about birds, collecting scrapbooks full of animal pictures cut from Sunday magazines. The Shell garage in the village – about thirty miles south of London – began giving away small brightly-coloured plastic-covered 3-D cards of endangered species. About two and a half inches long and two high, the pictures would change as I looked at them from different angles – the dolphins would leap out of water, the Przewalski's horses would wander across the steppe.

Each time my Mum or Dad pulled onto the forecourt, I'd gather another one. In due course I was given the album with its blank spaces where each card was to be stuck in. On the first page there was a large photo of Sir Peter Scott, founder of the World Wildlife Fund – for the whole venture was jointly run by Shell and the WWF. Eventually, to my delight, I had a full set of cards, a full album of animals that swam and galloped, swung and flew across the pages.

In about the same year (the dates of these things are unclear to me now), Jane saw pictures of the Biafran War on the television: black and white images on the evening news, emaciated children, mutilated bodies. She told me about this not long after we met, twenty-odd years later. She told me of her terror and her confusion. Of not sleeping. Of crying and asking her Dad to explain why such things happened. Of her Dad's calmness and patience as he tried to explain the cruelty of the world, presented by the BBC to that household on the northern fringes of London: Nigeria howling and wailing in the mind of a suburban girl.

Thirty-five years after these events, they don't seem so unconnected. Jane and I spend our lives together, and I wonder how the architecture of our imaginations is shaped, in some small way, by the effect of these memories. Nigeria in black and white, full of blood and starvation. Shell, in bright colour, all free gifts and a delight in the animals of the earth. How did the company, how did the media, construct the shelter of our minds?

At a cafe table, a man and two women in their sixties, strangers to me, are talking: 'It's all very well, but if we give them all this money, how do we know they'll spend it on the right things? The people in charge are so corrupt.' Only a few days to go now before Live 8 and the G8.

CHAPTER SIX

Does Corruption Begin at Home?

'What is going on in Nigeria today is not going on anywhere else. Nigeria today is the centre against corruption in the world.'

Nuhu Ribadu, Head of Nigeria's Economic and Financial Crimes Commission[1]

West Green Road in North London is not on the tourist trail and is a long, long way from the tidal creeks of the Delta. The road snakes west to east from Turnpike Lane to the Tottenham High Road. Equity House, Number 86, has a scruffy-looking black door. This dishevelled and shabby building is in the middle of a parade of shops, squashed between a halal butcher and a property service company.

But this nondescript building is the London office of a solicitor called Jeffrey Tesler. It has been his office for thirty years. It is Tesler who was working for the TSKJ consortium and who is now at the centre of a corruption scandal that is engulfing the $10-billion Bonny LNG plant, thousands of miles away.

Tesler's operations are now being investigated by France's leading anti-corruption judge, the Department of Justice in the US, the Securities and Exchange Commission in the US, the Serious Fraud Office in the UK, the Swiss authorities, and a Nigerian Parliamentary Commission: five countries investigating one gas plant in Nigeria, in a web of intrigue that stretches across continents, but whose heart is in London.

The TSKJ consortium is named after its different partners: the French firm Technip, the British firm M.W. Kellogg – owned by Kellogg, Brown and Root, which in turn is owned by Halliburton and Japanese Gas Corporation – the Italian company Snamprogetti and the Japanese Gas Corporation. In December 1995, the month after Saro-Wiwa's execution, TSKJ won the contract to build the first phase of the gas plant at Bonny.

As of August 2005 no one has been charged with corruption. Tesler is cooperating with the French investigating judge. He has refused to speak to journalists. When approached for an interview for this book he said, 'I am afraid I don't give interviews or deal with any such matters'. His lawyer has consistently denied that his client has done anything wrong.

The Tesler inquiry is just one of a number of investigations into corruption and tax evasion hitting Western companies in Nigeria. Some companies may try the excuse that corruption is just the cost of doing business in a country like Nigeria, and tax evasion is just good business sense . . . as long as you do not get caught. But times are changing.

'Things have changed,' argues Nuhu Ribadu, the energetic chairman of Nigeria's Economic and Financial Crimes Commission (EFCC). 'Things were bad. We did not handle our affairs properly. We are trying to get our act together. We are trying to correct the wrongs of the past. We are trying to see if we can establish a rule of law, fight corruption, and establish transparency.'[2]

The EFCC has been set up by President Obasanjo. Its mission is to 'curb the menace of corruption that constitutes the cog in the wheel of progress'. The task facing Nuhu Ribadu is nearly overwhelming in a country where corruption is rife. It is also highly dangerous. Ribadu says he is very conscious of the risks to his own safety. 'But I'm also aware that the work has to be done. We have no alternative but to do it.'

Ribadu works eighteen-hour days, which leaves him little time for his family or his love of films. He is already tackling internet fraud and government corruption. He has arrested his former boss, the Inspector General of Police, over fraud, attacked the Education Minister over bribery (who maintains his innocence), and arrested a Nigerian legislator for internet fraud.[3] Three Nigerian newspapers declared him Nigeria's Man of the Year in 2004. But one major problem facing Ribadu is that much of the corruption is not in Nigeria at all. Just as corporate lines of command are spread across the globe, so too are their financial webs.

London Weather Calling

The central allegation against 57-year-old London solicitor Jeffrey Tesler is that one of his companies, Tri-Star Investments, received at least $166 million for a 'slush fund' 'of allegedly corrupt payments' to help the TSKJ consortium win the various LNG contracts from Nigerian officials for the $10-billion Bonny gas plant.

Two of the partners in the TSKJ consortium told the *Wall Street Journal* that Kellogg managed the consortium. Snamprogetti declined to comment except to say it has been contacted by the Securities and Exchange Commission (SEC). Technip has also stated that a judicial investigation has been opened 'relating to certain contracts involving the construction of an LNG facility in Nigeria by the joint venture TSKJ.' Technip added that 'its standing policy is not to comment on affairs covered by judicial confidentiality'. Halliburton has made various statements to the SEC, detailed in this book.

The scandal began to unravel in October 2003, when a former director of Technip of France, one of the partners in TSKJ, told the French judge of the 'existence of a black box set up in Madeira', and accused Tesler's company Tri-Star Investments of being 'directly linked to corruption in Nigeria'.[4]

A 'train' is a section of processing capacity from gas to liquid. The Bonny plant had six proposed trains, sections of processing capacity from gas to liquid. TSKJ had just won the contract for the first two: the consortium set about winning the contracts for trains 3, 4, 5 and 6 as well. The partnership formed a company, TSKJ, based on equal 25 per cent shares. It was incorporated in the tax-haven of Madeira in Portugal, but the consortium was run from M.W. Kellogg's London office, Kellogg Tower, in Greenford near Heathrow airport, where a US flag flies on top of the building.[5]

In January 1996 construction started on the Bonny project. In March 1999, just months before civilian rule was restored, TSKJ controversially won the contract for the third train, in a deal reportedly signed at Schipol airport. A fourth train was won the following year. Train three is now working, train four is due in 2005 and train six by 2007. All these were, or are being, built by the TSKJ consortium, which had received about half of the $9 billion spent by September 2004.[6]

By the time the sixth train is completed in 2007, NLNG believes Nigeria will have the world's second or third largest liquified natural gas output, the majority of which is destined for Europe and the US. Gas for the first three trains goes to Europe, with almost two-thirds from trains four, five and six destined for the US.[7]

It is alleged both that payments were made to Nigerian officials and that kickbacks were paid to expatriate members of the consortium that coincided with each stage of construction at Bonny. Tesler denies the allegations of bribery, but has admitted receiving some $140 million that he says were legitimate consultancy fees on the oil project from 1994 to 2001.[8]

The investigators are looking into suggestions that Tesler received $60 million for the first contract, signed by Tesler on behalf of Tri-Star Investments in March 1995. The second contract, for $32.5 million, was signed by Tesler's business partner Michael Kaye, on behalf of Tri-Star Investments, in March 1999. The third contract, for $51 million, was in December 2001 and the fourth, for $23 million, in June 2002. Each payment to Tesler was reportedly made after the signing of the agreements between TSKJ and the NLNG officials. When asked about his involvement with Tri-Star Investments, Mr Kaye said, 'I don't want to discuss anything in relation to it.' He also pointed out that 'a solicitor often signs contracts on behalf of a client. It is quite normal. I do it all the time. I am not party in relation to any thing at all.' Kaye said that 'in no way at all' did he get involved with Tri-Star Investments dealings. When asked whether he still worked with Mr Tesler, Kaye replied: 'I am not goint to make any more comment.'[9]

In these contracts between a company called LNG Serviços and Tri-Star Investments (see below), Tesler agreed to 'promote and support the consortium' and 'assist in the maintaining of favourable relationships with the client and any other government and business representatives, when deemed desirable to further the securing of the EPC contract.' The contract also specified that payments were not meant to be paid to government officials.[10]

LNG Serviços is also central to the investgations. The TSKJ consortium created the subsidiary, also based in Madeira, that was half-owned by M.W. Kellogg The Portuguese were the first

European country to exploit the Niger Delta in the sixteenth century – now the country is an importer of Nigerian crude and LNG and its tax haven has become entangled in the Bonny Gas web.

LNG Serviços paid at least $166 million to Tri-Star Investments, a company incorporated in the British tax haven of Gibraltar, although it had accounts at the Swiss bank, Union Bancaire Privée, and at HSBC in Monaco.[11] A source close to the French inquiry also told *Le Figaro* newspaper that they were interested in the switch of banks from Switzerland to Monaco as 'this change in banks coincides with the start of a judicial procedure in Switzerland targeting Sani Abacha's assets there.'[12]

While it has subsequently been established that Tesler has only ever visited Nigeria once, the investigators found that he has a history of close connections with Nigeria's elite. These include General Sani Abacha, military ruler of Nigeria from 1993 to 1998, and his oil minister Dan Etete, who took office in March 1995 – two days before Tesler signed his first contract.

Giving evidence before the French judge, Renaud Van Ruymbeke, Tesler set out some of the background to his long-established connections in Nigeria. 'Since 1977, a period in which I started to work in Nigeria, I was the advisor of several important businessmen including a certain number of members of the Government,' he told the judge.

Tesler knew 'the Chief of Staff of the Navy, the Chief of Staff of the Air Force and a large number of officers who came to the War School in London because at the time it had a very good reputation. A large number of these officers asked me advices [*sic*] on all of their affairs. Not only commercial but also everyday (school, doctors, etc.). Many had children in London, had health care, their wives lived and shopped in England. They

are English-speakers and it is a former English colony.'[13] Tesler
has made millions exploiting the connections of our colonial
past. 'The big companies found out that this guy can deliver,'
argues Nuhu Ribadu. 'If you talk to him, it's as good as talking to
the President.'[14]

It is certain that some one approached one of Nigeria's Oil
Ministers. Patrick Smith from *Africa Confidential* recalls how he
spoke to Dan Etete's predecessor, Don Etiebet. 'He told me
someone rang him up and said "my name is London Weather
and we will set up an account for you, and every time I put
money into it I will phone you up and say London Weather is
calling". He told me that he'd turned down the offer.'[15] However there is no evidence linking Tesler to this offer.

Whitewash at the White House?

The corruption probes have political significance in the US,
because oil services giant Halliburton acquired Dresser, the parent
company of M.W. Kellogg, in a $7.7 billion deal in February 1998.
There is no evidence that Halliburton was aware of irregularities
at the Bonny plant at the time of purchase. The Chief Executive
Officer of Halliburton was Dick Cheney, now Vice-President. The
man named by Dick Cheney to head the new company known as
Kellogg, Brown and Root (KBR) was Albert Jack Stanley. Stanley
too became embroiled in the corruption scandal.[16]

Embarrassingly for Halliburton it has come to light that the
year after they took control of the company, William Chaudan,
the KBR representative on the TSKJ consortium, was pushing
for Tesler's contracts to be renewed. This 'raises questions over
what Mr Cheney knew – or should have known – about one of
the largest contracts awarded to a Halliburton subsidiary,' argues

the *Financial Times*. 'Mr Cheney's office did not respond to questions.'[17]

In his testimony before the French judge, Tesler admitted that between 1996 and 1998 he had paid $2.5 million into Swiss bank accounts held by the oil minister Mr Etete under a false name. Tesler claimed the money was for investments in offshore oil exploration, and that he did not know that Etete controlled the account.[18] Tesler was also reluctant to admit who were the real beneficiaries of some of the money. One account into which some of the money went was named 'Amal'. Tesler was asked who owned the account:

Tesler: 'I don't know exactly, I think something like the Fides Trust.'

Question: 'I didn't ask for the name of a financial establishment or accountant, I asked for the name of the actual beneficiary.'

Tesler: 'I don't know.'

After consulting his lawyer, Tesler then admitted: 'I believe that the final recipient of the Fides Trust account is Mr A.J. Stanley. I hesitated to mention it because of his links with Kellogg's. I think I met him in London around '94 or '95 to discuss the LNG programme.'[19]

Tesler admitted he had made payments to Chaudan as well as to Albert Jack Stanley.[20] Stanley received some $5 million in 'improper' payments from Tesler, who also placed $1 million into an account held by William Chaudan, although Halliburton 'has since learned that even larger sums may have gone into the accounts of Mr Stanley and Mr Chaudan'.[21]

An executive at Kellogg's working under Stanley's control was Wojciech Chodan, who now lives in Maidenhead, in the UK. It was Chodan who reportedly organized bank transfers relating to the Tesler contracts. Notes uncovered by Halliburton in an internal investigation found evidence of a meeting in November 1994, at which Chodan and Tesler 'discussed channelling $40 million to General Abacha through Tesler's firm Tri-Star'. There is however no evidence that the money was paid.[22] When asked by the *Guardian* newspaper about what had happened, Chodan replied 'I reported to Jack Stanley'.

In June 2004 Halliburton announced it had 'terminated all relationships with Mr Stanley and another consultant and former employee of M.W. Kellogg. The terminations occurred because of violations of our Code of Business Conduct that allegedly involve the receipt of improper personal benefits in connection with TSKJ's construction of the natural gas liquefaction facility in Nigeria.'[23] William Chaudan was also sacked. Neither Stanley, Chaudan or their lawyers have made any comments on the allegations. Stanley was later issued with a subpoena by the Securities and Exchange Commission (SEC).

By February 2004 the House of Representatives in Nigeria had authorized the Public Petition Committee to examine the bribery allegations. That same month, Halliburton announced that the Houston-based law company Baker Botts, which has close ties to the Bush family, would carry out its internal investigation. In August 2004 Chudi Offodile, chairman of the Nigerian committee, criticized the TSKJ consortium for being 'evasive'.

His interim report was published the following month and recommended that 'all companies forming part of the TSKJ consortium and all Halliburton companies in Nigeria should be excluded from new contracts and new business in Nigeria pending the outcome of the ongoing investigations.'[24] Offodile states he has 'no doubt in my mind that the payments to Tri-Star/Tesler were improper and could be classified as bribes'.[25]

When representatives of TSKJ and Halliburton finally testified before the Nigerian committee in October 2004, their 'failure to co-operate' was criticized by Nigerian MPs. Chairman Chudi Offodile argued that the companies' behaviour was an admission of guilt. 'The companies need to come clean,' he insisted, and 'Western governments need to encourage them to come clean.'[26]

By October 2004 Halliburton was facing inquiries into its operations in Iraq, Iran and Nigeria. The company made a discreet admission in its Security and Exchange Commission filing in the US: 'As a result of our continuing investigation into these matters information has been uncovered suggesting that, commencing at least 10 years ago, the members of TSKJ considered payments to Nigerian officials.'

The company also admitted that 'payments may have been made to Nigerian officials'. At its request, 'TSKJ has suspended the receipt of services from and payments to TSKJ's agent, Tri-Star Investments, of which Jeffrey Tesler is a principal, and is considering instituting legal proceedings to declare all agency agreements with Tri-Star terminated and to recover all amounts previously paid under those agreements.'[27]

Picking Up the Tab

British taxpayers' money is also intertwined with the scandal. In late 2002 the Minister for Trade and Industry, Baroness Symons, announced a £133-million guarantee for M.W.

Kellogg to help build the Bonny plant. The loan was financed by the Export Credit Guarantee Department (ECGD) who championed it as a prime example of the department's 'Good Projects in Difficult Markets (GPDM) initiative'.[28] The loan was finalized in January 2003.[29]

Despite this, Chudi Offodile believes that the British should have known about the scandal as the bribery allegations 'were public knowledge before the contract was signed. They ought to have done due diligence,' he says. 'If they had done so, I'm sure these things would have come up.'[30]

Dr Susan Hawley, from the British NGO, Cornerhouse, that has undertaken a two-year investigation into the ECGD, agrees. Speaking in May 2005 she argued that 'I think it is pretty clear that if the ECGD had asked the right questions . . . they should have picked up that there were serious problems and serious red flags that should have alerted them to the potential of bribery at least.' She continues: 'If they had asked the name of the agent and where the payment of the commission was to be made, they would have found that it was being paid to Tesler in a Monaco bank account, and that automatically should have raised suspicions. Normally you would employ a local agent, and you would not pay the money into an off-shore bank account.'[31]

A month later, in June 2005, the *Financial Times* published details of correspondence between the ECGD and Halliburton, obtained under the Freedom of Information Act. It concluded that the ECGD had done 'little to investigate serious allegations of bribery'. The documents also raised questions about whether M.W. Kellogg 'was entirely candid' in its application to the ECGD.[32]

Despite this, exactly a year earlier, in May 2004, the British Trade Minister, Mike O'Brien, had written that there was 'no suspicion of corruption'. He said he had been reassured by Halliburton officials that they were 'not under investigation themselves and that they believed this was entirely a French investigation into the actions of a French company'. Halliburton subsequently denied this, saying the company had 'advised the individuals at ECGD that there were investigations in the US and France'.[33]

It is not just the Nigerians who have criticized the British. The French investigating judge, Van Ruymbeke, calls Britain a 'haven' for corruption.[34]

There is growing concern as to how much Shell knew or should have known. 'We are yet to establish categorically that Shell was in the know,' said Chudi Offodile in June 2005, a month before the publication of his final report. 'But Shell was the technical adviser to the project and worked out the cost components.'[35]

Another person concerned about Shell's role is Patrick Smith. 'I don't find their "see no evil, hear no evil, do no evil" excuse very convincing at all,' he says. 'I had long, long discussions with them [Shell] which really involved them saying absolutely nothing. I said to them, you are equity holders in this business. You cannot absolve yourselves from responsibility. You award a contract to a consortium and the consortium behaves in a corrupt manner. Shell has an absolute interest in ensuring the integrity of the project and they clearly haven't done that. There is an issue of negligence at the very least on Shell's part.'

Smith also asks why Shell did not investigate the corruption: 'When British journalists, Nigerian journalists, Nigerian politicians all knew how corrupt the project was, why did Shell not get involved and try and stop it, as a major share-holder in the project?'[36]

Could the company have worked out cost components without knowing about the corruption? Has it been negligent? The corruption scandal started in 1995, just as Saro-Wiwa's trial got under way. Many people feel that Shell, in the capacity of technical manager, should have known that something was amiss. In 1997, in part because of Saro-Wiwa's death, Shell updated the group's Business Principles to categorically state that 'The direct or indirect offer, payment, soliciting and acceptance of bribes in any form are unacceptable practices.'[37]

It could be argued that the three chairman in charge of Shell during the duration of the scandal – Cor Herkstroter, Mark Moody-Stuart and Phil Watts – all bear some responsibility, as it happened on their watches. Moody-Stuart and Watts had also headed Exploration & Production at Shell, and they had direct responsibility for Nigeria.

Shell responds that the company is just the technical adviser to the project, maintaining that its work has been 'rigorous, well documented and impartial. Shell has no contractual relationship with TSKJ.' It also feels that it has not been negligent.[38]

Taxing Times

The Bonny LNG scandal is not the only time Halliburton has been in trouble with the Nigerian authorities. The company has also been embroiled in a tax-evasion scandal that has nothing to do with the gas plant. In its May 2003 Securities and Exchange Commission submission, Halliburton admitted that its subsidiary KBR had 'made improper payments of approximately $2.4 million to an entity owned by a Nigerian national who held himself out as a tax consultant when in fact he was an employee of a local tax authority.' The company noted that several employees had been fired as a result, and said that as much as $5 million in taxes could be outstanding.[39]

Two months later, in July 2003, Ribadu's EFCC declared that an employee of Halliburton, an American named Michael Sylva, was wanted for questioning in connection with the tax scandal.[40] In early 2005 the EFCC began to broaden its inquiries to investigate allegations of tax evasion by multinational oil companies in collusion with government officials.[41] Ribadu now says that 'In the case of Halliburton, we have just taken them to court for those who are involved in diversion and fraud.'

He adds that there is 'a lot of tax evasion' in the oil sector in Nigeria. But 'it is just a reflection of what has been going on in the country. Things are beginning to change now.'[42]

Nor is Halliburton the only company to be caught evading taxes in Nigeria. Willbros, another major international oil and gas construction company with a long-standing presence in Nigeria, is Shell's main sub-contractor onshore in the Delta, doing much of the actual work on the oilrigs and pipelines. In 1993 the company was embroiled in a fatal shooting incident in Ogoni, while trying to lay a pipeline. The person in charge at the time was James Ken Tillery.

Some twelve years after that incident, in January 2005, the company announced the resignation of Tillery, who was now President of International Operations. It also announced that Willbros's Audit Committee had retained independent, outside legal counsel and forensic accountants to begin an investigation into the conduct of Tillery and other Willbros personnel.[43]

In May 2005 Willbros announced that 'Mr. Tillery and other Willbros International employees or consultants may have directly and indirectly promised to make, made, caused to be made, or approved payments to government officials in Bolivia,

Nigeria and Ecuador, and possibly to client personnel in one or more of those countries.' In shorthand, here was another company admitting to bribery. Worse still, Willbros also admitted that it had been involved in 'illegal' tax accounting practices in both Bolivia and Nigeria.[44]

In a submission to the Securities and Exchange Commission, Willbros announced a reduction of income of up to $5 million in 2002, including $1.2 to $1.7 million related to underpayment of Nigerian payroll taxes and 'other accounting adjustments'. For 2003, Nigerian underpayments were between $0.5 and $0.8 million, with a further $0.4 to $0.7 million for the first three quarters of 2004: a total sum of $2.1 to $3.2 million.

If this were not bad enough, the company announced that 'In addition to the restatement amounts noted above, full year 2004 results were negatively impacted by: increased reserves for accounts receivable and warranty work, primarily in Nigeria; reductions of estimated contract margins on work in progress at year-end in Nigeria.'

Finally Willbros announced that 'the Company is withdrawing its guidance for the remainder of 2005 due to the following uncertainties associated with its operations this year', including 'Potential negative impact on contract margins in Nigeria due to changes in management, business relationships and business practices'.[45]

These revelations led to Willbros being named in a class-action lawsuit in the US. The complaint alleges that the company, in violation of the Foreign Corrupt Practices Act, engaged in illegal activities including the execution of related party transactions and the bribery of government officials in Bolivia, Nigeria and Ecuador.[46]

Nuhu Ribadu expects to see other companies in court for tax

evasion. 'Assuming there is something criminal in terms of forgeries or destruction of documents, then they will go to court,' he says. 'Or if the money has been diverted to pockets of individuals instead of government coffers.'[47]

See-Through Oil

Just as the person alleged to be at the centre of the Nigerian corruption scandal was in Britain, the firm commissioned to undertake an audit of Nigeria's oil industry is British, based in Aylesbury in Buckinghamshire. This is the home of the Hart Group, awarded a $2.3-million contract to undertake an audit of Nigeria's oil and gas industry from 1999, the year that President Obasanjo came to power, to 2003. It is a parallel investigation to the work being undertaken by Ribadu's EFCC.

It has been described as the most comprehensive energy sector transparency audit ever conducted.[48] The crucial, unanswered question is whether it will deliver, and whether it will uncover the corruption of Nigeria's oil industry. Accountant Chris Nurse, Managing Director of the Hart Group, said the audit will also examine flows of money between the government and oil firms. 'The intention is to get a lot of the information which was previously regarded as commercially secret into [the] public domain,' he told the press.[49]

The Hart Group was chosen from some dozen short-listed contenders who had submitted bids to the Working Group set up to push forward Nigeria's own version of the Extractive Industries Transparency Initiative, known as the EITI. The EITI had been announced by Prime Minister Tony Blair at the World Summit on Sustainable Development in Johannesburg, in September 2002. Its aim is 'to increase transparency over payments by companies to governments and government-linked entities, as well as transparency over revenues by those host country governments'.[50]

In a move designed to show that Nigeria was beginning to tackle corruption head on, in February 2004 President Obasanjo launched Nigeria's own version of the EITI – called NEITI. 'I personally have no doubt that Africa's era to be clean, open, transparent and accountable is now,' said Obasanjo. 'I rejoice greatly that Nigeria is, and will continue to be, at the helm of the continent's new transparent dawn.'[51]

One of those speaking at the conference along with Obasanjo and Paul Boateng – the Financial Secretary at the British Treasury – was Egbert Imomoh, ex-Deputy Director of SPDC. It was Imomoh who had requested military assistance in Ogoni in 1993 (see Chapter 3). He was now a Senior Corporate Advisor for Shell International in London.[52]

Once again Nigeria is taking the lead on the African continent, trying to return to the role it had played in the 1970s. But in trying to create this new dawn, Nigeria faces an awesome task, as the work of the EFCC shows. The EFCC believes that some £220 billion has been wasted, squandered or looted by Nigeria's rulers between Independence in 1960 and the present. Some $100 billion in private Nigerian assets is currently sitting in Western bank accounts, in London and Switzerland.[53]

General Sani Abacha, the military ruler who signed Saro-Wiwa's death warrant, presided over audacious looting of the Nigerian treasury. In one single incident his national security advisor, Ismaila Gwarzo, is said to have presented a note from Abacha to the Nigerian Central Bank and walked out with $4.5 billion. He was reported to have immediately passed half of it to Abacha's son, Abba,[54] who currently awaits trial in Switzerland, charged with aggravated money laundering, participation in a criminal organization, and embezzlement.[55] Abacha's Finance Minister is also thought to have embezzled $2 billion from the external debt service account alone.[56] Shortly after Abacha died in 1998, his family were forced to return over 66 billion Naira ($500 million).[57]

Today, the Nigerian authorities are still seeking the return of billions of dollars of Abacha's money from bank accounts in London, Switzerland, Liechtenstein and Luxembourg. 'We are only now beginning to come to grips with some of what he did,' said Osita Nwajah, a spokesperson for the EFCC, in June 2005.[58]

General Ibrahim Babangida, Abacha's predecessor as military ruler, is also widely seen as having looted the till. During his eight-year reign between 1985 and 1993 vast quantities of cash were embezzled, stolen or frittered away on prestige industrial projects that were famously unproductive. An investigation took place in the late 1990s into the disappearance of over $12.4 billion generated from the spike in oil prices during the first Gulf War, supposedly invested in various projects. The investigators confirmed the disappearance of the $12.4 billion, and that the projects were of doubtful viability. It was a 'gross abuse of public trust', according to the chairman of the investigation.[59] Babangida has never been called to account, and today is considering a bid for the presidency in 2007.[60]

With this kind of past, there are those who feel the fact that Nigeria has even initiated some kind of process of transparency is a cause for cautious optimism. 'Nigeria has been held up as a model within the EITI,' says Henry Parham, the co-ordinator of the Publish What You Pay Coalition, which aims to help citizens of resource-rich developing countries hold their governments accountable for the management of revenues from the oil, gas and mining industries. A coalition of some 250 NGOs, it is funded by global financier George Soros.[61] 'It's taken quite a lot of time to get to where they are. However, they have now enshrined the EITI into Nigerian law and this is a very strong statement of commitment.'[62]

Much, in the short term, will depend on the Hart Group and on the person in charge of the NEITI Secretariat, Dr Oby Ezekwesili, the charismatic and experienced former chair of Transparency International in Nigeria, known as 'Mrs Due Process'.[63]

Ezekwesili chairs what is called NEITI's National Stakeholders Working Group, composed of some 28 representatives, mainly from the Nigerian government but also from Shell, Chevron, NGOs and the media. Dr Edmund Daukoru, the Special Adviser to the President on Petroleum and Energy, who became the new Minister of State for Petroleum Resources in July 2005, is also a member of the Working Group.

As with many government committees, members from civil society are in the minority. There are other problems too. Henry Parham argues that the NEITI bill is 'very flawed' and gives too much control to Obasanjo. The NEITI Secretariat is housed in the presidential villa, under Obasanjo's control. He argues that the Working group 'should have more of a central role in monitoring and guiding the EITI process. There should be accountability mechanisms built in, also giving parliament more oversight, rather than just the Presidency.'

Other problems have appeared too. Minutes of the first meeting show that the Working Group 'touched on the problem of a fundamental lack of understanding of the way the oil industry operates'.[64] In their second meeting the Working

Group discussed appointing a consultant to assist them in their task. They 'discussed the issue of conflict of interest, noting that the best consultants are already working for the oil industry. [They] resolved to tackle the problem by selecting a consultant with the least conflict of interest issues relative to their appropriateness for the assignment.'[65] The challenge of finding a disinterested consultancy is common in the oil industry, especially in relation to countries such as Nigeria, where oil commands so much of the industrial economy.

The lack of co-operation from the oil industry is also a problem. At the third meeting: 'The Group noted the continued absence of Multi National Oil Company Stakeholders, particularly Shell, Chevron and Nigeria LNG at its meetings.' The 'Group averred that their absence was not only denying their firms the opportunity to participate, but also denying others in their constituency the chance to contribute.'[66] Shell's lack of attendance contrasts to SPDC's latest Annual Report, in which the company says it 'supports' the Initiative and was 'delighted' to be asked on to the Working Group.[67]

Based on the bids of lowest cost, in October 2004 the Working Group chose the American consultants Goldwyn International Strategies (GIS) to act for the Group.[68] Britain's Department for International Development paid for the cost of the advisors. Goldwyn International is run by David Goldwyn, seen as a leading expert on oil transparency, who has been instrumental in pushing the importance of African oil to US policy makers.

In January 2005 Goldwyn was named as a Senior Advisor to the Center for Strategic International Studies in the US, a leading neo-conservative think-tank. A former CIA agent, Robert Ebel (see Chapter 7), runs the Energy Programme.[69] So the person advising the Nigerian government is paid for by the British and works for a think-tank with links to the CIA.

Goldwyn's first task was to advise the Working Group about the appointment of a consultancy to undertake the audit of the oil industry. The audit would be in three parts: first a Physical Audit, designed to give a complete picture of the amount of oil and gas that has been produced, lost, refined and exported in the given period of review; secondly, 'financial flows' to show 'who has paid money, how much and who to?'; and thirdly, a 'Process Audit: a critical examination of crucial extractive industry processes' that would include recommendations for the future.

After the first consultancy chosen for all three audits 'failed to meet subsequent deadlines' during negotiations, the Hart Group was chosen in March 2005.[70] Hart Group calls itself 'a UK-based consulting organization with a large network of local and international associates and a 16-year track record of work mainly in underground resources (minerals and oil and gas) sectors'.[71] Its managing director is Chris Nurse, a chartered accountant whose experience includes 'industrial restructuring and financing'. Nurse used to work for Price Waterhouse Coopers, which is now one of Shell's two accountancy firms.

Other partners to the Hart Group include the Nigerian accountancy firm S.S. Afemikhe & Co., which has worked on Nigerian upstream operations, as well as two British-based companies, Chris Morgan Associates, based in the affluent town of Tunbridge Wells in Kent, and TRACS International from the Scottish oil capital, Aberdeen.[72]

The Devil is in the Detail

Although the oil industry has promised the EITI co-operation in theory, its response has been different. Hart soon ran into difficulties over the issue of aggregation/disaggregation of data. The Working Group had called for both 'Aggregated and Disaggregated reports (disaggregated by company/institution) in a manner suitable for publication and public comprehension'.[73]

As the old saying has it, 'the devil is in the detail': specific figures are needed to show what money goes where. To see 'who has paid what to whom', detailed accounts that remain 'disaggregated' are required. The more the figures are massed together – the more they are 'aggregated' – the harder it is to 'follow the money'. A company using aggregate data can add everything up and hide payments or bribes in gross figures. Disaggregated payment data leave everything plain for all to see.

'Not surprisingly,' says Stan Rerri from the NEITI Secretariat, 'due to the opaque nature of the oil industry there is an industry reluctance to fully disclose all information and data (wellhead by wellhead) regarding their operations.' Rerri also says that the 'Oil companies tend to hide behind dated Confidentiality Clauses that they claim prevent them from full disclosure.'[74] His concerns are reflected by ex-*Financial Times* journalist Michael Peel, who wrote a report on the Niger Delta for Chatham House in July 2005: 'In my experience and that of other journalists,' wrote Peel, 'the companies' attitude reflects a wide pattern of non-disclosure and piecemeal and partial disclosure in the industry in Nigeria.'[75]

The Hart Group had a tricky meeting with the oil companies including Chevron, Shell, ExxonMobil and Total to discuss this issue. Although they are required to 'present non-aggregated financial data' to the Working Group, in a progress report the Hart Group admitted that the oil companies had 'not bought into that proposition' as it 'might harm their competitive position'.

Hart noted that the oil companies were 'reluctant' to hand over disaggregated figures to their investigation and definitely not to the Working Group. If disaggregated information were to be given to the Hart Group, it would be in confidence, and on the understanding that it would not be passed on to the Working Group. The oil companies wanted the Hart Group to act as 'an independent and professional repository of information and present only aggregated information'. The Hart Group noted, however, that what the oil companies wanted was 'at variance with our contract'.[76]

The industry's insistence on aggregated figures was evident when Chevron's Vice President for Business Development, Sam Laidlaw, spoke in London at an important EITI conference in March 2005. He noted that Chevron saw just two aggregated figures, for gross revenues paid and received, as 'sufficient to meet the necessary EITI purpose'. If this were indeed the case, there is no way investigators could work out whether Chevron had been paying bribes or involved in tax evasion. This is the attitude of a company that prides itself on being one of the first signatories to the EITI.[77] ExxonMobil even characterized the EITI as just a 'government-to-government dialogue'.[78] There was no need for companies to disclose anything.

Despite comments like these, Chris Nurse from the Hart Group is loath to criticize the companies. He says they 'are acting entirely reasonably' and that their 'own business is essentially their own business'.[79]

The Hart Group expects a team of 65 auditors to take about a year to uncover the web of intrigue that surrounds the oil industry in Nigeria. Experts on tax and on Nigeria in the United Kingdom are concerned that even this commitment of time and resources will prove inadequate.

Although the Hart Group may begin to get to the bottom of some misdoings, the vast complexity of the web of tax evasion and corruption that spans continents will not be easily unravelled. It would be the work of years for anyone to look not just at the companies but at their web of accountants, of subsidiaries, of bank accounts both in Britain and in numerous tax havens. And that would just be the financial investigation.

'I am terribly sceptical,' says Patrick Smith from *Africa Confidential*. 'You have layers upon layers of commercial and political vested interest there. They may uncover some stuff. It's going to be inordinately tough. People will try and take them out if they get too close to the truth. It's not just a bit of pilfering. It's billions and billions of dollars of pilfering. To get to the bottom of the illegal bunkering [see Chapter 1] – you would need an armed security company to do that properly. It's not something for forensic accountants alone.'[80]

Smith also alleges that the oil companies or their accountants sometimes have 'two sets of accounts. They will show you the set of accounts they want the government and officials to see. There will be another one locked away.' Others agree with him. John Christensen is a former senior economic advisor on tax to the Jersey government, now a co-ordinator of the Tax Justice Network that arose out of meetings at the European Social Forum in Florence in 2002 and at the World Social Forum in Porto Alegre in 2003. The Network is a 'response to harmful trends in global taxation, which threaten states' ability to tax the wealthy beneficiaries of globalisation'.[81]

John Christensen says he was also told by 'a source' that some 'foreign companies routinely cheat Nigerian tax authorities by keeping three sets of books: one for the parent company, which includes bribes, called "commissions" or "remunerations"; one for the local company, which has operational but not financial autonomy, which records expenses for kickbacks and pays remarkably little taxes; and one for the government, which does not admit to paying kickbacks inside the country.'[82]

Christensen works closely with Prem Sikka, the Professor of Accounting at the University of Essex, founder of the Association for Accountancy and Business Affairs, who is a well-known public critic of the ethics of the accountancy profession. Professor Sikka is worried about the oil industry wanting to present only aggregated data: 'It means that you can't study the real guts, which is what you really want to do. You'll get a "global" overall kind of approach, rather than say this company is doing this or that.' Christensen agrees. 'He believes that the oil industry is actually particularly collegial in the way it works. They may appear to be in competition, but they are all in JVs [joint ventures] with each other, they all know what is going on. The whole point of a transparency initiative is to be transparent – it's not a non-transparency initiative!'

Both men feel that the Hart investigation will be too limited to really get to the bottom of what is going on. Sikka argues that financial intermediaries, accountancy firms and the company's global affiliates need to be looked at. 'An organization does not exist within the four walls of a building, an organization is a network and a series of relationships,' he says.[83]

However, Stan Rerri from the NEITI secretariat issues a warning to the oil companies: 'The oil companies no longer have any excuse for not fully disclosing information and data on the Nigerian Oil and Gas Industry,' he says, adding that when the NEITI Bill is passed, 'hindrances and lack of co-operation would be a criminal offence and would be reported to the Economic and Financial Crimes Commission.'[84] If the oil companies do not play ball, they will have to answer to Mr Ribadu.

Tricks of the Trade

But even the EFCC may have difficulty getting to the bottom of tax evasion. Sikka explains in more detail some of the ways oil companies avoid paying tax in a country like Nigeria. 'Oil companies have hundreds of subsidiaries and affiliates and they also run a lot of joint ventures. So in principle oil could be extracted from a well in Nigeria and then sent to a refinery. You might say that is a simple transaction, but it may not be because that oil on paper can be sold to an affiliate in Italy, Switzerland, Jersey or anywhere really, and then eventually brought back again on paper to Nigeria. On the way, everyone is supposed to have "added value", which is a euphemism for saying they got a commission of some kind; the profits are then geographically dispersed.' This is what is known as 'transfer pricing' in the accountancy profession.

He continues: 'Profit is essentially laundered. The overall impact of that on the companies will be zero, because the overall profit is still retained within the group, but because it is reported in different jurisdictions it results in a lower tax bill, and along the way you are actually also taking away wealth because Nigeria is effectively worse off.'

Sikka gives an example of tax avoidance by an oil company in the North Sea. 'Basically they were extracting from the North Sea and sending the crude around the world on paper before selling to their refinery [in the UK]. They were then selling this through their service stations. To the UK tax authorities, the oil company was making hardly any profit from the entire set-up. All profit was made by the company's subsidiaries abroad.'

Christensen agrees with Sikka. 'The oil industry is particularly well set up for all this because it is totally integrated,' he says. 'Trade is done within the company right from extraction, to transportation, through to refining, through to selling to the consumer. At every step on the way, transfer pricing can be used.'

Richard Murphy, Director of Tax Research Limited, who once worked for KPMG says there are other ways the companies could abuse the system. The first is 'loading of costs': 'For a lot of oil concessions there is a cost-sharing agreement of some sort [between the company and the state],' says Murphy. 'In these agreements there is the "cost oil" and then there is the "profit oil". This means that the company that develops the concession is allowed to recover all costs of developing it up to and including, the point that it breaks even. Then the "profit oil" is split between the company and host country. So there is the obvious opportunity to load your costs on an inter-group basis to up your "cost oil" and therefore reduce the "profit oil",' he says. 'You therefore reduce the amount you have to pay to the host country.'

He suggested that there are three ways the companies can 'load' their costs and so extract profit from an operation and reduce tax paid to the host country. The first is to overcharge for physical assets supplied, the second to make a service charge, and the third to make a financial charge. A company might over-price the physical transfer of assets into the country. 'So if you are transfer-ring exploration equipment into a country, you might over-price it when it comes in,' he argues. Secondly, 'you might load costs onto the price of services supplied from outside the country for such things as the supply of staff, and management services.'

A finance over-charge is achieved by something called thin capitalization, by which a company might put in a massive loan facility to finance its operation in Nigeria, which is charged for at a high rate of interest from another part of the same company. 'The price might be much higher than the company would be charged for the same loan in somewhere like the UK, for example. It would be justified by the supposedly high-risk nature of the operation in Nigeria. This increases costs in Nigeria and reduces taxes and profits there. Worse still, the loan will be made from a tax haven like Jersey, and when the interest is paid there, it might well be tax-free.'

There is also the issue of a tax on reserves. 'A country like Nigeria has offered tax incentives to explore for and locate reserves of oil,' argues Murphy. 'The amount of tax you pay can be dependent on the amount of reserves you find.' Murphy and others believe it possible that some oil companies may have over-stated their reserves in order to reduce the taxes they paid. It was the taxing of reserves that was behind Shell's reserves fiasco in Nigeria.

Economist Jedrzej George Frynas has studied the oil industry in Nigeria for years. He argues that 'the control over operating costs by foreign oil companies is probably the key to the understanding of high profits in the Nigerian oil industry.'

Shell does not disclose its financial results for Nigeria, but argues that once the Nigerian government has taken its cut, the remaining partners share out only '$1.87' per barrel, as long as the price of a barrel of oil is over $30 dollars,[85] which of course it is. While this amount may seem small, 'the real benefits to Shell may be much higher,' argues Frynas, 'since the rules for the calculation of profits within a company are not publicly known. Shell as a multinational company sets prices and administrative charges between affiliate companies in order to reflect the services performed by its multinational system. The company may at times inflate costs, if it chooses to do so.' The fact of the matter is that TNCs have the power to manipulate internal pricing, although there is no evidence that Shell has done so.

Speaking in general about oil company activity, one former chief executive of the Nigerian National Petroleum Company has stated that: 'Proper cost monitoring of their operations has eluded us, and one could conclude that what actually keeps these companies in operation is not the theoretical margin, but what returns they build into their costs.'[86]

Another thing that may elude the investigators is the use of tax havens. Take for example the company Bonny Gas Transport, established in 1989 to ship gas from the Bonny plant. The company was set up in Bermuda, not Nigeria. Bonny Gas Transport owns six of the vessels used to transport the gas; a seventh is chartered on a long-term basis from Shell Bermuda Overseas Limited, with an option to buy.[87] So one company based in Bermuda charters a ship from another company in Bermuda, although the ship is based in Nigeria, and is funda-mental to Nigeria's energy exports.

Shell argues that the reason for siting the company in Bermuda is as follows: 'In line with other first-class ship owners the ship is flagged in Bermuda, and like many international companies it is also registered in Bermuda ... The majority shareholder in NLNG is the state oil company of Nigeria,

NNPC, with the other shareholders being Total and Agip. Registration of BGT in Bermuda was a shareholder decision.'

We also asked the company the following question: 'Tax experts have suggested that leasing capital equipment from subsidiaries in tax havens such as Bermuda is a way of minimizing a company's tax burden. Would Shell like to comment on this?' Shell replied simply: 'No.'[88]

It would take years for accountants to pick through the myriad of company structures and complicated tax networks to see just how much money the international oil companies have made at the expense of Nigerians. The network spreads from London to Jersey, Switzerland to Washington, Bermuda to Bonny.

Hidden in Western banks will be money that has left the country, in a pattern that ensures that Nigeria stays poor and the companies stay rich. So shareholders in Surrey or Virginia pocket a handsome dividend, while families in Nigeria have little. The efforts of the EFCC and NEITI in trying to bring the oil industry to account are a commendable but small first step in unravelling the web of corruption and tax evasion that surrounds the industry in Nigeria.

In many ways these efforts are about Nigeria trying to wrestle back some kind of regulatory and financial control of the oil industry from the companies. But just as Nigeria tries to control more of its own destiny, it is becoming increasing intertwined with the destiny of the United States. America needs Nigeria's oil and gas, whether Nigeria likes it or not.

Changing Perceptions

ANDY ROWELL

It is 7 July 2005. A day to concentrate. But it is hard. It is the day of the terrorist attacks in London, when four bombs ripped through our capital. There is blood and carnage everywhere.

Today is a day of changing perceptions. A day when the false sense of security that had descended over London has been shattered. The paranoid days post-September 11, when we feared that we might be next, had receded. We had begun to believe that the next bomb might not be ours. But it was not to be. The bombs were a sickening reminder that has shattered the illusion that London, as Madrid before it, is a safe place to be.

In writing this book I have to challenge some of my own inherited perceptions that London is safe, Lagos is not. Britain is free of corruption, but Nigeria is not. I am forced to look again, to remind myself that this is not true. Much of the corruption stems from London or Washington. Many of the mechanisms that keep Nigerians poor – the networks of offshore bank accounts that companies use to bleed Nigeria dry of its profits – are based in tax havens that were set up by the British and other colonial powers.

I am struck by what the Tax Justice Network say in their book *Tax Us If You Can*, that half the tax havens in the world are in the British Commonwealth. Many were established with the encouragement of the Foreign and Commonwealth Office. These tax havens are used to keep the rich and powerful rich, and the poor desperately poor, but I didn't hear tax havens being mentioned by the G8 leaders in their communiqué on Africa today. European and American banks continue to be conduits of exploitation as they allow money to move to these tax havens, with no questions asked. The G8 did not talk about them, either. That would be too close to home.

I blank out the bombings and finally speak to Nuhu Ribadu, the Chairman of Nigeria's EFCC. I have been trying for some time. But finally I am put through. The man in charge of Nigeria's huge anti-corruption drive still finds time to talk.

Ribadu expresses his sorrow and outrage at the bombings. We move on to corruption. For too long some British and American companies have been corrupt and have fleeced Nigeria. But more than changing perceptions, Ribadu is actually changing reality, by rooting out corruption.

Now, because of people like Nuhu Ribadu, things are changing. Here is a man who is changing perceptions of his own country. A person who is prepared to take on the rich and powerful, the people who thought they were untouchable. The days of people seeing Nigeria as a corrupt country 'are over', he says. Ribadu's task will not be easy, but I come away hoping he is equal to the challenge. Have the corrupt met their match? Are those that have been evading taxes going to be caught? It would not be before time.

CHAPTER SEVEN

The Next Gulf

'What I see now is a spiralling cost of oil. The American policies that have had a doubtful success in the Middle East, have therefore focused their attention around the Gulf of Guinea. It is not people-centred. It is just barrel-centred. Clearly you will bring more discontent and that discontent will be counter-productive.'

Ledum Mitee, President MOSOP[1]

The Admiral of the Fleet

The year is 1911. A young politician named Winston Churchill has just been promoted to be First Lord of the Admiralty, the top civilian post for the British Navy, at the age of thirty-seven. Churchill was a rising political star who had made his name in his twenties as a war reporter witnessing some of the most brutal battles of the British Empire in Africa. His family had married into the Colonial Administration when his mother wed Montague Phippin Porch of the British Civil Service in Nigeria, as her third husband.[2]

By 1911 Churchill believed that war between Britain and Germany was inevitable, and he was on the brink of a decision that changed British energy policy forever. 'His charge was to ensure that the Royal Navy, the symbol and very embodiment of Britain's imperial power, was ready to meet the German challenge on the high seas,' recalls Daniel Yergin, in his book *The*

Prize. 'The issue was whether to convert the British Navy to oil for its power source, in place of coal, which was the traditional fuel.'

When Churchill arrived at the Admiralty, some of the Navy was already running on oil, but the pride of the fleet – the battleships – still burned coal. Coal meant a safe, secure supply from the huge coalfields under Britain. Oil meant insecure fields in faraway lands. But coal required many men to keep the ship running, and coal gave engine speeds far slower than oil. Oil was fast. Britain and its Empire lay under a growing threat, and Churchill was dedicated to keeping the Empire intact. 'The whole fortunes of our race and Empire, the whole treasure accumulated during so many centuries of sacrifice and achievement,' said Churchill, 'would perish and be swept utterly away if our naval supremacy were to be impaired.'

Although British admirals were resisting the move to oil, for over a decade they had been under increasing pressure from the founder of Shell, Sir Marcus Samuel, to make the switch. Shell's heavy oil from Borneo was ideally suited for use as fuel oil for ships' engines. A close friend of Churchill's, Admiral Fisher, who was known as Churchill's 'dry nurse', urged Churchill to work with Samuel and Shell. 'He's a good tea-pot,' Fisher wrote to an unconvinced Churchill, 'though he may be a bad pourer!'

Shell eventually won the day as Churchill was persuaded, although he remained suspicious of the company's motives. 'Mastery itself was the prize of the venture,' said Churchill as he chose oil to power the fleet's battleships.

But mastery came at a price, and that price was to ensure continuation of supply. Churchill established a committee to examine such issues as price and security of supply, and in July 1913 he made a statement to Parliament: 'If we cannot get oil, we cannot get corn, we cannot get cotton and we cannot get a thousand and one commodities necessary for the preservation of the economic energies of Great Britain.' He added: 'On no one quality, on no one process, on no one country, on no one route, and on no one field must we be dependent. Safety and certainty in oil lie in variety and variety alone.'[3]

The concept of energy security being dependent on a diversity of supply, or energy diversity as it was then called, was born. Energy diversity did not mean different types of energy, but relying on more than one country for supplies to ensure that the oil never dried up.

Strength through Diversity

America is a thirsty country. Although it has just 4.5 per cent of the world's population, it consumes 25 per cent of the world's oil and gas. That is vastly more than any other country. This gas-guzzling country is used to being able to consume as much as it wants. However, in the months before George W. Bush became President, America was rocked by a series of rolling power-cuts and oil and gas shortages. These were politically embarrassing, and potentially financially crippling for America, were they allowed to continue.

Since the 1860s America has been one of the world's great oil producers, but by 2000 falling US domestic oil production and increasing consumption meant that for the first time in US history, oil imports had risen to over 50 per cent of total consumption. This was causing great anxiety about US energy security. To the fledgling President, addressing America's energy crisis seemed his first and most pressing task.[4]

He was not the first American president to face an energy

crisis. After the volatile years following the oil crisis in 1973, President Jimmy Carter gave his last State of the Union address in January 1980. Carter specifically articulated that any 'attempt by an outside force to gain control of the Persian Gulf region will be regarded as an assault on the vital interests of the United States', and pledged to defend that interest by 'any means necessary, including military force'.[5]

Twenty years on, America remains locked in anxiety over the security of oil supplies. In his second week in office, President George W. Bush instigated a major review of energy policy, to be undertaken by a committee chaired by Vice-President Dick Cheney. On his election, President Bush had turned to one of his father's old mentors to be his Vice-President. Cheney had served under both President Ford and Bush Senior. He was also the ex-President of Halliburton, the global construction company that is an inherent part of the oil industry.[6] As outlined in Chapter 6, it is also implicated in a major corruption scandal in Nigeria. Investigators are still trying to establish whether Cheney is in any way involved.

Cheney is not alone in Bush's cabinet in being connected to the oil industry. Condoleezza Rice, Bush's National Security Advisor in his first term of office and Secretary of State in his second was a Chevron Director for a decade from 1991 until 2001.[7] She also chaired the company's public policy committee from 1999–2001. In the early nineties Chevron was accused of perpetrating a number of human rights abuses in Nigeria (see Chapter 1). Rice had a Chevron tanker named after her; it was quietly renamed the *Altair Voyager* after she moved into the Bush administration.[8]

Bush's Commerce Secretary and close friend Don Evans was the CEO of Tom Brown, a natural gas company with fields in

Texas, Colorado and Wyoming, for over a decade. Nor do connections to the industry end there; they go through layers of the administration, and also extend to Bush's financiers. Of the top ten 'lifetime contributors' to Bush's election war chests, six either come from the oil business or have ties to it, according to the Center for Public Integrity. Chevron too had made sizeable donations to Bush's campaign.[9]

In May 2001 Cheney's Energy Committee report was ready. President Bush convened a cabinet meeting around the famous oval mahogany table in the Cabinet Room of the White House, the gift of President Nixon. The Cabinet Room, where all important meetings take place, is next to the Oval Office and overlooks the White House rose garden. On that May morning, portraits of former presidents looked down on the young Texan President as he made his announcement on energy policy. An unfinished painting of the signing of the Declaration of Independence hung above the marble fireplace.

Beneath the grand chandeliers, Bush had taken his usual position at the centre of the table, in the presidential chair a symbolic two inches taller than those of the rest of the cabinet. Sitting opposite him was Cheney with his copy of the 'National Energy Policy Report'. The policies it contained would change millions of lives for people the world over – poor people without access to political power, but whose resources the powerful wanted. Bush was naturally enthusiastic about the document. 'It provides over a hundred proposals to diversify and increase the supply of energy,' he said. 'I am really pleased with the work the Vice-President and his folks did.'[10]

The report was heavily criticized by environmentalists for being in favour of the oil and nuclear industries, and for advocating the opening up of areas currently off-limits for oil drilling, such as ANWR – the Arctic National Wildlife Refuge in Alaska, seen as America's last pristine wilderness. 'The Bush plan would despoil the environment, threaten public health and accelerate global warming,' retorted the environmental group Natural Resources Defence Council.[11]

Even if ANWR were to be drilled it would provide only a temporary stop-gap for this guzzling nation. America's thirst for oil and gas means that the country is going to become increasingly reliant on imports. Diversification of American supplies away from the volatile Middle East is needed. 'Concentration of world oil production in any one region of the world is a potential contributor to market instability, benefiting neither oil producers nor consumers . . . Greater diversity of world oil production remains important,' the report stated.

One of the areas flagged in the report as being key to oil and gas diversity was West Africa, expected to be 'one of the fast-growing sources of oil and gas for the American market'. The document urged the US to 'deepen bilateral and multilateral engagement to promote a more receptive environment for US oil and gas trade.' It also recommended the President 'improve the climate for US oil and gas trade, investment, and operations, and to advance our shared energy interests'.[12] Washington was eyeing up Africa as part of its diversification plans.

Some four months later, on the morning of 12 September, Bush was once again back in the Cabinet Room, this time in very different and difficult circumstances, having convened a meeting of his security chiefs the morning after the terrorist attacks in New York and Washington. Bush declared that 'freedom and democracy were attacked'. He also talked about the need to protect national security.[13]

While September 11 led America to fight wars in Afghanistan and Iraq under the banner of protecting national security, it also led it urgently to seek new ways of protecting the country's economic security. For America, this means protecting its energy diversity. America's energy policy changed forever. Overnight, from being peripheral players in America's energy needs, West Africa and Nigeria moved to become central players, as the region became a potential counterbalance to the Persian Gulf – the Next Gulf.[14]

Bring the Oil Home

Washington's influential think tanks also have West Africa in their sights. Four months after the September 11 attacks, the Institute for Advanced Strategic and Political Studies (IASPS) held a symposium on African oil at the University Club just a few blocks north of the White House. This stately red-brick building faces the National Geographic Society. The IASPS is not the usual Washington think-tank vying to influence political policy. It is actually based in Jerusalem, with an affiliate office in the American capital.

Its current president, Robert Loewenberg, set up the IASPS in 1984.[15] Another key individual at the Institute is William Van Cleave, who is seen as a long-term advocate of increased military spending and a more aggressive US defence policy. Van Cleave was senior advisor to Ronald Reagan and a member of the Committee on the Present Danger that pushed for higher defence budgets to fight the 'Soviet threat'.[16]

In 1996 the IASPS published a document titled *Clean Break: A New Strategy for Securing the Realm*. It has been described as the 'result of one of the most dramatic cases of direct involvement in Israeli affairs by pro-Likud hardliners in the United States. It was produced as a policy memorandum for ultra-hawk Binyamin Netanyahu, the incoming Israeli Prime Minister and then leader of the Likud Party.'[17] The document talked about toppling Saddam Hussein as an Israeli rather than American war aim, as a 'means of foiling Syria's regional ambitions'. The document was produced/written by a group of neo-conservatives that included Robert Loewenberg, led by Richard Perle, the hawk's hawk, from the American Enterprise Institute.[18]

So in January 2002, with war against Iraq looming, the IASPS held its symposium at the University Club about shifting America's reliance on oil away from the turbulent Persian Gulf. The title of the symposium was 'African Oil: A Priority for US National Security and African Development'. Present were various US government officials and military representatives, as well as the ambassadors from Nigeria, Algeria, Congo Brazzaville, Namibia, Cameroon and Equatorial Guinea. The keynote speaker was Republican Congressman Ed Royce, the then chairman of the House International Relations Subcommittee on Africa.

Royce is the long-term congressman for Orange County in California and his priorities include, among others, 'protecting our homeland and supporting our troops and veterans'. He has since become Chairman of the Subcommittee on International Terrorism and Nonproliferation, too. 'I think that African oil should be treated as a priority for US national security post-9/11,' said Royce. 'I think that post-9/11 it has occurred to all of us that our traditional sources of oil are not as secure as we once thought they were.'[19]

This was to become an oft-repeated message throughout

Washington: post September 11, African oil was now a US national security issue. Although Saudi Arabia has lots of oil, after September 11 it was seen as a source of anxiety, not a source of security.

Walter Kansteiner III, who is seen as an African expert, rushed to the symposium from a meeting with his 'dear friend' Colin Powell. Two years before the release of Nelson Mandela, Kansteiner had written *Revolution or Reconciliation*, a book that characterized the ANC as illegitimate, violent revolutionaries engaged in 'unjustified', 'Marxist' struggle. At the time of the conference, Kansteiner was Assistant Secretary of State for African Affairs.[20]

His message was the same as Royce's. It was 'undeniable' that Africa 'has become a national strategic interest for us,' said Kansteiner. 'It's hard to get people that are used to just thinking Middle East, Middle East, Middle East as an oil source to really break out of the box and think that Africa has incredible potential, not only in its current reserves and production, but in the future. African oil is of national strategic interest to us, and it will increase and become more important as we go forward.'

The military were there too. Lieutenant Colonel Karen Kwiatkowski from the Office of African Affairs, Department of Defense emphasized how 'important Africa is to US defense policy and US security'. This oil has to be protected, she argued. She explained how the US had recently developed 'International Military Education and Training' in Nigeria. The number of defence attachés to Africa has doubled in the past three years. Kwiatkowski said the military were keen to understand the challenges facing US energy companies and investors in sub-Saharan Africa. 'The more we know, the more we might be able

to help.' She also added, 'We'd like to have improved relationships with US companies in Africa.'[21]

Out of the symposium a working group known as the 'African
Oil Policy Initiative Group' was formed. Its report was handed
to the House Energy and Commerce Committee on 12 June
2002 (See Chart 4). The Committee's then chairman, Billy
Tauzin, a Republican from Louisiana, said, '9/11 has reawakened
the awareness of the American public to our extraordinary
dependence on energy from the Middle East. It has taught us
the value once again of diversifying energy supplies. It is
important for us to build new relations with new sources of
supply and to look toward Africa and other regions of the
world.'[22] One of the report's key recommendations was that
'Congress and the Administration should declare the Gulf of
Guinea an area of "Vital Interest" to the US'.[23] This was the
exact language Carter had used to describe the Persian Gulf in
1980.

With language like that, the report received a lot of attention
from American oil companies. It also went down well with the
Nigerian government. One of the co-chairmen of the 'African
Oil Policy Initiative Group', Paul Wihbey, travelled to Nigeria,
where he met President Obasanjo. Although Obasanjo is
Nigeria's civilian president, his whole career has been in the
military, including training in Britain,[24] and he is a man who
believes in the importance of military intervention. 'Obasanjo
was very receptive to the idea of a US strategic role in the Gulf of
Guinea,' said Wihbey. 'A mantra in our meetings was the idea
that post-9/11, the Gulf of Guinea should replace the Persian
Gulf.'[25] Although the Persian Gulf still has the vast majority of
reserves, the Gulf of Guinea could help with both diversity and
security of supply.

US–UK Energy Dialogue

It is not just America that is worried about security and diversity of supply. For decades Britain and America have met to discuss joint issues to do with energy. Five days before the House Energy and Commerce Committee received the African report, the British and American governments met in secret to discuss joint collaboration on supply. At the meeting was the then US Secretary of Energy, Spencer Abraham, a former top aide to Vice President Dan Quayle under George Bush Senior, and a UK team led by Joan MacNaughton, the Director-General of the Energy Group at the Department of Trade and Industry.

The purpose of the meeting was to move forward the concept of the 'US–UK Energy Dialogue' that had been in development as a result of an agreement between President Bush and Prime Minister Tony Blair at their summit meeting at Bush's ranch in Crawford in April 2002. Although the build-up to war in Iraq had dominated the summit, officials had also been quietly working on the energy collaboration.

The overall aim of the Energy Dialogue is to 'bring together the separate strands of international energy policy and foreign policy to identify means to help diversify global energy production and meet security and diversity goals; and support developing countries in sustainable economic and energy developments'. In the short term, diversifying global energy production means finding oil from as many places as possible.

The Dialogue recognized that a 'large proportion' of future oil demand would be met by increased production in the Middle East, because of its vast reserves. But it also 'identified a number of key oil and gas producers in West Africa on which our two governments and major oil and gas companies could co-operate to improve investment conditions, good governance, social and political stability to underpin long-term security of supply.'

To this end, 'summaries of our diplomatic, commercial and technical assistance activities in Angola, Chad, Equatorial Guinea, Mauritania, Nigeria and São Tomé have been prepared and we have compared notes on specific areas where we could work together to leverage resources effectively and avoid duplication of effort.' A 'business group meeting' was then held in Washington in February 2003, at which a 'productive discussion' was had by all.[26] Companies involved in the US–UK Energy Dialogue included many operating in Nigeria: Shell, Chevron, BP, British Gas, and ExxonMobil.[27]

The two governments were also working on 'good governance and transparency' of the energy industry in Africa. The paper noted that 'increasing transparency' of developing countries' extractive industries was 'critical', and that the Prime Minister had 'launched an initiative to address this issue'.

In January 2003 a meeting was held in London between US Secretary of Energy Spencer Abraham and Patricia Hewitt, the then Secretary of State for Trade and Industry, to discuss elements of the Dialogue report. By July a 'Memorandum' was ready to be submitted to Tony Blair by Hewitt and to President Bush by Spencer Abraham and Don Evans, Bush's Secretary of Commerce. A native of West Texas, Evans is said to be a 'soul mate' of the President. He has raised money for each of Bush's political campaigns. According to the think-tank Foreign Policy in Focus, 'It was Evans who, after a George W. binge, steered the future president away from sin and toward Jesus.'[28]

The 'sensitive' document presented four key objectives for the UK and US for increased energy co-operation, the primary one being 'promoting the security and diversity of future international energy supplies'. The others were: 'integrating international energy investment with the development and social challenges of host countries'; 'developing clean energy technologies'; and expanding the US–UK trade relationship in the energy sector, 'using this whenever possible to advance the three objectives above'.[29] Once again, security and diversity topped the list.

Rising Stakes

There has long been a contradiction between Nigeria's OPEC production quotas and Shell and the US government's desire for increased production to satisfy their needs. In its quest to obtain more Nigerian oil, by early 2003 the US was putting pressure on Nigeria to leave OPEC. This would mean that Nigeria would be free to produce as much oil as it wanted – or as much oil as America wanted it to.

But rather than production increasing in the spring of 2003, as a result of the ongoing violence in the Delta some 40 per cent of Nigerian production was shut down. This was causing great concern in Washington, as it was in London. America had reason to be worried. Just under a third of Nigerian production – some 30 per cent – was being exported to America at the time.[30] Any prolonged shutdown would have serious consequences for America's economy.

In April 2003 the first of two ships donated to the Nigerian Navy by the US Government had arrived in Lagos; a further five were to follow. Part of the reason for their donation had been to stop the oil-bunkering trade that was threatening legitimate supply.[31]

By now the issue of African oil was becoming a recurring

theme on the agenda of Washington's influential right-wing, neo-conservative think-tanks. In May, the Center for Strategic and International Studies (CSIS) waded into the debate, alarmed at the growing violence in the Delta. CSIS is a neo-conservative think-tank on K Street in Washington, two blocks north of the White House, a street famed as the home of lobbyists (see Map 7).[32] The fact that the chairman of CSIS's energy and oil programme, Robert Ebel, worked for the CIA for 11 years[33] has led many to ask how close CSIS is to America's security and intelligence establishment.

'The persistent crisis in the Delta region impinges increasingly on US interests and should become a significant element in the US–Nigeria bilateral dialogue,' wrote the director of the CSIS Africa Programme, J. Stephen Morrison, along with two staff. 'The United States should work with the Nigerian and other regional governments to trace and eliminate the source of illegal arms and commodity flows that have already wreaked havoc in much of West Africa and now threaten to undermine the stability of its largest member, Nigeria.'[34] Morrison had served in the Clinton administration in the Secretary of State's policy planning staff, where he was responsible for African affairs.[35]

Two months later CSIS instigated a 'Task Force on Rising US Energy Stakes in Africa', co-chaired by Morrison and David Goldwyn. The ex-Assistant Secretary of Energy for International Affairs under Bill Clinton runs Goldwyn International Strategies, who call themselves 'the world's leading expert on extractive industry revenue transparency' (see Chapter 6).[36] Members of the Task Force came from the US government and from NGOs as well as from Halliburton, Chevron, Shell Oil, and included Malik Chaka from the Subcommittee on Africa.

Reporting in March 2004, the Task Force concluded: 'The

United States has vital – indeed rising – national interests in West and Central Africa, concentrated in, but not restricted to, Nigeria and Angola.' This 'complex, unsteady zone' was identified as being critical to the 'security and diversification of US energy supply'.[37]

'Clearwashing' Exploitation

The Task Force argued that in order to exploit West African reserves, it was necessary for the US to 'pursue sustained, high-level engagement to promote transparency and reform' in Nigeria broadly consistent with the Extractive Industries Transparency Initiative and Publish What You Pay Initiatives. They called for an annual African Energy Summit and for increased military 'education and training' and 'expanded maritime security programs'. Finally, they argued that debt relief was an important tool to help keep President Obasanjo in power.[38]

Debt relief should be an aim for everyone, in order to end endemic African poverty. But here the Task Force was saying that debt relief would keep Obasanjo in power. Obasanjo is a man Washington and London can do business with – a military general, educated in London; a man they can trust, even though his people may not trust him. So debt relief is seen to be not only a tool for reducing poverty, it also becomes a tool for resource exploitation.

Similarly, in arguing for transparency the Task Force joined a growing chorus of voices demanding that the murky deals shrouding many oil industry contracts around the world should be subjected to clarification. Because of the perception of rampant corruption in Nigeria, it was becoming politically unacceptable for businesses to be seen to be operating there, unless there were to be some kind of reform. However, there are those who think the EITI will be ineffective.

A report recently released by Oil Change International, the Jubilee Debt campaign in the US and the British progressive think-tank, the Institute for Public Policy Research (IPPR) is wary of the initiative. 'We are highly sceptical of the ability of the current, non-mandatory, version of the Extractive Industries Transparency Initiative (EITI) to deliver on much, except to make oil companies and governments look good.'[39]

Any mandatory, rather than voluntary, moves to make transnational companies more accountable to their shareholders, wider stakeholders and civil society at large must be welcomed. However, it is worth remembering that much of the corruption in Nigeria may not originate in that country. The corruption scandal in Bonny and pervasive tax evasion by Western transnationals should deter us from any easy distinction between the law-abiding West and corrupt Nigeria (see Chapter 6).

Any initiatives that improve the lives of the people of the Niger Delta must similarly be welcomed. However, there is a danger that these initiatives will just become a way of facilitating America's exploitation of Nigerian crude without addressing the fundamental problems of the people of the Niger Delta.

Another call for transparency came from the Heritage Foundation, one of the most influential right-wing think-tanks in Washington, which held a seminar entitled 'Perils and Possibilities: Petroleum Opportunities in Africa'.[40] For years the Heritage Foundation was the conservative voice in Washington, reaching its peak with the Reagan administration.

On a stormy day in the American capital Ambassador Pamela Bridgewater, the then Deputy Assistant Secretary of State for African Affairs, the longest-serving US diplomat in South Africa, spoke. Bridgewater stood in front of the Stars and Stripes, in a dress that matched the yellow of the flag's braid. According to Bridgewater, US firms and money were 'key' in Africa's ongoing progress, and a 'linchpin' in developing the African oil sector. 'We believe that US energy security is advanced by sustained improvement in the investment climate of African nations and by ensuring that the African energy sector works as transparently and efficiently as possible,' she concluded.

Careful examination of Bridgewater's words reveals that what she is saying is that US energy security is advanced by transparency. Transparency thus becomes a means to an end, not an end in itself.

Also speaking at the Heritage Foundation was a staff member of the Subcommittee on Africa, Malik Chaka. An African specialist, Chaka served on both the 'African Oil Policy Initiative Group' and CSIS's Task Force. He had worked on the Africa Growth and Opportunity Act (AGOA), which he calls 'the most important US legislation targeted at Africa', though critics say it will force 'African countries to dismantle state support and privatize their economies in return for minimal concessions on trade and aid'.[41]

'America's interests are best served if African oil also fuels development,' argued Chaka. 'If it doesn't, you have US companies being targeted by angry citizens in oil-producing areas. They grow hostile and expect US oil companies to provide services, schools, clinics, clean water and roads that should be provided by government. . . . If new oil revenues are to advance development in Africa, the US and others must promote transparency and the rule of law in oil-producing countries.'

So African development could become a prerequisite for US energy security, and not a goal in itself. Transparency becomes a tool to make the exploitation of Nigerian oil acceptable to the wider world, even if the communities in the Delta do not want that exploitation. It is clear that many communities see the exploitation of their land as nothing more than a continuation of colonial exploitation, excluding them from the decision-making and the rewards, leaving them with the burden and the pollution. They are left poor partly because companies operating in Nigeria use an extensive network of tax havens to avoid paying tax.

Paul Wihbey, co-chairman of the African Oil Policy Initiative Group, was also a joint-author of a report titled *Breaking the Oil Syndrome – Responsible Hydrocarbon Development in West Africa*, published in July 2005. Its fundamental conclusion was that 'good governance, infrastructure and human development are the keys to the development, security and sustainability of oil-exports from West African states.'[42] But nowhere in any of the report's 38 recommendations was consultation with the communities of the Delta listed.

There is a danger that all these 'keys' and initiatives mean that it will become acceptable for oil exploitation with all its current problems to continue, but under a new guise. Just as 'green-washing' is the impression of environmental responsibility, this 'clearwashing' could be the impression of financial responsibility and transparency.

Oronto Douglas, the current Commissioner for Information for Bayelsa State, took part in early meetings on EITI, the Extractive Industries Transparency Initiative, but pulled out when it was suggested that transparency was the panacea for the oil industry's ills. 'It is absolutely not right if someone says that if oil is transparent, then everything is going to be OK,' argues Douglas.[43]

In their book *Shell Shock*, Ian Cummins and John Beasant note how 'transparency is a current Shell buzzword and is much used in PR documents'. A month after Shell had applauded President Obasanjo's announcement on transparency at an international conference in Berlin in 2002, 'Shell's senior managers were recommending [that] details of bonus negotiations and reserve problems in Nigeria be kept secret.'[44]

'We Drool Over São Tomé'

The keynote speaker at the conference to launch CSIS's Task Force report was Nigeria's Finance Minister, Ngozi Okonjo-Iweala. Other speakers included Ed Royce, along with General Charles 'Chuck' Wald, Deputy Commander of the United States European Command (EUCOM). Wald had led the American Air Force in the Afghan war and had seen combat in Vietnam, Cambodia, Laos, Iraq and Bosnia.[45] In a growing sign of the American military's changing preoccupations, Wald now spends half his time on African affairs. Africa has become a focus for US military policy, and Wald is the personification of that policy. Also speaking was Fradique de Menezes, the President of São Tomé, whom everyone knows by his first name. So what was Fradique doing in Washington?

Situated strategically on the Equator in the middle of the Gulf of Guinea are the two islands of São Tomé and Príncipe that make up the smallest country in Africa (see Map 1). These beautiful islands of ancient volcanoes, rainforests, beaches and crystalline waters were brutally controlled by the Portuguese, through first slavery and then forced labour. While still a Portuguese colony, they played a part in Shell's involvement in the Biafran War (see Chapter 3).

It was only in July 1975 that the islands became independent. The Portuguese left behind an impoverished nation, 90 per cent illiteracy and one doctor. The islands are now famous for some of the world's best coffee, Marilyn Monroe stamps, and the routing of sex chat-lines. Its colonial buildings slowly crumble under the unrelenting tropical sun.[46]

But one of the world's poorest and most indebted nations is now being courted by the richest, the USA, eager to exploit its oil and gain a strategic military foothold on the continent. São Tomé is seen 'as one of the largest untapped oil provinces in Africa' by the US government and foreign oil companies. Reserves of oil could be as high as 13 billion barrels.[47]

The country's oil reserves are being jointly developed with Nigeria in a 'Joint Development Zone' (JDZ) finalized in 2001. Ownership of the area in question was disputed by both countries, so the JDZ was a solution to the diplomatic quarrel. But 60 per cent of the resources go to Nigeria; 40 per cent to São Tomé.

Oil development had begun in the mid 1990s, before Fradique was elected and before the JDZ agreement. When Fradique came to power in 2001 he vowed to rip up the existing oil and gas contracts signed with Exxon and a company called ERHC. Since then, ERHC, or Environmental Remediation Holding Company, a US-listed company, had been taken over by a company called Chrome Energy.

Chrome Energy is in its turn owned by Emeka Offor, a Nigerian businessman close to both the former Nigerian President Abacha and the current President Obasanjo. The deal Chrome Energy and Exxon had secured with São Tomé has been described by the journal *African Energy* as so derisory as to be the 'modern equivalent of shiny beads and fancy cloth'. Gavin

Hayman of Global Witness, the NGO that has led the campaign for transparency in the oil industry, called it 'one of the worst in the oil industry's chequered history'.[48]

Fradique could not accept the contracts, and tried to renegotiate them, but still ERHC had preferential bidding rights in the new deal in the JDZ described by one oil analyst as 'ruinously unfavourable' to São Tomé.[49] The JDZ has not been without its difficulties, including quarrels over awards for licensing blocks, an attempted coup against Fradique, allegations of impropriety and corruption, and continued wrangling over ERHC's rights.

The JDZ's first licensing round in 2003 produced only one bid, from a consortium led by Chevron and ExxonMobil, triggering a front-end bonus payment of $123 million, of which São Tomé is due to receive $49 million. The more recent bidding round that ended in December 2004 was tightly fought. Since then there have been months of wrangling between Nigeria and São Tomé officials, who have clashed over the award of the blocks. São Tomé complained that Nigeria was proposing to give 20 per cent of the blocks to Nigerian companies, some of which had no experience in the oil industry.

For many years, dominated as it was by Shell and the other international companies, Nigeria had no domestic oil companies, but that has changed in recent years, with more indigenous companies bidding for concessions. When the results of the latest round of bidding were announced in late May 2005, ERHC Energy, as it is now called, and its partners were awarded two blocks. This caused outrage in São Tomé, contributing to the resignation of the Prime Minister of Fradique's government, leaving Fradique 'isolated' and the country 'biting the bullet' over losing out to Nigeria; Fradique had already lost his oil minister, who had resigned over the affair.[50]

Those advising Fradique believed the situation was a 'mess'.[51] It had been intended that the island should be an example of model oil development, a place where oil could help development, rather than be a curse, but already it has caused bitter infighting and allegations of corruption. The signs are not good.

There was rejoicing in Nigeria, however, especially over the concept of domestic companies beating their multinational counterparts. 'Nigerians are wiser now,' suggested an article in the Nigerian newspaper *This Day* in June 2005. 'The era when the oil majors, with headquarters in the United States, threw their weight around government offices in Nigeria and got cheap oil concessions are over. Nigerian entrepreneurs are rising to their feet, and they will give everybody a tough competition in future. No blackmail can roll back that momentum.'[52]

Dr Edmund Daukoru, President Obasanjo's adviser on Petroleum and Energy, was also enthusiastic about the potential of the JDZ (see chapter 4). 'The JDZ is unique not only as part of the Gulf of Guinea, but an extension of the Nigerian deepwater where the potential for major production capacity addition has already been established beyond doubt,' he said. 'We are at the threshold of major oil and gas development in our region in partnership with a consortium of world-renowned major oil and gas companies to explore and exploit our common resources for the benefit and emancipation of our peoples.'[53]

In an echo of their colonial past, it is likely that the islands will also become some kind of base for the American military. There have been persistent rumours that the US military are interested in building a regional command centre, something the São Tomé government are keen to encourage. The concept was also put forward by the African Oil Policy Initiative Group. An integral part of their plan to make the Gulf of Guinea an area of vital interest to the US was to establish a regional sub-command, similar to that in South Korea.

Speculation concerning US military intentions increased when General Fulford, a four-star general, Vietnam veteran and General Wald's predecessor at European Command, visited the islands. Fulford is currently director of the Africa Center for Strategic Studies, part of the Pentagon's National Defense University. Fulford said the US would train the island's under-equipped armed forces. The following month Fradique was reported as saying that he had received a phone call from the Pentagon telling him that the issue of a military base on the island was being studied, although the US denied this.[54]

Fradique was in New York in 2002 for the international commemorations held on September 11. Speaking to a breakfast audience at the Waldorf-Astoria Hotel in New York, that included President Bush, he argued that São Tomé was 'strategically situated in the most important petroleum area in the world today: the deep water off the western coast of Africa in the Gulf of Guinea'. He mentioned Vice-President Cheney's Energy Report and the importance of oil outside the politically volatile Middle East.

Before he left the US, Fradique had meetings with World Bank officials, congressmen and oil executives. He discussed the idea of a naval base with Condoleezza Rice's deputy for Africa, Jendayi Frazer, and Walter Kansteiner III, the Assistant Secretary of State for African Affairs.[55] The following month Kansteiner visited São Tomé as part of a trip to the region.[56]

In 2003 General 'Chuck' Wald became 'the most senior American official to visit the island'.[57] Wald has said he 'drools' over São Tomé, as it is a 'potentially ideal site' for the US military, and compares it to the Indian Ocean island of Diego

Garcia, which was used by US forces for attacks during both the Iraq and Afghanistan wars. Wald said São Tomé could become a US Forward Operating Location, which are used temporarily by American forces during conflict.[58]

Not surprisingly, in early 2004 the US Trade and Development Agency announced it would finance feasibility studies into the development of a deep-water port and expanded airfield facilities on São Tomé. A US military liaison officer was sent to the island on a one-year assignment on behalf of the European Command, to co-ordinate and develop security co-operation programs with São Tomé. These included 'not only military education and training for São Toméan forces, but also military equipment sales and transfers'.[59]

In August that year General Wald visited the country a second time, with Chuck Hagel, a Republican Senator from Nebraska who is chairman of the Senate Foreign Relations International Economic Policy committee. A staunch Republican, Hagel had once been considered as President Bush's running mate for Vice-President. The two Chucks stressed the 'strategic importance of São Tomé for American interests in Africa'. The trip also included a stop in Nigeria, where 'US instructors were reported to be training Nigerian counter-insurgency troops in the oil-producing Niger Delta'.[60]

Wald told reporters in Nigeria that he had talked with 'military leaders about having a way that we could co-operate together in monitoring the waters of the Gulf of Guinea'. His comments came at the same time as increased US–Nigerian naval exercises took place in the region as part of a new African Coastal Security Program.[61]

Leave No Continent Behind

In April 2004 both General Fulford and General Wald were in Washington for an important conference on West Africa held at the American Enterprise Institute (AEI). Based on 17th Street, just north of the White House, the AEI is one of the most influential think-tanks in Washington and a bastion of neo-conservatism. It is where corporate interests and conservatism meet. Its Board of Trustees includes the CEOs of such companies as ExxonMobil, Motorola, American Express, Merck & Co., Dell, and Dow Chemicals.[62] Because of this it has been called the 'granddaddy of the big corporate front groups'.[63]

AEI is intricately linked to the Bush administration. 'At the American Enterprise Institute, some of the finest minds in our nation are at work on some of the greatest challenges to our nation,' said the President at the Institute's Annual Dinner in 2003. 'You do such good work that my administration has borrowed twenty such minds.'[64] One of those 'great minds' belongs to Dick Cheney, who was a Visiting Fellow at the AEI. His wife Lynne is still a senior fellow.

There is a crossover too between the AEI and the Project for the New American Century (PNAC), also housed on 17th Street, whose members include key neo-conservatives and hawks such as Defense Secretary Donald Rumsfeld, William Kristol, Richard Perle and Paul Wolfowitz. PNAC led the call for the 'removal of Saddam Hussein's regime from power' to 'secure the interests of the US and our friends and allies around the world'.[65]

One person who straddles both organizations is Thomas Donnelly, the Resident Fellow in Defense and Security Policy Studies at AEI, who is also a senior fellow at PNAC. Donnelly's career is in defence and he has worked on *Defense News, Army*

Times, and *National Interest.* In 2002 he was also Director of Strategic Communications and Initiatives at the Lockheed Martin Corporation, the largest arms manufacturer in the world.[66]

At the AEI in April 2004 Donnelly and his Defense Studies Programme organized a conference called 'Leave No Continent Behind – US National Security Interests in Africa'.[67] The conference summary said it all: 'America is growing increasingly reliant on African oil, which already accounts for 15 per cent of US imports and is expected to become even more important in the decade ahead . . . Can African oil and gas reserves save the United States from dependence on the Middle East?'[68]

'Today's conference would be unimaginable in a pre-September 11th world,' Donnelly said as he opened the conference. He told delegates that the concept of 'US national security interests in Africa' had been an oxymoron for far too long with the US defence community. 'We must account for the fact that the United States will soon import a greater slice of its oil from West Africa than from Saudi Arabia,' he said. The US 'may have to understand that Africa, like Central Asia, like South Asia, like Southeast Asia, has got to be considered part of the greater Middle East'.[69]

One government official conceded that Africa would provide up to 30 per cent of US oil in the next ten years. Nigeria alone currently provides just over 10 per cent of America's oil, and is the country's fifth most important supplier after Canada, Venezuela, Saudi Arabia and Mexico.[70]

Strategically Important

James Burkhard, from the American oil industry analysts Cambridge Energy Research Associates (CERA), spoke too, as he had at the Heritage Foundation conference. He reiterated the importance of West African oil. But just as he had at the Heritage conference, Burkhard returned to the theme of Winston Churchill and gas. 'Forget about oil for a moment,' he said. 'The US will become much more dependent on imported natural gas to 2010, and certainly even beyond that out to 2020,' he argued. 'West Africa will become an increasingly important supplier of natural gas . . . We're simply not producing as much natural gas as we consume.'

Burkhard likened America's switch to dependence on gas as being similar to the British Navy's change to oil a century before. 'The US has made a bet on natural gas that is similar to the bet that the British Navy made on oil about 90 years ago,' he said. 'The British Navy made an explicit bet on oil, but the US has made an implicit bet on natural gas. And the reason for that is [that] most of the growth in power generation capacity in the United States over the next decade, the vast majority of that growth, is going to be gas-fired power generation. The concrete has been poured, the turbines are going to be built.' He reiterated that West Africa is very well placed to supply LNG to both Europe and the United States.

One of the companies strategically positioned to exploit gas in Nigeria is Chevron. George L. Kirkland, Vice President of Chevron and ex-managing director of Chevron Nigeria, was at the conference. Chevron, like Shell, is investing heavily in Africa, having put in about $5 billion over the last five years and with $20 billion more planned with its partners.[71] Chevron has substantial associated and non-associated gas reserves (some 15 per cent of Nigeria's reserves), predominantly offshore.[72] It was Kirkland who responded on behalf of Chevron when the military intervened in the Ilaje community protests in 1998, in which two people were killed (see Chapter 1). He had interrupted a fishing holiday in Florida to be at the AEI conference.

Kirkland argued that 'diversity of supply' for the US was critical, and that Africa was 'central to that diversity'. Kirkland continued: 'for our own vital interests, I believe the US government must continue to view Africa as a region of strategic importance' that is 'fundamental to America's energy security'.

Kirkland talked about the potential for African gas that has 'been a resource looking for a market' for years. 'In the US, natural gas demand provides yet another reason why Africa is destined to play a bigger role in energy security for the US. While US natural gas demand is expected to increase by nearly 50 per cent by 2020, traditional North American supply sources will be able to meet only 75 per cent of the nation's long-term needs.' Africa 'provides the potential to meet the energy demands of the United States'. Nigerian LNG, he said, was 'very, very important'. Kirkland concluded by arguing that 'Africa is rapidly expanding natural gas development and America is rapidly expanding on its demand. This offers powerful reasons to strengthen US relationships with Africa.'

George Bush too has been trying to strengthen the relationship between Chevron and Nigeria, by doing all he can to promote the image of Chevron as a 'responsible corporate citizen' in Nigeria. On a presidential visit to Abuja in July 2003, Bush hailed Chevron's commitment to 'corporate social responsibility'. He personally praised Chevron's CEO, Dave O'Reilly, who 'understands the definition of corporate responsibility' and expressed his appreciation for 'the leadership of Dave and Chevron. Their job is not only to make a return for their shareholders, their job is to show compassion, as well.'[73]

Three months later, in October 2003, O'Reilly and Chevron-

Texaco were once again being rewarded by the Bush administration, this time formally. At a ceremony at the State Department O'Reilly, on behalf of ChevronTexaco, received the US Secretary of State's Corporate Excellence Award. 'We applaud Chevron Nigeria's commitment to its employees and to the people of the Niger Delta. More than a good corporate citizen, Chevron Nigeria is a good neighbour, and a model of excellence and trust,' said Colin Powell, handing over the award in a ceremony that was beamed to US embassies around the world, including Nigeria.[74]

The award came to Chevron despite 'its previous record of complicity with human rights violations in the region', notes Anna Zalik from Cornell University, who is studying the social welfare programmes of the oil industry in the Delta. Zalik calls the award 'absurd'. 'Despite the violent context surrounding Chevron installations, US congressional attention to Chevron's complicity in killings by Nigerian Mobile Police, and charges of corrupt relations with local authorities, why was Chevron Nigeria granted this State Department award?' asks Zalik. The answer she gives is that this award 'is often granted to those seeking to improve on a tainted history'. Zalik also points out Condoleezza Rice's former role in Chevron, and the company's payments to Bush's election campaign.[75]

Nigeria is not just strategically important to the US, it is of vital importance to the major oil companies – such as Chevron, Shell and Exxon – who are based in the US or have major interests in the country. Some \$30–40 billion will be invested in Nigeria and Africa in the next decade, on which some 100,000 US jobs will be supported.[76] Shell is the largest developer of LNG worldwide, and its Nigerian gas reserves and interest in the Bonny plant is key to its commercial ambitions.

Exxon's gas reserves are significantly less, although its oil is important. The company currently produces just over half a million barrels per day in Nigeria, about 9 per cent of the company's global production. It plans to invest $11 billion between 2003 and 2011, more than doubling production to 1.2 million bbl/d.[77]

It is not just the oil majors that are involved in Nigeria. Some 300 Houston-area companies do business there, including 24 with Nigerian subsidiaries, the most important being Conoco-Phillips, Halliburton, Willbros, Baker Hughes, J. Ray McDermott and Transocean (see Chapter 4).[78]

Such companies spend millions on lobbying in Washington. The oil industry has spent some $440 million over the past six years on politicians, political parties and lobbyists in order to protect its interests in Washington. ExxonMobil was the industry leader, spending $55 million from 1998 to 2004. Next came Chevron ($32 million), BP ($28 million), and then Shell ($27 million).[79] Engaging the government in power is vital to the oil industry.

All the companies lobby on a whole host of issues, but Nigeria and Africa feature strongly. Congressional lobbying records show that Exxon has lobbied on Nigeria, Nigerian Oil, São Tomé, and the African Growth and Opportunity Act. One of Shell's PR companies, Stuntz, Davis and Staffier, has lobbied on measures that would help the company import LNG tankers from Nigeria. The Shell Oil Company, Shell's US subsidiary, has also lobbied on Nigeria, the 'Liquified Natural Gas Import Terminal Development Act' and the Africa Trade Bill. Chevron's PR company BKSH and Associates, the communications arm of Burson-Marsteller, has lobbied on behalf of Chevron's 'International Operations'.[80]

No wonder Shell is lobbying on LNG legislation – it is eager to increase America's import capacity. There are only four LNG import terminals in operation today in the US, located in Everett, Massachusetts; Lake Charles, Louisiana; Cove Point, Maryland and Elba Island, Georgia. Intriguingly, the last two are in states that received the slave ships from the Delta. Slowly a new Atlantic Triangle is emerging, one in which the US and Europe both finance and consume Africa's resources (see Map 9). This time it is oil and gas, but again the lucrative triangle has to be defended. Nigeria's multi-billion dollar LNG facilities have been called 'conspicuous new potential targets' for terrorists.[81] They have to be protected at all costs.

Military Might

At the AEI Conference in April 2004, Thomas Donnelly chaired a session on 'US Strategic Engagement in Africa' at which General Fulford spoke. 'Nigeria, in my estimation, needs to be at the very top of US security concerns in Africa. We should use every bit of leverage we have, diplomatic and military and economic.' Fulford argued that America 'should be on the inside helping to professionalize their military'.

'We need special forces,' added General Fulford. 'We need Marines, we need soldiers, we need airmen who can go down with their counterparts and not only train effectively, but also provide that mentorship on what it means to be a professional military in a democratic, civilian-controlled society. The US military are the only ones that can carry that message effectively, and I think we need to rebuild that capacity.'[82]

The keynote address was given by General Wald from European Command (EUCOM): 'As a matter of fact, we get more oil from Western Africa today than we do the Middle East. It's a huge, important area.' Wald's boss, General James Jones, head of EUCOM (including NATO's Forces in Europe) has been outspoken about Africa's potential as a 'terrorist breeding ground' and is concerned about the possible convergence of Islamic fundamentalism and oil wealth in West Africa.[83] Beginning in 2004 and carrying into 2005, EUCOM began the development of a coastal protection system in West Africa named the Gulf of Guinea Guard,[84] an echo of the Royal Navy squadron at Fernando Po in the nineteenth century.

According to EUCOM, the attacks of September 11 'forced EUCOM to look at the region in a counter-terrorism context, and that's driving our security strategy there'. EUCOM now believes that West Africa is of 'emerging strategic importance' in relation to terrorism. 'As terror networks are disrupted/pushed out of the Mideast, they seek sanctuary in the ungoverned spaces of North and West Africa,' argues Lieutenant Colonel Pat Mackin, the Deputy Director of EUCOM's Public Affairs. 'The largely Muslim population is vulnerable to extremism, given their perception of weak/unresponsive governments and lack of economic opportunities.'[85]

To counter this threat, General Jones has proposed a series of 'bare-bones' camps with airfields close by where a military brigade, some 3,000 to 5,000 troops, could be stationed in Africa to provide a 'significant military presence'. Although not advocating permanent bases, EUCOM is seeking 'forward-operating sites' and 'co-operative security locations' in the region. Here 'US forces would be granted access to landing, refueling, and possible staging of US aircraft, ships, and/or troops in the event US forces were required in the region – either as a humanitarian response or as part of military operations/exercises.'[86]

According to Lieutenant Colonel Pat Mackin, 'there are no direct military measures' to protect US oil and gas installations in the region. Instead, EUCOM's strategy is 'to enhance the security of individual countries and the region as a whole'. This will be done through a whole host of measures including military partnerships and training, and support to regional African security organizations.

EUCOM also wants to serve as a 'regional "enabler"' to bring countries together to address regional security issues' and to dissuade government corruption and other illegal activity. It believes it can do this by 'providing humanitarian assistance programs', and by 'encouraging international organizations (NATO, EU) and the international community to address the issues there'. EUCOM sees 'the security of the oil industry there as a by-product of overall regional security. It's in the interest of the US, Europe and the region.'[87]

As part of its engagement strategy, in March 2005 the African Center for Strategic Studies, run by General Fulford, held a five-day conference in Abuja on 'Energy and Security in Africa: Meeting the Challenge in Petroleum Producing States'. General Fulford and John Campbell, the US Ambassador to Nigeria, opened the conference. Senior Nigerian officials were there including the Minister of Defence, as well as senior officials from the US government and EUCOM; as were Stephen Morrison from CSIS and Dave Goldwyn, also now from CSIS and also now advising Nigeria on its transparency initiative.

Michael Achu from Shell's External Security Liaison Department was there too, as was Donald Boham from SPDC. Paul Barker, Chevron's 'Regional Security Adviser', was also in attendance, along with representatives from 16 African countries. Goldywn once again outlined why African oil was so important to the US: because it meant diversity of supply away from the Middle East; because of the large level of investment planned; and because of the jobs it supports.

Alisdair Walker, the Political Officer in charge of 'Energy Security' at the Foreign & Commonwealth Office, represented British interests at the conference. The FCO has also been increasing its interest in the region, and recently created a new position for an 'energy expert for West Africa', to be stationed in London. Britain too has signalled its intent to increase its military intervention in the area. Two months previously Britain's then Africa Minister, Chris Mullen, had also been in Abuja. He said that Britain would 'look favourably' on any request by Nigeria on issues such as military training and technical support in the Niger Delta.[88]

The week after the Abuja conference in March 2005, General Jones, the head of EUCOM, suggested it might have to change its name from 'US European Command' to 'US European and African Command'. Jones said that Africa 'will figure in our national interests in the foreseeable future'.[89]

Three months later in June 2005, General Wald attended yet another major conference on oil and gas, this time the 'West Africa Oil & Gas 8 – Gulf of Guinea & Beyond' conference at the Waldorf-Hilton Hotel in London. Shell, Chevron and Vanco sponsored the conference.

There were sessions on Nigeria and São Tomé. During the sessions entitled 'unlocking the Gulf of Guinea' Wald spoke on 'Measures to protect oil operations in the Gulf of Guinea'. Other speakers talked about the need for energy security too.[90] Baroness (Lynda) Chalker, a senior adviser to the Commonwealth Business Council and former Minister for Overseas Development at the British FCO, spoke on 'Strategies to deepen the benefits of West Africa's oil and gas reserves'.[91] The same week, Baroness Chalker was appointed a non-executive director of Equator Exploration, an organization that was looking to secure £60 million to fund oil exploration in the Gulf of Guinea. It has rights in both Nigeria and São Tomé.[92]

The seminar was held just before the G8 Summit at Gleneagles in Scotland. While the G8 attracted the world's attention to debt relief and aid to Africa, the oilmen were once again getting down to business – the business of exploiting Africa's resources and thereby ensuring energy security and diversity for America, defended by the muscle of American might.

Just days before the Gleneagles summit, Patrick Naagbanton, Director of the Niger Delta Project for Environment, Human Rights and Development, was in London for the Shell AGM. He expressed concerns about an increased American presence in the Delta that included arms for the military. 'There is clearly an increase in US weapons in the hands of the Nigerian army and navy,' he said. Interestingly, he had also noticed 'a greater presence of US media people . . . whereas a year or so ago you never saw them'.[93] If news editors in Washington believe that the Niger Delta is important, it is a reflection of the true importance of the Niger Delta to America.

The day after Shell's AGM, the US admitted to a fresh troop deployment in Nigeria's coastal waters: the USCG *Bear*, part of the Sixth Fleet, was undertaking 'maritime security operations' off Nigeria.[94] On top of these manoeuvres key players continue to push for a greater military presence.

General Carlton Fulford, Malik Chaka and representatives from Chevron, Exxon, Shell and BP were all members of the new CSIS Task Force on 'Gulf of Guinea Security' that published their report in July 2005. The Task Force was chaired by Republican Senator Chuck Hagel, with co-chairs J. Stephen Morrison and David Goldwyn. Nigeria's Vice-President, Atiku Abubakar, gave the keynote speech at the conference to launch the report. Also speaking was Rear Admiral Frank Rennie, from EUCOM, who had flown from Europe for the event.

The Task Force recommended that the US should 'make security and governance in the Gulf of Guinea an explicit priority in US foreign policy'. To this end it recommended a 'special assistant to the President and Secretary of State to co-ordinate US policy in the region'. It also recommended that the Gulf of Guinea should become a regular item on the agenda at the G8 meetings, and in talks with China, whose interests in the region are growing fast, a fact worrying the United States.[95]

'EUCOM can play a leading role in regional stabilization,' David Goldwyn told the assembled delegates, 'and their British and French equivalents can help too.'[96] The concept of the old Imperial powers once again coming together to protect their strategic interests is one that Winston Churchill would have been proud of.

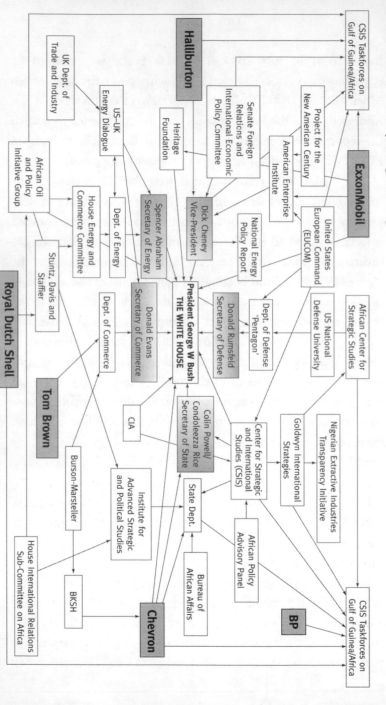

Chart 4. The Niger Delta in Washington – the web of institutions and companies related to the oil industry in Nigeria, 2005

In the Shadow of the Gulf

JAMES MARRIOTT

I remember the Oil Crisis of 1973. My father bought a bicycle and declared that, if necessary, he would cycle the several miles to the station in order to catch the morning train to London. I'd never seen him on a bicycle before, and I swear I never saw him use it for commuting. But he did trade in the car for a more fuel-efficient model.

Since then the Persian Gulf has woven its thread in and out of my life. 'The Fall of the Shah' in lurid pictures in *Time* magazine. Television footage of the bewilderingly brutal battles of the Iran–Iraq War. The First Gulf War, the images of Cruise missiles hitting Baghdad, and my sense of furious powerlessness on the protest marches. Eleven years in which the desperation of Sanctions drifted in and out of my consciousness. The unbelievable hope of the march against the War on Iraq. And now this . . . this bloody Occupation.

In truth, it seems that the thread through my life has been a halter around my neck, dragging me this way and that. Living in the shadow of seemingly endless wars. The Middle East presented as a place of constant threat.

Is this the fate of the Gulf of Guinea? From here, it seems hard to believe that it could so fill the imagination of the coming generation. But then, at some point in time the Middle East must have had little resonance in the lives of my parents or grandparents. I guess the moment of switch might have been the

Suez Crisis of 1956, when my father was 26, my mother just 19. Was that when the sense of threat began?

What will be the Suez of the Gulf of Guinea? What will be the moment of switch? Could it be that Nigeria will be presented as a place of threat? Will our desperation for what they have turn West Africa into the next battleground?

CHAPTER EIGHT

Six Months in the Making of History

'I repeat that we all stand before history. I and my colleagues are not the only ones on trial. Shell is here on trial . . . but its day will surely come and the lessons learnt here may prove useful to it. There is no doubt in my mind that the ecological war that the Company has waged in the Delta will be called to question sooner than later and the crimes of that war be duly punished.'

Ken Saro-Wiwa, the closing statement to Military Tribunal, 1995

The Threshold of History

In February 2005 in Abuja, President Obasanjo made the inaugural address to Nigeria's National Political Reform Conference (NPRC), known as the 'Confab'. In dark robes and a traditional blue-and-white Nigerian hat, the President opened the conference by talking about his deep sense of responsibility.

'We are once again at the threshold of history,' said Obasanjo. 'History has presented us with the opportunity to reassess, refocus, redefine and redesign our political landscape.' He hoped the process would strengthen the bonds of unity, and enhance the values that promote democracy, good governance and good neighbourliness, so that all Nigerians 'feel that they are part of the evolving political process and socio-economic advancement'.[1]

The Confab was just one of a number of conferences and meetings convened in the first half of 2005 that had the potential to shape the future of the Niger Delta. Ten years after the death of Saro-Wiwa, in London, Washington, Abuja and Lagos, the future of the Delta and of Nigeria was being discussed, and the forces that will shape this future were revealed in these meetings. What happened at these conferences and what happens in the second half of 2005 will impact the future of the Niger Delta and its peoples over the coming decades. The future of the next generation hangs in the balance.

The first chapter of this book examined the ten years of violence and pollution in the Delta that have passed since the executions in Port Harcourt. The question that decade poses to the present is, will the next ten years be any different? Will 2015 find the communities and ecology of the Delta in a similar position, or a worse one? Or will a new path have been embarked upon?

Part of the answer might have been found in the Confab. The Confab is the latest in a long history of constitutional conferences in Nigeria's history, from the pre-Independence meetings in the late 1950s to the constitutional conferences of the late 1970s and mid and late 1990s. It was the pre-Independence debates that Chief Dappa-Biriye attended in the 1950s. Ken Saro-Wiwa was arrested while campaigning to be the Ogoni representative at the constitutional conference in the mid 1990s, having failed to win election to two in the 1970s.

Huge issues of political, judicial, socio-economic and electoral reform were supposed to be on the agenda of the Confab. It was an attempt to help Nigeria rid itself of the shackles of its colonial and military past and the endemic corruption of its present. The idea was to try to 'strengthen its democracy' – to be at the threshold of history – to map out a new constitution, a new structure for the country that should set the new generation on the road to recovery.

But making this new start was not going to be easy. At stake, said the organizers, was the whole unity, stability and security of the Nigerian Federation. To these must be added issues of nationality, identity, liberty, social justice, and minority rights.[2] Each one is a tinderbox waiting to be ignited between different ethnic groups and factions from North, South, East and West, from the drylands of the North to the tidal creeks of the Delta.

Into this potential conflagration went Ledum Mitee, the President of MOSOP, and Oronto Douglas. Douglas had by now been appointed Commissioner for Information and Strategy in the government of Bayelsa State, arguably the most important of the six Niger Delta states in terms of the oil industry. Some had questioned Douglas's motives for moving from outspoken critic of government into the lions' den of holding a government office. Some in the Delta went as far as to say he had 'sold out'.

Douglas replies that he is still a critical and outspoken advocate for the people of the Delta and for the environment, this time working from the inside, not shouting from the outside. 'We must not relent, we must continue to speak out. We must continue to seek peace and justice,' he says. 'The moment you stop speaking out you are dead.' The day he no longer feels comfortable with what he is doing, he will leave his government post, he says. But there is no doubt that Douglas walks a fine line in trying to appease both his critics and his new bosses.

'Oil has a very violent characteristic inherent in it,' Douglas said in June 2005. 'No matter what transparency measures you put on it, the implication and impact of oil is huge. It is not just on the present generation, but the future generations. We are talking about a resource that destroys the present and destroys the future. The sooner we consign it to the dustbin of energy history, the better for all of us. It is not going to lead us to the promised land of energy security. There is nothing about sustainability in an oil economy or an economy based on oil.'[3] Powerful words from a government minister of a state which produces a significant proportion of Nigeria's oil.

A Peaceful Future?

As the delegates at the Confab in Abuja started thrashing out the details, another conference was held in Washington in February. Rather than addressing the challenges facing Nigeria or West Africa as a whole, this meeting concentrated specifically on the Niger Delta. It was jointly hosted by the Bureau of Intelligence and Research at the US State Department, and the National Intelligence Council. The meeting was chaired by Lannon Walker, former US Ambassador to Côte d'Ivoire, Nigeria and Senegal. Although speakers talked about plans for reconciliation in the Delta, one delegate was particularly struck by the number of American military personnel present at the conference.[4]

Some two weeks later, an altogether different conference on the Delta took place in Lagos, Nigeria's largest metropolis. In late February and early March 2005 the global coalition against the oil industry known as OilWatch held a 'Conference on Oil, Resource Conflicts and Livelihoods in Africa'. It was hosted by Environmental Rights Action, with which Oronto Douglas had been associated for so long.[5]

Nnimmo Bassey, chair of OilWatch-Africa and executive

director of Environmental Rights Action, spoke to delegates from Ghana, Nigeria, Cameroon, Chad, Mozambique, South Africa, Sudan, Congo Brazzaville, Latin America, North America and Europe. 'The announcement of an oil discovery in any territory is comparable to the declaration of war against the territory,' he said. 'Oil destroys the environment, contaminates water and air, and it also contaminates the social structure, destroys forests, destroys life and livelihoods and holds nothing sacred.'

In a communiqué issued at the end of the meeting, OilWatch called the 'growing militarization of the Gulf of Guinea by the United States and some European countries fuelled by their desire to control African oil and gas resources' a 'declaration of war'. The communiqué demanded:

- immediate halting of American and European military build-up and their unconditional pull-out from the region. They should equally halt military support to governments of the region;
- a moratorium on exploration and development of new oil and gas fields on the continent as a short term measure, and that efforts should be made to develop alternative energy sources and the long term ban on fossil fuel exploitation;
- a change in the relationship between African governments, international financial institutions and governments of oil and gas resource endowed African governments;
- the restoration, compensation and sanction for the social and environmental damage as a step to recognize ecological debt.[6]

Three days after this communiqué, representatives from the US State Department, EUCOM and the US Department of Energy, along with delegates from Denmark, France and the United Kingdom, gathered for a heavyweight conference in Abuja that was poles apart from the OilWatch event. It was the Africa Center for Strategic Studies conference hosted by retired General Fulford, and co-sponsored by the Nigerian government.[7]

Whereas OilWatch had called for an immediate halting of American and European military build-up, these delegates discussed ways of increasing military co-operation to secure the Gulf of Guinea's 'strategic' oil and gas reserves.[8] Lannon Walker, the former US Ambassador to Côte d'Ivoire, Nigeria and Senegal, was there too.

Here under discussion were two different visions of the future that could hardly be further apart, one in which the communities have a say in a de-militarized sustainable post-oil future, the other in which governments and companies want increased production guaranteed by military might. The first would be a radical break with the 'business as usual' path, the second no more than a continuation of the colonial policy started by the British and the Royal Navy over three centuries ago.

The Future of Resource Control and Derivation

Meanwhile, the Confab continued. By May 2005, after four months of talks, tensions were becoming unbearable. There were specific rumours of the President's hidden agenda, trying to increase the length of his Presidency in the new draft constitution, and of secret meetings and special deals. There were grave splits between the communities of the North and

South. There were continuing divisions between the major ethnic groups.

One of the main stumbling-blocks was the long and embittered issue of resource control and derivation – who has legal control over the oil and gas, and who derives income from their exploitation. These issues cannot be separated from the current conflict in the Niger Delta – in fact, they are at the heart of that conflict. The people of the Delta have long argued that the oil under their feet is theirs and not the Nigerian government's or the oil companies'. The Ogoni, Ijaw, Itsekiri and other groups have never controlled the revenue that flows from beneath their land. It is a recurring theme.

This issue had been a central part of the speech Saro-Wiwa made in 1990 when he launched his book *On a Darkling Plain* at the Nigerian Institute of International Affairs in Lagos: 'The notion that the oil-bearing areas can provide the revenue of the country, and yet be denied a proper share of that revenue because it is perceived that the inhabitants of the area are few in number is unjust, immoral, unnatural and ungodly,' he had argued. 'Why are they entitled to but 1.5 per cent of their resources? Why has this money not been paid as and when due?'[9]

The issue had been a central pillar of the Ogoni Bill of Rights signed by the Ogoni leaders in 1990, which argued that some $30 billion worth of oil had been drilled from Ogoniland, but in return the 'Ogoni people had received NOTHING'. The Ogoni elders now called for 'the right to the control and use of a fair proportion of Ogoni economic resources for Ogoni development'.[10]

And it had been a central pillar of the Kaiama Declaration signed by the Ijaw in December 1998: 'That the political crisis in

Nigeria is mainly about the struggle for the control of oil mineral resources which account for over 80 per cent of GDP, 95 per cent of national budget and 90 per cent of foreign exchange earnings. From which, 65 per cent, 75 per cent and 70 per cent respectively are derived from within the Ijaw nation. Despite these huge contributions, our reward from the Nigerian State remains avoidable deaths resulting from ecological devastation, and military repression.'[11]

Explaining the issue, Oronto Douglas argues that derivation is all about money from the oil industry – from royalties and rent. Currently, oil revenue provides the Federal government with some 91.5 per cent of revenue. Theoretically, 13 per cent of the oil revenue is redirected back to the Delta states. After Independence it was 50 per cent; in 1975 it had been reduced to 20 per cent. By 1982 it had been reduced even further, to 1.5 per cent. This money went to a Commissioner, appointed by the military government, who was then responsible for its distribution. This meant in practice that those who had connections with the military government, or were in favour with the government, received a disproportionate share of the funds.

A decade later, under pressure from the Delta communities, the 1.5 per cent was raised to 3 per cent. But it was not enough: 'We cannot accept three per cent of our property in return for one hundred per cent of the pollution,' Saro-Wiwa wrote.[12] It was then increased to 13 per cent. Even so, this sum was only theoretical; much of the income never reached the Delta, but was siphoned off en route. To rectify this, the 'South–South Delegation' of the six key Delta states at the Confab were pushing for 50 per cent derivation. As part of this strategy, they were arguing for at least 25 per cent to start with, with a 5 per cent increase every year for five years to make it up to 50 per cent.

In parallel with the issue of derivation, Douglas advocates 'total resource control, which is about allowing the communities and the people to be in charge of their lives. If Shell wants to come and exploit oil in my community they will have to come and seek permission from us. If the communities do not want oil drilling, because our lives are sacred, they should accept that.' He says that 'resource stewardship is what we are looking at. Communal rights to protect, to defend, and enjoy the rights that god has given to us.' The communities have been denied resource control 'by the cruelties of colonialism, successive dictatorships and bad government that has engulfed our country and continent for decades'.[13]

The communities of the Delta have never made the decisions about resource control. The Colonial Office in London in essence made these decisions for the 46 years following the promulgation of the Mineral Oil Ordinance in 1914, and has been replaced by the Nigerian Oil Ministry for the 45 years since Independence. The struggle over how much control of resources should be held at a local level and how much should be held at a national level takes place in many states across the world – it could be seen in the arguments between Shetland, Edinburgh and Westminster as North Sea oil was developed in the 1970s. However, in Nigeria it is made particularly acute because the very existence of Nigeria as a multi-ethnic state has been constantly under debate since the 1950s – constantly, and often violently – and because the communities in which oil extraction occurs suffer so acutely from the impact of that industry operating in the midst of their villages and farms – as opposed to Shetland, where the oil developments have taken place far offshore.

Now Douglas and his colleagues are arguing that decisions about resources should lie in the hands of the communities in which the oil is produced – the concept of communal resource stewardship. Others support him too. Ledum Mitee, head of MOSOP, argued: 'The owner of farmland that has been polluted or taken over by oil exploitation is not compensated by more money from local government or state government or even a water project in the village. But nothing is said about that. We need a say in how oil exploration is done. If you put an oil well in front of my house – shouldn't I have a say?'

The two issues of resource control and derivation were central to a 'Minority Report' that Douglas, who sat on the Committee on Environment and Natural Resources, presented to the Confab. The report also advocated that a 'five-year moratorium on mineral resource exploration and exploitation be put in place in the Niger Delta and its adjoining continental shelf, so as to enable the area presently under aggressive and violent resource exploitation to recover. The break will also enable Nigerians to put in place a framework that will eventually break the cursed spell on our over-dependence on unsustainable hydrocarbon resources.'[14]

Even if the South–South states were to win a higher derivation level at the Confab, there are those who believe that this would not be the answer. 'I oppose it,' said Patrick Naagbanton, an Ogoni, and Director of the Niger Delta Project for Environment, Human Rights and Development. 'My trouble is with account-ability and good governance. It is OK to have greater derivation, but not if it is under the same governance system. Then there is no point, as the people will never see any of the money. Suddenly, there is a big euphoria that this Confab process will bring about the solution to all the problems. I don't think so.'[15]

The Future of Ogoni

In late May 2005 attention was drawn back to Ogoni when the government announced that it had appointed a Roman Catholic priest, the Reverend Father Hassan Kukah, Joint Co-Secretary of the Confab, to facilitate a reconciliation between the Ogoni and Shell.

One morning Ledum Mitee, who was at the Confab as head of MOSOP, noticed that Kukah was curiously late turning up to the meetings. Although he knew that talks about reconciliation were under way, he did not know that an announcement was imminent. He heard it from Kukah during a tea break. 'I had to leave the Confab, to respond,' he said.

In the announcement, President Obasanjo declared that Kukah would be assisted by the International Centre for Reconciliation (ICR) at Coventry Cathedral in the UK, one of the world's oldest such centres, which began its work after German bombers destroyed Coventry and its cathedral in November 1940.

Kukah is a man who bridges Africa and Britain. Born in Southern Kaduna in Nigeria, he went to university in Nigeria, but undertook Peace Studies at Bradford University. He served as Secretary on the Oputa Human Violations Investigation Commission, and in 2002–3 was a Senior Fellow at St Anthony's College, Oxford.

But can he bridge the huge chasm between the Ogoni and Shell? Eager to return to the oil fields they had had to abandon in 1993, Shell has made four attempts at reconciliation in the intervening 12 years. All of these have failed.

'Without peace, you do not give development a chance,' said Obasanjo. 'I sincerely want to put this conflict in Ogoni behind us so that we can have the environment necessary for development.'

Canon Justin Wallaby, a Director of the ICR, said the announcements regarding reconciliation 'are not a final resolution of the Ogoni conflict, let alone of the problems in the Niger Delta as a whole. They represent a significant first step, and recognize the commitment to non-violence by the leaders of MOSOP as well as many other Ogoni leaders. The statements confirm the beginning of a process that will simultaneously manage present sources of conflict, seek a just resolution to the past, and plan a more prosperous and successful future for all the Ogoni people.'

Basil Omiyi, Managing Director of Shell Companies in Nigeria, said: '[We] warmly welcome the statements today by the President, the Rivers State Governor, and the Movement for the Survival of the Ogoni People. We will continue to do everything we can to ensure that a lasting reconciliation amongst and between Ogonis and Shell is achieved, to the benefit of all stakeholders.'[16]

After the announcement, Mitee's mobile phone started ringing before he could get back to his hotel room, with journalists eager to hear the Ogoni response. MOSOP issued a press release, in which Mitee welcomed 'the effort being made by the Federal Government to engage in a dialogue which we hope will be sincere and will recognize the need to redress abuses which have affected every village in Ogoniland'. But he added that 'It is critical that people do not misinterpret a willingness to talk as anything more than a first step.'[17]

Others, like Douglas, were also sceptical. 'Any announcement about reconciliation is fine, but knowing the Nigerian government and Shell and their penchant for public relations and propaganda, I think this statement was put out because of the global mobilization towards the Tenth Anniversary of the killing of Ken [Saro-Wiwa],' says the lawyer, showing that even in government his forthrightness has not been diminished.[18]

Indeed by late June 2005, within a month of the statement, MOSOP had accused Shell of trying to 'destabilize' the Ogoni with 'divide and rule' tactics. Shell's 'Ogoni Re-entry Department' had begun a 'familiarization' tour of Ogoni, with the company making 'undisguised attempts to divide Ogoni communities' using Shell's 'community development projects' as 'baits', said MOSOP. It was 'equally concerned about the related activities of persons who may be acting on the company's behalf, or in its interest, who are embarking on recruiting some Ogoni youths to sign a declaration inviting Shell to resume oil operations in Ogoni'. Shell denied the allegations.[19]

The issue of reconciliation has also run into problems with the Wiwa family: 'I look at all this reconciliation process and it all seems very hasty to me,' says Saro-Wiwa's son Ken Wiwa. 'The family haven't been consulted. It just strikes me as the same pattern of "Well, they are irrelevant, if you take Ken Saro-Wiwa out of this we can deal with this." It is just the same as saying "If we take Ken Saro-Wiwa and put him in prison and kill him, then we can have our way in Ogoni." They are doing the same thing again with this reconciliation process.'

Wiwa argues that the reconciliation has not dealt with the issue of what happened on 21 May 1994 when four Ogoni chiefs were murdered. Nor has it dealt with the fact that his 'father is still, on the statute books, a murderer. How can I sign up for reconciliation when my father remains a murderer on the statute books?' he asks. 'As far as the family is concerned, it tells us that these guys are not serious, they just want to repeat the mistakes of ten years ago.'

Saro-Wiwa's brother Owens also believes that there has to be an official pardon before movement can be made. 'The issues that would facilitate the enthronement of peace are exoneration of Ken and the eight others, resource control and some level of political autonomy for the Ogoni within Nigeria and Rivers State,' he says. 'If that is done, I think that the path is clear for the resumption of oil drilling in Ogoni by an acceptable company to the majority of Ogoni people.'[20]

Both Owens and Ken Wiwa believe that as far as the Ogoni people are concerned, Shell can never return to their land. Peace in Ogoniland and elsewhere in the Delta will only be possible if the legitimate demands of the people for respect and fair treatment are met. The Wiwa family took Shell to court in the US in 1996, arguing the company's complicity in Saro-Wiwa's death. Nine years later, the legal case is still ongoing.

A Violent Future?

On 10 June 2005 the Nigerian press reported that 'For the third time this week, the National Political Reform Conference was thrown into a bedlam over the issue of resource control . . . Trouble started again yesterday when Mr Oronto Douglas threatened that the Niger Delta would use any method to ensure that it controls its resources.'[21]

By now all the state governors in the South–South delegation had endorsed the minimum derivation level to 50 per cent. However, the conference decided that only 17 per cent was on offer, up from the present 13 per cent. This caused the delegation to walk out in the 'rowdiest session' so far seen at the conference.[22]

'I was the first person to walk out – I started the walk-out,' says Ledum Mitee, who reiterates Saro-Wiwa's point that the Delta states receive too little money in return for too much pollution. He asked whether it was 'seventeen per cent of the suffering of the pollution of the gas flares, or just of the benefits' the Delta states were to receive. Mitee is worried that if the issue of derivation is not sorted out at the Confab, then 'it will send a message to some people in the Delta, who are not as peaceful as we are [that] they [the Confab] do not want to listen.'[23]

As if to illustrate Mitee's point that violence is now never far from the surface in the Delta in Nigeria, the *Financial Times* reported, five days after the walk-out, that 'Nigerian militants kidnap oil workers'. The newspaper gave details: 'a militant group in Nigeria's oil-producing Niger Delta said it kidnapped two German oil workers and four Nigerians yesterday to press for a series of social and economic demands. Oil services company B & B said six of its staff were abducted while travelling by boat from Delta State to Bayelsa State, where the ethnic Ijaw militant group is based. T.I.T. Manse, leader of the little-known Iduwini National Movement for Peace and Development, said the kidnappings were aimed at putting pressure on the local unit of Royal Dutch Shell. He said B & B was a Shell subcontractor.'[24] Once again it is the outsourced oil service providers that bear the brunt of the hostility to Shell.

A week later the Ijaw Youth Council told the Nigerian Press that they were considering closing down oil operations in their area, citing the refusal of other delegates to meet their demand for an increase in derivation from 13 to 25 per cent as a reason.[25]

Not only does the prospect of Shell returning to Ogoni look unlikely, but until the Nigerian government and companies such as Shell take the aspirations of the communities seriously, instead of pushing ahead with their production targets regardless, it is unlikely that violent elements will desist. In order for the violence and the mistrust that feeds it to die down, derivation, resource control and political self-determination all need to be addressed. In the absence of a resolution of these issues, the ten years since Saro-Wiwa's death have seen an increase in violence. And if these issues are not addressed, this may well be the pattern of the next decade.

In July the Confab collapsed, after the South–South delegation failed to get what they wanted. 'We came with a mandate from our people to demand 100 per cent resource control. We conceded to merely accepting 25 per cent in the interim, which has been denied. Therefore we can no longer participate in the proceedings of this conference,' said one South–South delegate. This huge issue, on which the people of the Delta have fought so long, remains unresolved.[26]

The Financier's Future

The day after the walk-out from the Confab in Abuja, the finance ministers of the G8 countries were meeting in London, prior to the G8 Summit. They announced their historic debt reduction deal for eighteen 'HIPCs' – most 'Heavily Indebted Poor Countries'. Their announcement outlined the conditions of the deal: 'We reaffirm our view that in order to make progress on social and economic development, it is essential that developing countries put in place the policies for economic growth . . . accountable and transparent institutions and policies . . . boost private sector development, and attract investment, a credible legal framework, and the elimination of impediments to private investment, both domestic and foreign.'[27]

So in return for cancelling debt, the finance ministers wanted all blocks to investment removed. What would be the primary investment of the G8 in Africa? Oil and gas. Where would this be? The answer is found a few paragraphs further down the communiqué: 'Nigeria is key to the prosperity of the whole continent of Africa . . . We are prepared to provide a fair and sustainable solution to Nigeria's debt problems in 2005.'[28]

Nigeria was not included in this first tranche of debt relief, but at the end of June the Paris Club of the richest nations also agreed to 'eradicate $31bn (£17.3 bn) of debts owed by Nigeria within six months'. However, the deal was pegged to Nigeria using its 'windfall' from rocketing global oil prices to pay off $6 billion and even buy back some remaining debt at a market-related discount. Nigeria's Finance Minister, Ngozi Okonjo-Iweala, was clearly delighted: 'We are thrilled by this news. It will mean more money for roads, rural electricity, health, education and HIV/Aids.'[29]

Once again the devil is in the detail. The debt that the Paris Club is 'forgiving' is debt that should never have been incurred in the first place. It represents money loaned to military rulers who squandered it and moved much of it to foreign bank accounts. The bulk of what is actually being forgiven is interest and penalties, as no money has been loaned by the Paris Club since 1992. Furthermore, the Paris Club is bearing no responsibility for lending to military rulers whom they knew, or should have known, would squander the money. Meanwhile, as we have seen, there are various ways in which the oil companies of the Paris Club countries (which include the US, UK, France and Italy) have worked to reduce their tax burden in Nigeria, thereby playing their part in keeping the country in debt.

Okonjo-Iweala's joy may be short-lived, however. The

report by Oil Change International, Jubilee, USA Network and the Institute for Public Policy Research highlights the fact that countries with higher oil exports tend to have higher debts. It offers a warning to Nigeria that its projected vast oil revenues, if not used wisely, could mean that mistakes of the past are repeated, and it concludes: 'If Nigeria increases its oil production from its current level of 2.5 million barrels per day to its projected 3 million barrels per day in 2006, and 4 million barrels per day by 2010, Nigeria's external debt will grow by 69 per cent, or US$21 billion, over that time period.'[30] This apparent paradox of debt coming out of rising oil revenues stems from states' habit of utilizing the revenues achieved at times of high oil prices to borrow heavily. Past experience in Nigeria shows that this borrowed capital has been mismanaged, and then, when the oil price drops, the state has been left heavily indebted. It is known as the Paradox of Plenty.

Shell will be at the heart of Nigeria's plans to increase production. At its last AGM in London, just days before the debt announcement, Shell had made a bold proclamation of investment in Nigeria. Malcolm Brinded, head of Shell International Exploration & Production, was speaking at the annual general meeting of Shell Transport & Trading in the Excel Centre in London's Docklands. In an aircraft hanger-sized room fit for 10,000 delegates, before an audience of just more than a thousand shareholders, Brinded emphasized the extent to which Nigeria would be a key part of the newly-merged company's future strategy.

The presentation by the board highlighted the impressive profits during 2004–5, but acknowledged that the reserves scandal had made it a difficult year. Shell managers told the audience – most of whom were pensioners – that there was still a lot of oil and gas in the ground that would be brought 'online' in good time. The Challenges such as climate change or the 'difficult operating environment' in the Niger Delta could be overcome with 'hard work and technological development'.[31] Nigeria remains a jewel in Shell's crown, despite all the crises the company has faced in the country.

At the AGM were several representatives from Shell's 'Fenceline Communities'. These are communities who live in the shadow of a Shell installation and who consider Shell to be a less than satisfactory neighbour. Some are from Texas and Louisiana, where predominantly poor African-American families live alongside refineries whose emissions impact upon their health.

Representatives of Fenceline Communities were there too from Durban in South Africa, Manila, Sakhalin Island in far eastern Russia, Northern Ireland, Brazil, the Dutch Antilles and, of course, the Niger Delta. Patrick Naagbanton, Director of the Niger Delta Project for Environment, Human Rights and Development, had come to question the board about gas flaring in the Delta. Malcolm Brinded defended Shell by attacking the Nigerian government. 'SPDC is 55 per cent owned by the government,' he said. 'We've invested $2 billion in collecting gas so far, and the reason there is still a lot to do is because the government has failed to deliver the $4 billion it is obligated to contribute.'

After all the 'Fenceline' people asked their questions, they stood up, and were seen to be wearing T-shirts reading 'Shell is Hell'. Singing a song in memory of Ken Saro-Wiwa, they were escorted out by security. One elderly shareholder grumbled, 'What are they going on about, who is Ken Sari-wawa?' Someone next to him explained. 'What the hell has that got to do with us?' he replied, grimacing.[32]

The Corporate Future

The final AGM of Shell T & T signalled not only the merger of the two companies, but a radical shift in the London stock market. Prior to June 2005, Royal Dutch had been quoted on the Amsterdam Stock Exchange while Shell T & T was quoted in London, where it constituted about 3.5 per cent of the London Stock Exchange. The merged entity is to be listed only on the London exchange. The move means that, at a stroke, Royal Dutch Shell is set to constitute approximately 9.5 per cent of the FTSE All-Share index, effectively 9.5 per cent of the UK stock market.

As the *Financial Times* points out, this is the most radical alteration of the London stock market for the best part of a decade. It has two significant effects. Many of the most stable pension funds and unit trusts hold shares roughly in proportion to the weighting of the stockmarket itself. These are called Tracker Funds because they track the FTSE indexes. The further up the indexes a company climbs, the more of that company's stock the Tracker Funds need to buy.

So if Shell nearly triples its value on the stock market, these funds and trusts need to nearly triple their holding of Shell shares. This means that investment and pension funds become more dependent on Shell. Millions of UK investors and pension fund holders need to be surer than ever of Shell.

Secondly, Shell's increase in the London stock market means that the percentage of the stock exchange that is tied to oil, gas and coal shares also increases. This in turn means that the percentage of the market whose income depends upon a continuous growth in these fossil fuels also increases.

Two days after the merger, Hilary Benn, the UK government's Minister for International Development, expressed his forthright views on the issue of climate change. He warned that the developed world is 'going to have to adjust' to prevent climate change becoming a global catastrophe.[33] The British government, as hosts of the 2005 G8 Summit in Gleneagles, had made climate a priority along with the issues of debt and aid. The battle was on to try to get universal approval for action on climate, but the Bush administration was reluctant even to accept that climate change was caused by human activity.

Since Bush came to office, Washington has refused to sign up to the UN Kyoto Agreement, whose principle is that each country calculates its carbon dioxide emissions, and then attempts to reduce these to pre-1990 levels and lower. Through this system of calibration, the 56 million citizens of the UK are judged to be responsible for 2.2 per cent of global emissions.

However, as a report published by Henderson Global Investors in June 2005 makes clear, if the emissions from corporations' production processes and the products that they sell are assessed, then the corporations are responsible for a substantial contribution to global emissions.[34] Just five oil and mining companies on the London Stock Exchange – Shell, BP, Scottish Power, Corus and BHP Billiton – contribute 10 per cent of global emissions of carbon dioxide, and Shell is responsible for 23 per cent of this total. This means that Shell's activities and the goods that it sells generates 2.3 per cent of total global emissions, more than all of the UK population combined.[35]

At the G8 Summit, President Bush and the US were widely

criticized for inaction on climate. However, some of the stron-
gest drivers of climate change are those hydrocarbon companies
clustered together in the heart of the City, London's financial
centre – companies such as Shell.

As part of the G8 Summit, Hilary Benn attended the Business
Action for Africa meeting in London chaired by Mark Moody-
Stuart, the current chairman of mining monolith Anglo American. Moody-Stuart had been head of Shell Exploration &
Production from 1991 to 1996, and Chairman of Shell from
1998 to 2000 – so that for nine years of his senior working life he
had had a pivotal role in the destiny of the Nigerian oil industry.
He had stood down as a Shell non-executive director the week
before at the company's AGM.

Business Action for Africa is part of Prime Minister Tony
Blair's 'Commission for Africa'. 'The role of the private sector as
the engine for growth in Africa is fundamental,' argues Blair.
You can see the kind of private sector growth that he is
advocating from the list of conference speakers: Jeroen van
der Veer, the current Chairman of Royal Dutch Shell; Jan du
Plessis, Chairman of British American Tobacco; and Steve Hayes
from the Corporate Council on Africa, the US lobby group for
big business in Africa.[36]

Blair's Business Action for Africa appears to be a replica of
other initiatives endorsed or supported by Washington and
London, such as the Africa Growth and Opportunity Act
(AGOA) passed by Congress, and the New Partnerships for
African Development, known as NEPAD, drafted by African
leaders in 2001. It has been readily endorsed by the G8 and by
Blair, who calls it 'an unprecedented opportunity for progress'.
But what kind of progress? Trevor Ngwane, the Secretary of
South Africa's Anti-Privatization Forum, argues that 'NEPAD is

being used as a bridgehead to bring privatization to Africa through South Africa.'[37]

All these initiatives see privatization and resource exploitation as crucial. At the same time, they all say they are committed to helping eradicate poverty, as did the Business Council, Hilary Benn, and the conference delegates.[38] What kind of future will it be for an Africa that is dominated by Western banks as well as Western mining, oil and tobacco companies?

This appears to be a continuation of colonial models of commerce, where the primary beneficiaries are western shareholders. There is little evidence from history that this will lift Africans out of poverty.

A Sinking Future?

Gas flaring from oil installations around the world is a constant source of carbon dioxide entering the atmosphere. As explained in Chapter 3, the oil industry in the Delta is one of the worst cases in the world of gas flaring. It has been estimated that the flaring in the Delta emits some 70 million tonnes of CO_2 a year, higher than the emissions for Portugal, Sweden and Norway. Shell's percentage of this is difficult to quantify because it gives its emissions as 'hydrocarbons' rather than CO_2, but it has been estimated to be greater than the individual emissions of over 100 countries, including Ecuador, Estonia, Sri Lanka and Bahrain.[39]

Today, according to a report by ERA and the Climate Justice Programme (CJP), 'More gas is flared in Nigeria than anywhere else in the world. Estimates are notoriously unreliable, but roughly 2.5 billion cubic feet of gas associated with crude oil is wasted in this way every day. This is equal to 40 per cent of all Africa's natural gas consumption in 2001, while the annual financial loss to Nigeria is about $2.5 billion. The flares have contributed more greenhouse gases than all of sub-Saharan Africa combined. The biggest culprit is of course the biggest producer: the Shell Petroleum Development Company.'

ERA and CJP point out that although Shell and the Nigerian government have said that they plan to phase out gas flaring by 2008, this is incompatible with the government's plan to increase production to 4 million barrels by 2010. Indeed, Shell's flaring of gas actually increased from 2002–3 by 22.8 per cent.

In May 2005 Shell conceded that flaring would not end until at least 2009.[40] 'It is difficult to see how most of the resulting increased amounts of associated gas will not be flared. We demand an immediate end to gas flaring, and an end to exploration and new oil field development until facilities are in place for the utilization of all associated gas,' ERA and CJP argue.[41]

In June 2005, ERA and CJP announced they were backing communities from across the Delta in a ground-breaking legal action. A legal suit was filed in the Nigerian Federal High Court against the Nigerian government, the Nigerian National Petroleum Corporation and Shell, Exxon, Chevron, Total and Agip to stop the gas flaring. One of the plaintiffs, Tare Dadiowei from the Gbarain community in Bayelsa State, commented: 'It is our hope that the laws of Nigeria will protect us from the continuous violations of our human rights and destruction of our livelihood by Shell. While Shell makes cheap excuses for the continuing flaring of gas in our communities, we bear the huge costs with our contaminated air and soil, diseases and death.'[42] Tare Dadiowei lives near Shell oil fields and therefore complains about them. But other plaintiffs make similar complaints about other oil companies in Nigeria.

The reality is that every flare that oil companies burn and every drop of oil and gas they drill causes climate change, and some places on earth are more susceptible than others to the effects of those climate changes. The sensitive fragile ecosystem of the Niger Delta is one of them.

President Obasanjo and Shell believe that drilling oil will lift the people of the Niger Delta out of poverty, but it will actually sink their homes in the process. It will be like killing someone in the process of setting them free.

The people of the Niger Delta have worried about this for some time. In the summer of 1992 Chief Dappa-Biriye, on behalf of the Rivers Chiefs and Peoples Conference, travelled to the United Nations Conference on Environment and Development in Brazil, the famous Rio Summit. At the conference Dappa-Biriye presented a report on 'The Endangered Environment of the Niger Delta'.

A key element of this report focused on the impacts of climate change. 'If we superimpose the predicted sea level rise on the gradually subsiding Niger Delta (subsidence exacerbated by oil and gas extraction), the net effect is that within the next two decades . . . about a 40km-wide strip of the Niger Delta and its peoples would be submerged and rendered extinct. Thus the very existence of the indigenous people of the Niger Delta and adjoining coastal zone is seriously threatened by environmental degradation caused by petroleum industrial pollution,' said the report.[43]

Echoing Dappa-Biriye's report, the World Bank specialist David Moffat and Professor Olof Linden from Stockholm University published a study in December 1995 in which they estimated that 80 per cent of the Delta's population will have to move due to sea-level rise, at a cost of $9 billion.[44]

The concept that climate change will undermine African poverty eradication was at the heart of a presentation made by Dr Anthony Nyong, from the University of Jos in Nigeria, at the Scientific Symposium on Stabilization of Greenhouse Gases. The Symposium was called by Tony Blair to gauge scientific opinion on climate change in the run-up to Britain's presidency of the G8. It attracted 200 of the world's leading climate scientists, including Dr Nyong. The Symposium was held at the shiny new Meteorological Office building in Exeter in early February 2005, just days before the opening of Nigeria's Confab.[45]

'Global warming is already happening, with its impact being felt most by the world's poorest people, particularly those in Africa. Climate data for Africa for the last 30–40 years shows global warming has taken a firm hold,' Dr Nyong warned. 'There will be more extreme events such as drought and floods, and the seasonal patterns will shift. Food production, water supplies, public health, and people's livelihoods are all being damaged and undermined.'

Dr Nyong also looked at the impacts of a 1-metre sea-level rise. This would not only displace millions of people in the Niger Delta, as Dappa-Biriye had predicted, but would also threaten some 75 per cent of Nigeria's agricultural land. Ironically, the sea-level rise also affects the oil industry: 'In Nigeria, and in particular in the Niger Delta, another concern are the oil fields. It was estimated that about 259 producing oil fields are located in the threatened areas, representing a value at risk of $10,790 million for a 1-metre sea level rise.'[46] So the more oil the industry produces, the more it kills itself. But the industry can move elsewhere, the people of the Niger Delta cannot.

In May 2005 the Report of the International Scientific Steering Committee from the Symposium was published. Africa warranted special attention. 'Alternative development pathways need to be taken into account in developing strategies to avoid dangerous anthropogenic climate change,' concluded the scientists: 'This was seen as particularly important if the potential impacts of climate change in Africa are to be avoided.'[47] By the time of the G8 Summit two months later, an alternative development path for Africa was nowhere to be seen.

Life without Oil?

It is the day after the Shell AGM. Ledum Mitee sits in a London pub in Southwark. Mitee had to endure his own horror when he was arrested and incarcerated along with Saro-Wiwa. Unlike Saro-Wiwa he had been set free, in a move that mystified many, including Mitee, at the time.

For years Mitee was in exile, finally returning home in the late 1990s. He still leads MOSOP, and talks about life now without Shell in Ogoni, about the 12 years since the company withdrew in 1993, after producing oil there for 35 years. 'Without Shell our communities have better, greener vegetation. The crop yields have been better. Some of the things we lost are coming back; for instance, our society was dislocated completely. The social dislocation when oil companies come to town, like prostitution, is enormous. It is far less now. We feel better as a community.'

He sips a cold lager and talks about the reconciliation process, about how MOSOP was approached by the reconciliation service at Coventry Cathedral when they were hired by Shell to look into the prospect of reconciliation. Last September, in 2004, Mitee met with President Obasanjo in Abuja. Obasanjo asked Mitee how the Nigerian government could get Shell back into Ogoni. 'I replied that the question would have been easier if it had been how do we get oil flowing back in Ogoni, because it is not only Shell who exploit oil.' Obasanjo's response to Mitee was stark: 'These Shell guys will make a lot of trouble if we were to kick them out.'

There is still great scepticism about the whole reconciliation process: 'We know that this is the Tenth Anniversary coming up,' Mitee continues. 'There is a lot of work being done to raise the issues of ten years ago, this is what happened and nothing seems to have changed. The timing of the announcement, when nothing seems concrete, reinforces the scepticism of the people that this is just a PR stunt. But we do not want to sound like we have killed [the initiative] before it has started. Generally the Ogoni people feel that we need to be convinced that the talks are going to be real and genuine and are not going to be used for a PR purpose.'

Mitee is also worried that Shell has not changed, arguing that although the company's PR 'rhetoric has changed', its practices have not. 'They have become more slick to hide some of the obvious things they are doing.' In fact, he says, 'I could say it could not be worse than what is happening now.'

Patrick Smith from *Africa Confidential* backs up Mitee's argument that nothing has changed. Smith calls the Shell PR during the era of Ron van den Berg, Managing Director of SPDC from 1997 until 2002, 'arrogant and inept in the extreme. My private encounters absolutely substantiated that. They were absolutely believing. Van den Berg himself believed his own propaganda. Which I think is extremely dangerous, because as far as they were concerned, the crisis in Nigeria was all about a bunch of opportunistic thugs' who wanted to make money out of Shell. Within the company, Smith says, Shell believed it was 'behaving extremely honourably. I think the problem is that they have never broken out of that in Nigeria.'[48]

Mitee continues: 'Shell has to break from the past,' otherwise 'I fear a situation [in which] there will be a very repressive attitude, serious human rights abuses in order to get a drop of oil. The whole of the Niger Delta will become very costly in terms of human rights abuses, [and] lives that will be lost. What I see now is a spiralling cost of oil. The American policies that have had a doubtful success in the Middle East, have therefore focused their attention around the Gulf of Guinea. It is not people-centred. It is just barrel-centred. Clearly you will bring more discontent, and that discontent will be counter-productive.

'At the end of the day, the place will become so messed up you will get very close to what you are getting in the Middle East,' he finishes. 'In the case of the Niger Delta, it could be worse. Because we are used to a situation where the social contract between the government and the people has broken down. There is now a very high level of arms in the area, the situation could become so bad that in five years' time it will be very difficult to get a drop of oil without a life.'[49]

Who Maps the Future?

At the end of June 2005 Ken Wiwa, the son of Ken Saro-Wiwa and now a dedicated campaigner for justice in Ogoni, reflects on the future too. He talks about the reconciliation process and how the family has not even been consulted. He talks about the fundamental need for an official pardon for his father and the others.

Wiwa moves on to the accountability of Shell. 'You know what annoys people in the South? The way that Westerners can commit crimes and violate the environment and human rights, and say "ah, we got it wrong" or "we have changed". No – if you got it wrong, where is the accountability?'

Wiwa continues outlining what further positive steps should be taken. 'We don't even know how much oil there is in Ogoni. Only the oil companies know that.' He argues that what is needed is a re-drawing of the oil company concession maps into cultural inventories. 'You figure out what the natural resources are, what the human resources are, what the in-digenous knowledge systems are. Produce an inventory of what these communities are. So when these communities engage with foreign direct investors, there is an inventory. Based on this inventory, this is who we are. You can come and invest in our community, but you must enhance the inventory. You must also be accountable.'

By this means, he says, you 'end up with maps that are drawn up by the local people, rather than maps drawn by Shell or maps drawn by a colonial entity' whose maps 'were drawn to reflect what their own ambitions were, not what the ambitions of the local people were.' These methods of cultural mapping are being developed in Canada, he explains.

It is also what Ken Saro-Wiwa was trying to do in Ogoni. 'If you look at my father's writings, he says that after thirty years of Shell we took stock of who we were, what we had lost and what we wanted. But that stock-taking exercise was stopped in 1993. We need to continue that. We can then say to Shell, this is who we are and your investment is jeopardizing the value of this community.'[50]

Wiwa's dream is far from the future being proposed in meeting-rooms in Washington, where American oil executives and politicians plan further US involvement in Nigeria as a way of reducing US dependence on Middle Eastern oil. Nor is it on the agenda of British officials in London who are engaged in the US–UK Energy Dialogue, which talks about Nigeria but does not consult its people.

Remember Saro-Wiwa

We have compiled a list of recommendations made by representatives of the communities of the Delta (see chapter 9). As you read the proposals, reflect that we – the citizens of the North and the past colonial powers – should not neglect our own role in determining which path the Delta takes into the future.

The first Atlantic Triangle, the slave trade and the slave plantations, existed as an economic and political system for the better part of 300 years. It was brought to a close by a number of factors – the abolition of the slave trade, the abolition of slavery itself, and the rise of the coal-fired Industrial Revolution, to name but three.

It is important to remember how this great change came about. It depended upon a vast range of actors, often unknown to each other, working in different theatres over a long period of time. These theatres included the resistance to enslavement that constantly took place in the villages of West Africa, the slave rebellions that repeatedly disrupted the economic life of the plantations in America and the Caribbean, and the movement for the abolition of slavery, which began at a meeting in the heart of the City of London on 22 May 1787.

The campaigners who established the Committee for the Abolition of the Slave Trade worked tirelessly for 51 years until slavery was formally abolished in the British Empire on 1 August 1838. Nearly four million slaves were freed on that day, the day British slavery died after 276 years. Another 26 years passed before slavery was finally abolished in the United States.

The Atlantic Triangle was as fundamental to the economic life of seventeenth- and eighteenth-century Europe as oil and gas are to our society in this and the last century. Yet the system of slavery was dismantled, and it offers a picture of how the system of oil and gas might be dismantled, how an emancipation from the empire of oil might be achieved.

The past ten years following the execution of Saro-Wiwa and the Ogoni Eight have essentially been blighted years of violence and pollution, of militarization and neglect. The question this provokes is, how do we – in the states that depend upon the Nigerian oil and gas industry for energy, employment and investment – meet the challenge of the next ten years?

What will the Delta look like in 2015, what will our relationship be with it in 2015? How do we assist the Delta communities in following the path that is loosely drawn in the list of recommendations, and ensure that they are not forced to go down the path that is being delineated in those meetings and conferences in Washington and London?

One recommendation from the Delta is that they wish to pursue a path that does not depend on increasing oil extraction. On the material level we can assist this by pursuing a development model for ourselves that reduces our consumption of oil and gas, increases the amount of energy we draw from local renewable sources, and removes the pressure to import crude and LNG from Nigeria.

Another recommendation from the Delta is that they wish to pursue a path that does not depend on the increasing militarization of the Gulf of Guinea. This military build-up is in part driven by the interlocking interests of the US and UK governments, the armed forces of the US, the investment banks, and the international oil companies – in particular Shell, Chevron and ExxonMobil. We can assist the desires of the Delta communities by persuading our governments not to pursue this course of militarization, and by weakening the bonds which bind the oil corporations to the government and the defence establishment.

A further recommendation from the Delta is that a process of creating cultural inventories should be undertaken by communities in the region, in order to effect the representation of the social, economic and cultural understandings of those communities. The pursuit of justice for the Delta communities could be assisted by increasing the cultural representation of those communities in centres of power such as London and Washington.

One step in this direction was taken in the spring of 2005. On 22 March the 'Remember Saro-Wiwa' initiative was launched at the City Hall in London by Ken Wiwa, the Mayor of London Ken Livingston, and Anita Roddick, formerly Director of The Body Shop. This campaign to create a 'living memorial' to Ken Saro-Wiwa in London is being led by a coalition of organizations and individuals, initiated and co-ordinated by PLATFORM, that includes African Writers Abroad, Amnesty International, Christian Aid, Friends of the Earth, Greenpeace, Human Rights Watch, Index on Censorship, and International PEN.[51]

Their collective intent is to ensure that the name of Saro-

Wiwa and the cause of the Delta communities are given the highest profile in the cultural life of London – to raise at the heart of the old and the new Atlantic Triangle a memorial to a figure who gave his life in the struggle for justice against that economic system.

At the City Hall launch there were readings from the Nigerian novelist Helon Habila, the poet Linton Kwesi Johnson, and Ken Saro-Wiwa's old friend the British novelist William Boyd. Ken Wiwa spoke at length about the current plight of the Delta and about his father. He closed with the lines: 'When people like Ken Saro-Wiwa are killed, their death issues a challenge to all of us. I remember walking out of the Steve Biko Memorial Gardens in South Africa a few years ago, and I will never forget the inscription at the top of the gates. It simply says: "I would rather die for an idea that will live, than live for an idea that will die".'

This is our Empire

JAMES MARRIOTT

June 2005. I am up at six to write. There is gentle breathing in the bed that I have left. The village too is asleep.

As the Earth turns, the sun's light falls upon it evenly. In anticipation the woods, fields and gardens burst into birdsong, a wave of sound that passes around the planet ceaselessly, night falls as dawn rises elsewhere. A singing planet.

Where I am sitting is due north-west of Umuechem, Soku and Isoku – Ijaw, Igbo and Urhobo villages. Dawn broke there just a little before it did so here. I try to imagine the birdsong in the mangroves, the creeks, the fields and forests, and how different it is from here.

But much of the birdsong would be familiar to me, for so many of the songbirds in my village migrate here from West Africa. The nightingale that sings in the blackthorn scrub at the end of the orchard, winters in Nigeria. Perhaps it spends half the year in the mangroves? The sounds of my summer nights depend upon the health of the Delta.

I try to imagine the roar of the gas flares – bright orange flames 100 feet long, as loud at dawn as they were at nightfall, as it was at midnight, as it will be at midday.

The rocks beneath the Delta farmland spew up their black gold, ceaseless, dismissive of night or day. The crude passes through flowlines, flowstations and pipelines. The liquid that moved beneath the rocks now courses through these steel veins above ground – bound for Bonny, Escravos, Forcados, Qua Ibo, Pennington and Brass.

At the terminals, I imagine the roar of the tugs' engines as they manoeuvre the tankers alongside and away from the loading-jetties. The night shift gives way to the day shift, the tankers arriving and departing at any time of day or night.

It is now dawn somewhere out in the Atlantic. Is there a big sea or is it flat calm? Are there whales and dolphins visible from the bridge 90 feet above the surrounding ocean? What is the captain doing as his crude-carrier, fully laden with thousands of tonnes of Bonny Light, ploughs through the waves. Is he awake or asleep? As watch gives way to watch, the ship – computer- and satellite-guided – heads for the night of America.

Does the tanker arrive at night or day? Whatever the hour, the tugs at the terminal of Port Arthur refinery, a hundred miles east of Houston in Texas, will be on stand-by – engines turning over – waiting to guide their charges.

The tanker will unload in the shadow of the vast complex, part refinery, part chemical works, of storage tanks and cracking towers, of product pipes and olefins plant. High above, from the towering stack, rises a sheet of orange flame and a cloud of black smoke. The refinery's flare burns night and day: Ijaw, Igbo, Urhobo geology filling the Texan air. I wonder, does it drown out the Texas birdsong?

And the plastics from these plants, do they build the foundations, and enable the workings of my laptop?

In this early morning, this is my Empire. Its working sustains my life. This is our Empire. We were born in it, we inherited it, its comforts and cruelties. This is our Empire, ours to retreat from, and ours to dismantle.

I try to imagine a life without oil.

CHAPTER NINE

Voices from the Delta – A Programme for Change

Below is a list of recommendations, based on voices from the Delta and other experts on Nigeria (for more details see Chapter 8). For some interactive recommendations on what you can individually do, go to the website: www.remembersarowiwa.com

Justice for the Past

- The Nigerian Government to issue a formal pardon for Ken Saro-Wiwa and the eight other Ogoni – Dr Barinem Kiobel, John Kpuinen, Baribor Bera, Saturday Doobee, Nordu Eawo, Paul Levura, Daniel Gbokoo and Felix Nuate. All their names to be removed from the statute books.

- The British government to release all official papers relating to the trial and execution of Ken Saro-Wiwa and the eight other Ogoni that they are currently withholding on the grounds that the 'information may prejudice the commercial interests of a British Company in Nigeria'.[1]

- As a first step in reconciliation, all the major international oil companies (Shell, Chevron, Agip, Total & ExxonMobil), the contractors and the oil service companies (Willbros, *et al*) to issue formal and public apologies for their involvement or implication in any human rights abuse and manslaughter in the Niger Delta perpetrated as a result of oil and gas extraction processes since 1987, since the first oil-related killings by the security forces at Iko.

- The International Criminal court to conduct a thorough investigation of human rights abuse in the Delta. Where appropriate this investigation to lead to the prosecution of foreign and Nigerian institutions and individuals.
- Ecological restoration and clean-up of all environmental damage produced by the exploitation of oil and gas in the Niger Delta since 1956. Compensation to be paid to all landowners and communities for all environmental damage and financial loss.
- An investigation by the Economic and Financial Crimes Commission (EFCC) in Abuja to be held into financial payments between all oil companies and oil service companies and the Nigerian military since 1987.

Respect in the Present

- An immediate halt to all flaring of associated gas at onshore wells in the Niger Delta area, and an assessment of the accumulated ecological debt accrued through the exploitation of oil and gas in the Niger Delta since 1956.
- A five-year freeze on new oil and gas development and exploration in the Niger Delta and Nigerian continental shelf, and a halt to the provision of finance capital (public or private) for such projects. While this is not a call for an end to current production, a freeze on new oil and gas developments should occur while issues of resource control, derivation, corruption, and demilitarization are worked out.

- As a direct result of the National Political Reform Conference (Confab) in Abuja, a process of demilitarization of the Delta region to be undertaken. A first step in this process could be either 'Zones of Peace' set up in specific areas of the Delta, or a Small Arms Treaty to include the whole Delta.
- Whatever demilitarization process is chosen, it should include all elements of the Nigerian military, security forces and police. It should also include all oil companies and the private security companies and police working for them. And it should include all the militias. International peace monitors, including representatives from recognized peace groups and civil society, should oversee the process.
- An international mission should be deployed as quickly as possible to provide independent monitoring of the entire electoral process and therefore help to reduce the risk of an escalation of armed conflict. It should provide technological assistance to the political parties on the conduct of their campaigns and to the Electoral Commission on overall procedures.
- Demilitarization of Nigeria and the Gulf of Guinea by US and European military forces. A freeze on any deployment of US and European military forces in the region, any permanent or temporary military bases.
- The EU Anti-Fraud Office should assist the EFCC's investigation into tax evasion. The investigation should look at the use of international tax havens to reduce tax burdens of foreign companies working in Nigeria.
- As part of this investigation, all tax havens and foreign banks to open up their books on all accounts over $1 million related to Nigeria and to fully investigate the

existence of embezzled funds and return them to a special
account dedicated to targeted development projects.

An End to the Empire of Oil

- International assistance to be provided to enable the
  communities of the Niger Delta to follow a sustainable
  development path which is not solely linked to the exploitation of oil and gas. A proportion of government
  revenue to be spent on renewable energy projects in the
  region and on enabling economic diversification to reduce
  dependency on oil.
- A process of creating cultural inventories to be undertaken
  by communities in the Niger Delta, in order to effect the
  representation of social, economic and cultural understandings and assets as perceived by the communities
  themselves rather than by outside agencies.
- After the cultural mapping process is complete, a fund for
  the Delta communities to be set up. Oil revenues should
  directly support sustainable development of the communities, with funding priorities identified by the communities through the cultural mapping process.

Maps

Map 1. Nigeria 2005, showing states and inset of São Tomé and Príncipe

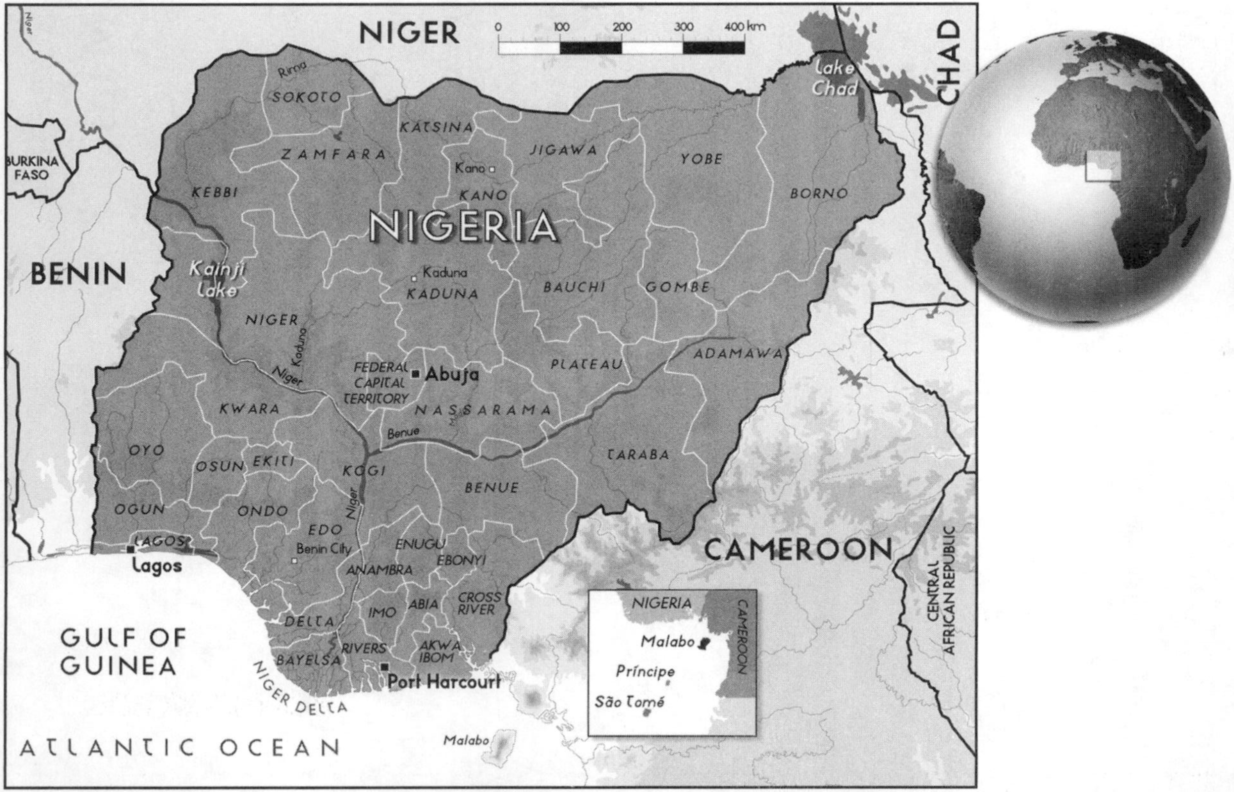

Map 2: The environmental zones of the Niger Delta

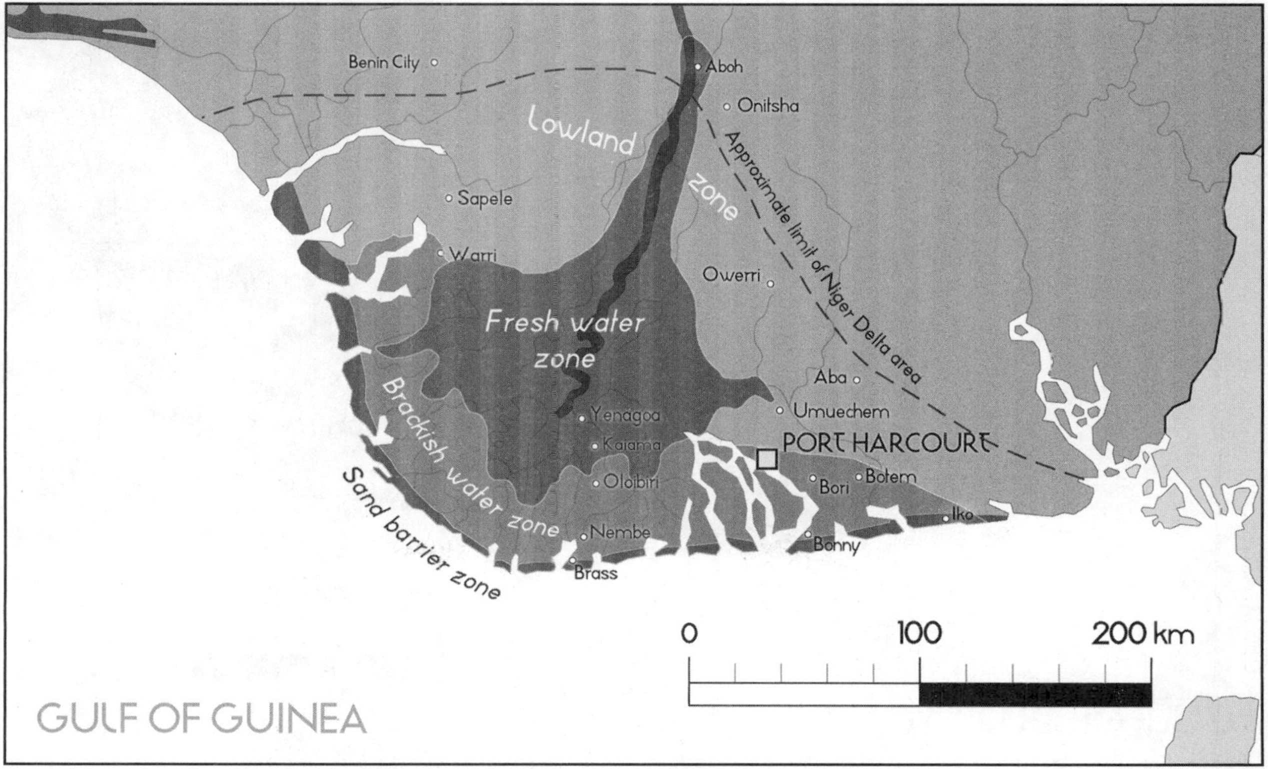

GULF OF GUINEA

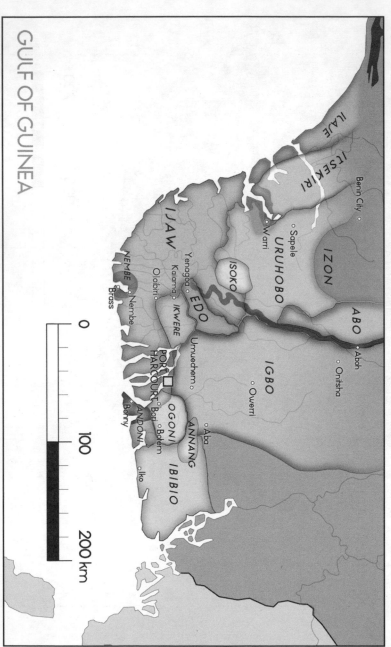

Map 3. Approximate boundaries of ethnic groups in the Niger Delta

Map 4: The Nigerian oil industry at the point of Independence, 1960 – showing discovered oil fields, pipelines and export terminal

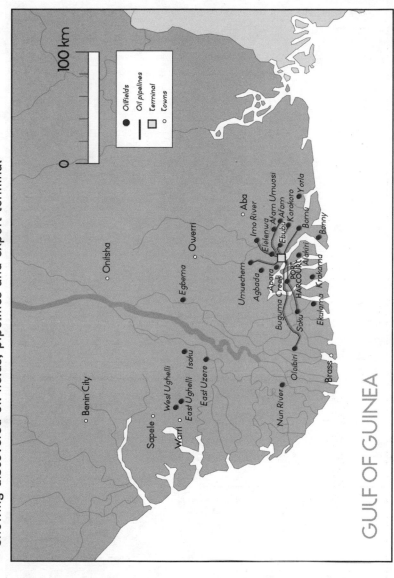

Map 5. The Nigerian oil industry today, 2005 – showing oil and gas

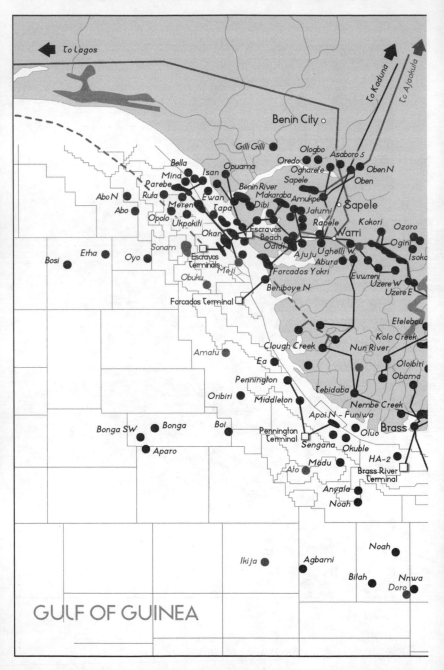

fields, pipelines, export terminals & offshore exploration blocks

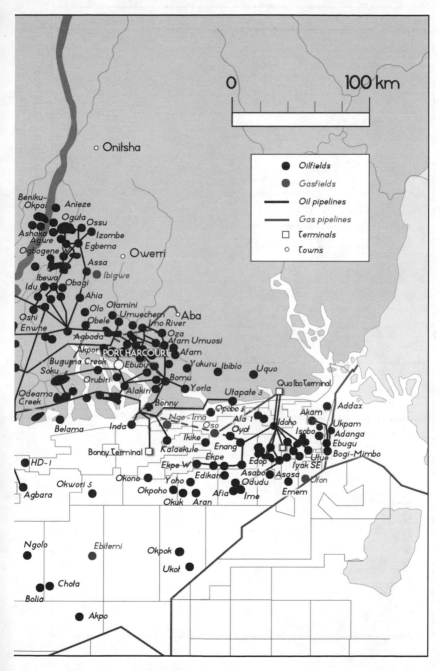

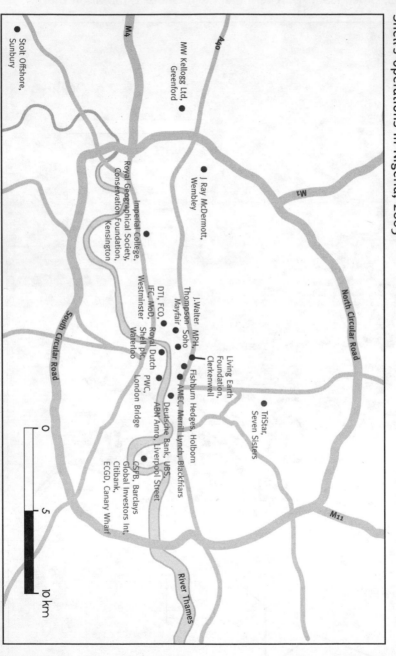

Map 6. The Niger Delta in London – map of some of the companies and institutions related to Shell's operations in Nigeria, 2005

Map 7. The Niger Delta in Washington – map of some of the institutions and companies related to the oil industry in Nigeria, 2005

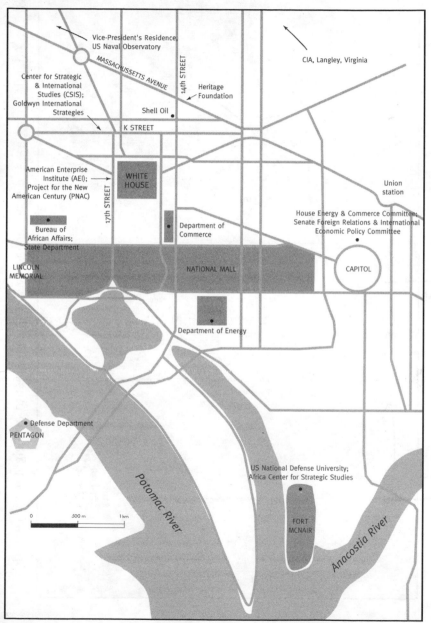

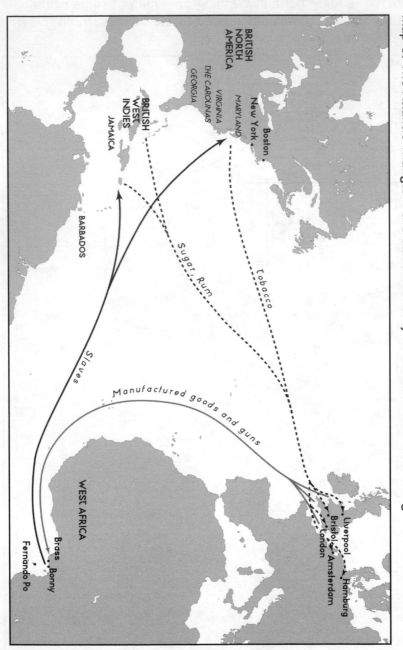

Map 8. The Atlantic Triangle – the slave economy in the seventeenth and eighteenth centuries

Map 9. The new Atlantic Triangle? The flows of oil, gas and money in and out of Nigeria, 1995–2005

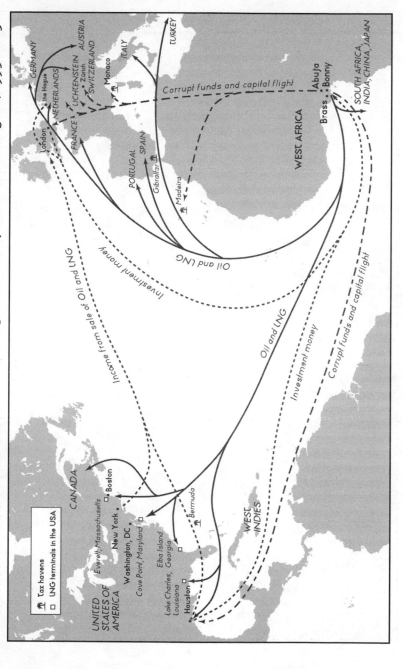

Glossary

Business and Oil Industry Technical Terms

AGM	Annual General Meeting
bb1/d	Barrels per day
CEO	Chief Executive Officer
CMD	Committee of Managing Directors, the governing body in Shell up to 2005
LNG	Liquified natural gas

Companies and Consultancies

AIOC	Anglo-Iranian Oil Company, forerunner of BP
BGT	Bonny Gas Transport
CERA	Cambridge Energy Research Associates Energy
ERHC Energy	Environmental Remediation Holding Corporation
GIS	Goldwyn International Strategies
KBR	Kellogg, Brown and Root
NLNG	Nigeria Liquified Natural Gas Limited
NNPC	Nigerian National Petroleum Corporation
Royal Dutch	Royal Dutch Petroleum Company, the Dutch arm of Shell
SCIN	Shell Companies In Nigeria
Shell-BP	Shell-BP Petroleum Development Company of Nigeria
Shell T & T	Shell Transport & Trading Plc, the British arm of Shell
Shell Mex & BP	Joint oil marketing company between Shell and BP in the UK, 1931–1974
SNEPCO	Shell Nigeria Exploration & Production Company
SNG	Shell Nigeria Gas Company
SNOP	Shell Nigeria Oil Products
SPDC	Shell Petroleum Development Company of Nigeria.
TSKJ	TSKJ consortium is known after its different part-

ners; Technip, Snamprogetti, MW Kellogg; and the Japanese Gas Corporation.

Oil Projects in Nigeria/Gulf of Guinea

JDZ	Joint Development Zone negotiated between Nigeria and São Tomé
WAGP	West African Gas Pipeline

Government Institutions, Governmental Organizations and Initiatives

AGOA	Africa Growth and Opportunity Act
ANWR	Arctic National Wildlife Refuge, Alaska
CIA	Central Intelligence Agency (US)
DTI	Department of Trade and Industry (UK)
DfID	Department for International Development (UK)
ECGD	Export Credit Guarantee Department (UK)
EFCC	Economic and Financial Crimes Commission (Nigerian)
EITI	Extractive Industries Transparency Initiative
EU	European Union
EXIM	Export-Import Bank (US)
FCO	Foreign and Commonwealth Office (UK)
GPDM	Good Projects in Difficult Markets - A project of the ECGD
HMG	Her Majesty's Government (UK)
MI5	The British Security Service
NEITI	Nigerian Extractive Industries Transparency Initiative
NEPAD	New Partnership for African Development
NPRC	Nigeria's National Political Reform Conference, also known as 'Confab'
OPEC	Organization of Petroleum Exporting Countries
SEC	Securities and Exchange Commission (US)
UK	United Kingdom
US	United States of America
USCG	United States Coast Guard

NGOs, Civil Society Groups and Think-tanks

AEI	American Enterprise Institute
CJP	Climate Justice Programme
CSIS	Center for Strategic and International Studies
ERA	Environmental Rights Action
FOWA	Federation of Ogoni Women's Associations
IASPS	Institute for Advanced Strategic and Political Studies
ICR	International Centre for Reconciliation
IPPR	Institute for Public Policy Research
MOSOP	Movement for the Survival of Ogoni People
NGO	non-governmental organization
NYCOP	National Youth Council of Ogoni People
PNAC	Project for the New American Century
UN	United Nations
UNDP	United Nations Development Programme
UNEP	United Nations Environment Programme
UNHCR	United Nations High Commissioner for Refugees

Military

Lt Col	Lieutenant Colonel
EUCOM	United States European Command
MPF	Mobile Police Force
NATO	North Atlantic Treaty Organization

Reference Notes

Preface

1 See www.platformlondon.org
2 See www.remembersarowiwa.com
3 D. Rowan (2005) 'Africa Made Me a "Bloody Pinko Liberal" ', 29 June, *Evening Standard*, p. 49.

Chapter 1: A Span of Ten Years

1 C. Duodo (1995) 'Hanged Activists Were Starved', *Observer*, 19 November, p. 24.
2 K. Maier (2000) *This House Has Fallen – Nigeria in Crisis*, Penguin, pp. 81, 83, 89–90.
3 http://www.africaaction.org/docs95/nig9511.htm; Human Rights Watch/Africa (1995) '*Nigeria – The Ogoni Crisis – A Case Study of Military Repression in Southeastern Nigeria*', July, Vol. 7, No. 5, p. 26.
4 M. Birnbaum (1995), *Nigeria: Fundamental Rights Denied: Report of the Trial of Ken Saro-Wiwa and Others*, ARTICLE 19 in Association with the Bar Human Rights Committee of England and Wales and the Law Society of England and Wales, June, p. iii.
5 M. Birnbaum (1995), *Ibid.*, June, Appendix 10: Summary of Affidavits Alleging Bribery.
6 S. Buerk (2005), Email to Andy Rowell, 11 July.
7 Restricted document (1995), Subject My Tel. No: Trial of Ken Saro-Wiwa, February.
8 Mainly taken from A. Usen (1998), 'To Set the Captives Free', *Africa Today*, November, pp. 8–11; A. Duval Smith (1998), 'Hymns of Death', *Guardian*, 26 October, G2, pp. 2–3; also C. Duodo (1995), 'Hanged Activists Were Starved', *Observer*, 19 November, p. 24; F. Aigbogun (1995), 'It Took Five Tries to Hang Saro-Wiwa', *Independent*, 11 November, p. 10; I. Black, O. Boycott, J. Vidal (1995), 'Nigeria Defies World With Writer's "Judicial Murder" ', *Guardian*, p. 1.

9 W. Boyd, Forward in K. Saro-Wiwa (1995), *A Month and A Day*, Penguin, p. vii.

10 P. Adams, G. Hepple, J. Davison (1995), 'Pariah – Nigeria Drops into Darkness', *Sunday Times*, 12 November.

11 Z. Saro-Wiwa (1995), 'Sorrow of the Saro-Wiwas', *Telegraph Magazine*, 16 December, pp. 20–7.

12 Catma Films (1996), *In Rememberance – Ken Saro Wiwa*, shown on Channel 4, 9 November; G. Whittel (2000), 'Justice and Oil', *The Times*, 16 November.

13 Lagos TelNo 542 and Your Tels Nos 29 and 30 to UKDel CHOGM Auckland (1995) *Subject: Nigeria: Saro-Wiwa/Ogonis: Death Sentences*, 9 November.

14 K. Wiwa (2005), Interview with Andy Rowell and Lorne Stockman, 29 June.

15 N. Rufford (1995), 'Feuding Commonwealth Finds Unity', *Sunday Times*, 12 November, p. 19; S. Crawshaw (1995), 'Hangings Plunge Summit into Crisis', *Independent*, 11 November, p. 12.

16 K. Wiwa (2005), interview with Andy Rowell and Lorne Stockman, 29 June.

17 http://www.shell.com/static/nigeria/downloads/pdfs/ 2004_rpt.pdf

18 http://www.csis.org/africa/0507_GulfofGuinea.pdf; *US Fed News* (2005), 'Energy Information Administration Issues Country Analysis Brief On Nigeria', 18 April.

19 *Ibid.*

20 J. Bearman (2003), 'Perils and Possibilities: Petroleum Opportunities in Africa', Address to Heritage Foundation Conference, 8 May; http://www.heritage.org/Press/Events/ev050803b.cfm

21 *US Fed News* (2005), 'Energy Information Administration Issues Country Analysis Brief On Nigeria', 18 April; S. A. Khan (1994), *Nigeria – The Political Economy of Oil*, Oxford University Press, pp. 56–7.

22 http://www.shell.com/home/Framework?siteId=nigeria&FC2=/ nigeria/html/iwgen/about_shell/shell_companies/spdc/ zzz_lhn.html&FC3=/nigeria/html/iwgen/about_shell/shell_companies/spdc/dir_spdc_1203_1027.html

23 http://www.shell.com/home/Framework?siteId=nigeria&FC2=/ nigeria/html/iwgen/about_shell/shell_companies/spdc/ zzz_lhn.html&FC3=/nigeria/html/iwgen/about_shell/shell_companies/spdc/dir_spdc_1203_1027.html

24 http://www.shell.com/home/Framework?siteId=nigeria&FC2=/ nigeria/html/iwgen/leftnavs/zzz_lhn3_0_0.html&FC3=/nigeria/

html/iwgen/about_shell/shell_companies/dir_indexshell-comp_1405_1621.html

25 http://www.shell.com/home/Framework?siteId=nigeria&FC2=/nigeria/html/iwgen/leftnavs/zzz_lhn3_0_0.html&FC3=/nigeria/html/iwgen/about_shell/shell_companies/dir_indexshell-comp_1405_1621.html

26 K. Hamilton (1995), 'Under Fire', *Sunday Times*, p. 3.

27 Advert in *Observer*, 19 November 1995.

28 J. Sweeny and C. Duodu (1999) 'Nigeria? Carry on Trading Chaps', *Observer*, 5 November, p. 21.

29 D. Pallister, M. Milner, D. Atkinson (1995), 'Few Qualms in Big Business of Kickbacks', *Guardian*, 13 November, p. 8.

30 Human Rights Watch/Africa (1996) *Nigeria, 'Permanent Transition', Current Violations of Human Rights in Nigeria*, Vol. 8, No. 3, September, pp. 37–8.

31 Catma Films (1996), *In Rememberance – Ken Saro Wiwa*, shown on Channel 4, 9 November.

32 Human Rights Watch/Africa (1996) *Nigeria: 'Permanent Transition'*, Human Rights Watch/Africa, Vol. 8, No. 3(A), September, p. 42.

33 P. Sisler (1996), 'US Sees Worsening Abuses in Nigeria', *United Press International*, Washington, 6 March.

34 Catma Films (1996), *In Rememberance – Ken Saro Wiwa*, shown on Channel 4, 9 November; Report of the Fact-Finding Mission of the Secretary-General (1996), 23 April.

35 *Reuters* (1996), 'EU Parliament Seeks Oil Embargo Against Nigeria', Strasbourg, France, 23 May.

36 *Reuters* (1996), 'Environment Award Given to Nigeria's Ken Saro-Wiwa', Nairobi, 29 May.

37 Shell International Limited (1996), *Shell Nigeria Offers Plan for Ogoni*, 8 May.

38 MOSOP (1996), *MOSOP Response to Shell's 'Plan for Ogoni'*, Press Release, 12 May.

39 A. Isomkwo (1996), 'Komo Urges Shell Back to Ogoniland', *Daily Sunray*, 1996, 29 July.

40 E. Ibagere (1996), 'Nigeria Shell Talks to Ogonis to Restart Work, Port Harcourt', *Reuters*, Nigeria, 11 September; *IPS* (1996) 'Nigeria – Environment: Oil Firms Back Environment', 17 September.

41 MOSOP (1996), Press Release, 2 October.

42 MOSOP UK (1997), *Summary of Events since October 1996*, Feb. 26, electronic correspondence.

43 http://www.westafricareview.com/vol2.1/mwalilino.html

44 C. Ake (1994) *Interview With Catma Films*, January; A. Rowell

(1996) *Green Backlash – Global Subversion of the Environment Movement,* Routledge, p 288-399

45 A. Rowell (1996) *Green Backlash – Global Subversion of the Environment Movement,* Routledge, p 288–399

46 Lieutenant Colonel Okuntimo (1994) RSIS Operations: Law and Order in Ogoni Etc, Memo From the Chair of the Rivers State Internal Security (RSIS) to His Excellency, The Military Administrator, Restricted, 12 May.

47 M. Birnbaum (1995) *Nigeria: Fundamental Rights Denied: Report of the Trial of Ken Saro-Wiwa and Others,* ARTICLE 19 in Association with the Bar Human Rights Committee of England and Wales and the Law Society of England and Wales, June, pp. 9

48 A. Rowell (1996) Interview with Claude Ake, 1 November.

49 MOSOP UK (1997), *Summary of Events Since October 1996,* Feb. 26, electronic correspondence.

50 MOSOP (1997), *Ogoni Must Survive,* Press Release, 4 January.

51 World Council of Churches (1997), *Ogoni – The Struggle Continues: WCC Publishes Report,* Switzerland, 3 January.

52 E. U. Imomoh (1997), *The Journey Towards Reconciliation in Ogoni,* 7 January.

53 Federation of Ogoni Women Association (1997), *Ogoni Women Tell Shell to Stay Out,* 25 April.

54 D. Wiwa (1997), 'The Role of Women in the Struggle for Environmental Justice in Ogoni', *Delta Magazine,* October, pp. 11–12.

55 *Delta Magazine* (1997), 'Oil Producing Communities Unite At Rally', October, pp. 5–6.

56 http://www.informationclearinghouse.info/article4066.htm

57 O. Douglas (1997), interview with Andy Rowell, 29 September.

58 Environmental Rights Action (1998), *Environmental Testimonies,* Number 5, 10 July.

59 http://www.informationclearinghouse.info/article4066.htm

60 K. Howe (1998), 'Human Rights Group Investigates Chevron – 2 Nigerians Killed in Offshore Protest', *San Francisco Chronicle,* 19 November.

61 Environmental Rights Action (1998), *Environmental Testimonies,* Number 5, 10 July; http://www.informationclearinghouse.info/article4066.htm

62 Environmental Rights Action (1998), *Environmental Testimonies,* Number 5, 10 July; K. Howe (1998), 'Human Rights Group Investigates Chevron – 2 Nigerians Killed in Offshore Protest', *San Francisco Chronicle,* 19 November; http://www.information-clearinghouse.info/article4066.htm

63 Essential Action and Global Exchange (2000), *Oil For Nothing: Multinational Corporations, Environmental Destruction, Death and Impunity in the Niger Delta*, http://www.essentialaction. org/shell/Final_Report.pdf

64 K. Maier (2000), *This House Has Fallen – Nigeria in Crisis*, Penguin, p. 127.

65 http://www.ijawcenter.com/kaiama_declaration.html

66 http://www.ijawcenter.com/kaiama_declaration.html

67 O. Douglas (1998), Email, December.

68 *P.M. News* (1999), 'Curfew Lifted, More Die In Delta', 4 January; Niger Delta Human & Environmental Rescue Organization (1998), *Field Report Of The Looming Niger Delta Crisis*, 30 December; *Reuters* (1999), 'Focus – Nigerian Oil Terminal Clash Kills 19', 1 February.

69 ERAction (1999), 'Dirty War', January–March, pp. 21–3.

70 Ijaw Youth Council (1999), *On Kaiama We Stand*, Press Briefing, 18 January.

71 C. Ikwunze (1999), 'Ijaw Youths Amputated', *Vanguard*, 27 April.

72 O. Wiwa and A. Rowell (2000), 'Some Things Never Change', *Guardian*, http://www.guardian.co.uk/guardiansociety/story/0,,3 93913,00.html

73 ERA ALERT (1999), 'Soldiers Attack Oil Communities – Traditional Ruler, Others Feared Killed', 7 January.

74 K. Jhumra (1999), 'Pouring Oil Over Troubled Waters: Chevron Funds Nigerian Village Projects', *Earth Times News Service*, 24 June.

75 BBC News Online (1999), 'Nigeria Embraces Civilian Rule', 29 May; http://news.bbc.co.uk/1/hi/world/africa/355850.stm; K. Maier (2000), *This House Has Fallen – Nigeria in Crisis*, Penguin, pp. xxii, 1–3.

76 O. Wiwa and A. Rowell (2000), 'Some Things Never Change', *The Guardian*, http://www.guardian.co.uk/guardiansociety/story/ 0,,393913,00.html; Human Rights Watch (2003), *Letter to Shell Petroleum Development Company of Nigeria*, 7 April; http:// www.hrw.org/press/2003/04/nigeria040703shell.htm

77 Environmental Rights Action (1999), 'Voices From Odi', Testimonies, 15 December, http://www.essentialaction.org/shell/era/ Testimony14.html

78 K. Maier (2000), *This House Has Fallen – Nigeria in Crisis*, Penguin, p. 142.

79 Catma Films (2000), *Lying in Wait*, shown on Channel 4; O. Wiwa and A. Rowell (2000) 'Some Things Never Change', *Guardian*, 8 November; http://www.guardian.co.uk/guardiansociety/story/0,,393913,00.html

80 Catma Films (2000) *Lying in Wait*, Shown on Channel 4; O. Wiwa and A. Rowell (2000) 'Some Things Never Change', *Guardian*, http://www.guardian.co.uk/guardiansociety/story/0,,393913,00.html

81 International Forensics Program (2004), 'Remains of Nigerian Activist Ken Saro-Wiwa Returned to His 100-Year-Old Father; Six of the Ogoni Nine Identified, One Body Still Missing and Two Bodies Await DNA Identification', 30 November; http://www.phrusa.org/research/forensics/news_nigeria–2004–11–30.html

82 O. Wiwa and A. Rowell (2000), 'Some Things Never Change', *Guardian*, 8 November; http://www.guardian.co.uk/guardiansociety/story/0,,393913,00.html

83 A. Detheridge (2000), 'Letter to Ian Mayes', *Guardian*, 8 November.

84 J. Frynas (1999), *Corporate and State Response to Anti-Oil Protests in the Niger Delta*, paper presented at the African Studies Association Annual Conference, Marriott Hotel, Philadelphia, 11–14 November.

85 MOSOP (1999), *MOSOP Files 8,000 Cases Before Human Rights Panel*, Press Release, 13 August.

86 A. Emeanua and Y. Oni (2001), 'Ken Saro-Wiwa's Father Shuns Oputa Panel As Commission Resumes Sitting in Port Harcourt', *This Day*, 16 January.

87 *AFX News Limited* (2001), 'Shell Denies Charges Of Human Rights Abuse In Nigeria', Port Harcourt, 2 February.

88 Human Rights Watch (2002) 'No Democratic Dividend', October; http://www.hrw.org/reports/2002/nigeria3/Nigeria1002.htm#P62_897;http://www.thisdayonline.com/archive/2002/01/22/20020122news 12.html

89 O. Wiwa and A. Rowell (2000), 'Some Things Never Change', *The Guardian*, 8 November; http://www.guardian.co.uk/guardiansociety/story/0,,393913,00.html

90 Human Rights Violations Investigation Commission (2002), *Synoptic Overview of HRVIC Report: Conclusions and Recommendations*, presented to President Chief Olusegun Obasanjo, May.

91 Human Rights Watch (2002), 'No Democratic Dividend', October; http://www.hrw.org/reports/2002/nigeria3/Nigeria1002–04.htm#P418_137673

92 FCO (2003), *Violence Affecting Oil Production in the Niger Delta*, restricted document, 25 March.

93 P. Naagbanton (2005), Interview with Lorne Stockman, 28 June.

94 M. Peel (2005), *Crisis in the Niger Delta: How Failures of Trans-*

parency and Accountability are Destroying the Region, Chatham House, July, pp. 2–3.

95 Human Rights Watch (2003), 'Nigeria: Government and Oil Firms Should Act on Delta Violence', London, 9 April; http://www.hrw.org/press/2003/04/nigeria0409.htm

96 Human Rights Watch (2003), *Nigeria: Delta Violence, a Fight Over Oil Money*, New York, 17 December; http://hrw.org/english/docs/2003/12/16/nigeri6616.htm

97 WAC Global Services (2003), *Peace and Security in the Niger Delta – Conflict Expert Group Baseline Report*, Working Paper for SPDC, December.

98 *Ibid.*

99 From www.shell.com, 8 June 2004

100 M. Peel (2005), 'Oil in Troubled Waters', *Financial Times Magazine*, 26 March; WAC Global Services (2003), *Peace and Security in the Niger Delta – Conflict Expert Group Baseline Report*, Working Paper for SPDC, December.

101 C. Boyd (2004), *Africa Trip Report*, Business Executives For National Security, September.

102 M. Peel (2005), 'Oil in Troubled Waters', *Financial Times Magazine*, 26 March, pp. 16–20; Human Rights Watch (2005), *Rivers and Blood: Guns, Oil and Power in Nigeria's Rivers State*, February; http://hrw.org/backgrounder/africa/nigeria0205/1.htm

103 K. Ebiri (2005), 'Six Feared Dead In Rivers Communal Clash', *Nigerian Guardian*, 8 March; J. Ighodaro (2005), 'Six Feared Dead in Communal Clash', *Vanguard*, 8 March.

104 I. Okonta (2005), 'Death of Pa Jim Wiwa', *This Day*, 16 April; http://allafrica.com/stories/200504180479.html

105 O. Wiwa (2005), Interview with Andy Rowell, 11 May.

106 *Ibid.*

107 K. Wiwa (2005), Interview with Andy Rowell and Lorne Stockman, 29 June.

Chapter 2: The Colonial Company

1 Bandung Film Productions (1995), interview with Ken Saro-Wiwa on *The Hanged Man*, broadcast on Channel 4, November.

2 N.A.M. Rodger (2004), *The Command of the Ocean: A Naval History of Britain 1649–1815*, Allen Lane. p. 67.

3 J. Walvin (1992), *Black Ivory – A History of British Slavery*, Fontana, pp. 32–3; P. Fryer (1984), *Staying Power – The History of Black People in Britain*, Pluto pp. 20–1.

4 K. Maier (2000), *This House Has Fallen – Nigeria in Crisis*, Penguin, p. 119; M. Anderson and P. Peek (eds) (2002), *Ways of the Rivers*, UCLA, pp. 67–8.

5 *Ibid.*, p. 60.

6 J. Walvin (1992), *Black Ivory – A History of British Slavery*, Fontana, p. 30; J. Rawley (2003), *London – Metropolis of the Slave Trade*, University of Missouri, p. 4.

7 V. Carretta (2003), *O. Equiano, The Interesting Narrative And Other Writings*, Penguin, pp. 46–61.

8 J. Walvin (1992) *Black Ivory – A History of British Slavery*, Fontana, p. 30; J. Rawley (2003), *London – Metropolis of the Slave Trade*, University of Missouri, p. 14.

9 V. Carretta (2003), *O. Equiano, The Interesting Narrative And Other Writings*, Penguin, p. 62.

10 P. Fryer (1984), *Staying Power – The History Of Black People In Britain*, Pluto, p. 44.

11 Channel 4 Productions (1999), interview with Robin Blackburn on *Britain's Untold Story*, broadcast on Channel 4, autumn.

12 H. Zinn (2003), *A People's History of the United States*, Perennial, p. 33.

13 J. Walvin (1992) *Black Ivory – A History of British Slavery*, Fontana, p. 309.

14 Major A.F. Mockler-Ferryman (1900), *British West Africa – its Rise and Progress*, Swan Sonnenschein, pp. 290–1.

15 M. Anderson and P. Peek (eds) (2002), *Ways of the Rivers*, UCLA, pp. 86–8.

16 *Ibid.*, p. 264; I. Okonta and O. Douglas (2001), *Where Vultures Feast – Shell, Human Rights and Oil in the Niger Delta*, Sierra Club, pp. 10–12; Major A.F. Mockler-Ferryman (1900), *British West Africa – its Rise and Progress*, Swan Sonnenschein, pp. 305–6.

17 I. Okonta and O. Douglas (2001), *Where Vultures Feast – Shell, Human Rights and Oil in the Niger Delta*, Sierra Club, p. 1.

18 Major A.F. Mockler-Ferryman (1900), *British West Africa – its Rise and Progress*, Swan Sonnenschein, p. 450.

19 *Ibid.*, p. 280.

20 K. Appiah (1998), *Ogoni's Agonies – Ken Saro-Wiwa and the Crisis in Nigeria*, Africa World Press, pp. xix–xx.

21 K. Saro-Wiwa (1992), *Genocide in Nigeria – The Ogoni Tragedy*, Saros International, p. 15.

22 M. Anderson and P. Peek (eds) (2002), *Ways of the Rivers*, UCLA, pp. 39–59.

23 *Ibid.*
24 T. Falola, A. Mahadi, M. Uhomoibhi, U. Anyanwu (1991), *History of Nigeria 3*, Longman Nigeria, p. 79.
25 *Ibid.*
26 *Ibid.*, pp. 1–14; J.F. Frynas (2000), *Oil In Nigeria*, Lit Verlag, p. 9; W. Engdahl (2004), *A Century of War – Anglo-American Oil Politics And The New World Order*, Pluto, p. 25.
27 J.H. Bamberg (1994), *The History of the British Petroleum Company*, CUP, vol. 2, p. 119, p. 172; J.H. Bamberg (2000), *British Petroleum and Global Oil 1950–1975*, CUP, pp. 109–13.
28 D. Yergin (1991), *The Prize*, Simon & Schuster, pp. 269–71.
29 *Ibid.*, pp. 271–9.
30 J.H. Bamberg (1994), *The History of the British Petroleum Company*, CUP, vol. 2, p. 119, p. 172.
31 J.H. Bamberg (2000), *British Petroleum and Global Oil 1950–1975*, CUP, pp. 109–13.
32 *Ibid.*
33 *Ibid.*
34 J. F. Frynas (2000), *Oil In Nigeria*, Lit Verlag, p. 12.
35 J. Bearman (2005), 'Shell Set to Rise Again With Nigerian Gas', *African Energy*, Issue 87, June, pp. 8–9.
36 Personal diary of Cyril Pyke, property of S. Marriott; Intelligence Department of the Colonial Secretary's Office, Southern Nigeria (1912), *Southern Nigeria Handbook 1912*, Waterlow, pp. 165–8.

Chapter 3: Crisis After Crisis

1 Quoted in K. Saro-Wiwa (1992), *Genocide in Nigeria – The Ogoni Tragedy*, Saros International, p. 71.
2 *African Concord* (1990), 'Oloibiri: In Limbo', 3 December, pp. 28–32.
3 A. Rowell (1996), *Green Backlash – Global Subversion of the Environment Movement*, Routledge, p. 291.
4 Environmental Rights Action & Climate Justice Programme (2005), *Gas Flaring in Nigeria: A Human Rights, Environmental and Economic Monstrosity*, June, p. 25.
5 *Ibid.*, p. 4.
6 *Ibid.*, p. 5.
7 A. Edemariam (2005), 'The Boat is Sinking', *Guardian*, 15 June, G2, pp. 6–7.
8 J. Wilson (1970), Nigeria, 5 April, FCO 65/806

9 S. A. Khan (1994), *Nigeria – The Political Economy of Oil*, Oxford University Press, p. 5.

10 K. Maier (2000), *This House Has Fallen – Nigeria in Crisis*, pp. 123–5.

11 I. Okonta and O. Douglas (2001), *Where Vultures Feast – Shell, Human Rights and Oil in the Niger Delta*, Sierra Club Books, p. 21.

12 Prime Minister's Personal Minute (1969), Foreign and Commonwealth Secretary, 29 July; FCO 67/212.

13 A. Sampson (1981), *The Seven Sisters – the Great Oil Companies and the World They Shaped*, Coronet, p. 225; *Daily Telegraph* (2002), Obituary of Sir David Barran, 3 June.

14 M. Stewart (1969), Military Aid and Assistance for Nigeria, to Prime Minister, 4 August; FCO 67/212.

15 West Africa Department (1969), Biafran Attacks on Shell/BP Installations in Africa, 31 October; FCO 67/212.

16 Carless (1969), Correspondence to FCO, 26 May; FCO 67/212.

17 B. Barder (1969), Hand-written notes on Shell's Operations in São Tomé, 5 June; FCO 67/212.

18 J. Wilson (1972), Re: Nigerian Oil, Letter to Sir Cycil Pickard, Lagos, 16 March; FCO 65/1226.

19 From File FCO 65/806.

20 J. Wilson (1970), Nigeria, 5 April, FCO 65/806.

21 K. Saro-Wiwa (1992), *Genocide in Nigeria – The Ogoni Tragedy*, Saros International, pp. 63–4.

22 K. Saro-Wiwa (1995), *A Month and a Day*, Penguin, p. 53.

23 K. Saro-Wiwa (1992), *Genocide in Nigeria – The Ogoni Tragedy*, Saros International, pp. 44–57.

24 J. Spinks (1970), Oil Operations in Ogoni Division, Letter to HE Military Governor, Rivers State, 9 June.

25 Dere Youths Association (1970), *A Protest Presented to Representatives of the Shell BP Dev. Co. of Nig. Ltd. By the Dere Youths Association, Against the Company's Lack of Interest in the Sufferings of Dere People Which Sufferings Are Causes As a Result of the Company's Operations*, quoted in K. Saro-Wiwa (1992), *Genocide in Nigeria – The Ogoni Tragedy*, Saros International, pp. 64–6.

26 K. Saro-Wiwa (1992), *Genocide in Nigeria – The Ogoni Tragedy*, Saros International, pp. 80–1.

27 P.W. Heap (1970), Visit to Port Harcourt, 13–14 November; FCO 65/807.

28 A.C. Hunt (1970), Letter to H. J. Arbuthnott, Lagos, 4 September; FCO 65/807.

29 J. B. Johnston (1970), Letter to W. Wilson, 6 July; FCO 65/807.

30 Biography taken from Debrett's *People of Today*.
31 Royal Dutch/Shell (1970), British Policy in Africa – Implications for the commercial interests of the Royal Dutch/Shell Group, 2 July, FCO 65/807.
32 Oil Department, FCO (1970), Record of Conversation Between the Foreign and Commonwealth Secretary and the Managing Director of Shell, 27 July, FCO 65/807.
33 S.A. Khan (1994), *Nigeria – The Political Economy of Oil*, Oxford University Press, p. 22.
34 J. Wilson (1972), Call by Chairman of Shell on Secretary of State on 29 March, 28 March; FCO 65/1227/ 1228.
35 FCO (1972), Record of a Conversation Between the Foreign and Commonwealth Secretary and Sir David Barran, Chairman of Shell, FCO, 12 April.
36 P. Grattan (1972), Letter to Lord Bridges, 23 May; FCO (1972), Nigerian Oil, 23 May; PREM 15/595 and PREM 15/1836.
37 Lord Rothschild (1972), BP Note to Mr Armstrong, 30 May; PREM 15/595 and PREM 15/1836.
38 RTA (1972), Prime Minister, 31 May; PREM 15 / 595 and PREM 15/1836.
39 I. Okonta and O. Douglas (2001), *Where Vultures Feast – Shell, Human Rights and Oil in the Niger Delta*, Sierra Club Books, p. 55.
40 Environmental Rights Action (1995), s*Hell in Iko – The Story of Double Standards*, 10 July; A. Rowell (1996), *Green Backlash – Global Subversion of the Environment Movement*, Routledge, pp. 294–5.
41 R. W. Tookey (1992) Letter to the *Ecologist*, 1 December; E. Nickson (1996) Letter to P. Brown and A. Rowell, 6 November
42 WAC Global Services (2003) *Peace and Security in the Niger Delta – Conflict Expert Group Baseline Report*, Working Paper for SPDC, December
43 J. R. Udofia (1990), 'Threat of Disruption of our Oil Operations at Umuechem by Members of Umuechem Community', Letter to Commissioner of Police, 29 October.
44 Hon. O. Justice Inko-Tariah, Chief J. Ahiakwo; B. Alamina; Chief G. Amadi (1990), *Commission of Inquiry into the Causes and Circumstances of the Disturbances that Occurred at Umuechem in the Etche Government Area of Rivers State in the Federal Republic of Nigeria.*
45 R. Tookey (1993), Letter to Mrs Farmer Concerning Shell's Operations in Nigeria, 11 June.
46 E. Nickson (1996), Letter to Paul Brown and Andy Rowell, Shell International, 1996, 5 November.
47 Human Rights Watch/Africa (1995) *Nigeria – The Ogoni Crisis –*

A Case Study of Military Repression in SouthEastern Nigeria, Vol. 7, No. 5, pp. 10–11

48 Catma Films (1994), *The Drilling Fields*, Channel 4, 23 May; Amnesty International (1993), *Possible Extrajudicial Execution / Legal Concern*, 19 May; Unrepresented National and Peoples Organization (1993), Developments in Ogoni, January–July 1993, Nigeria, Office of the General Secretary, The Hague, 26 July; A. Rowell (1996), *Green Backlash – Global Subversion of The Environment Movement*, Routledge, p. 300.

49 J.K. Tillery (1993), Re: Work Progress Up-Date Bomu Area TNP Contract No E-1C61: Letter for the Attention of Mr J.R. Udofia, 3 May.

50 R. Boele (1995), *Report of the UNPO Mission to Investigate the Situation of the Ogoni of Nigeria February 17–26*, Unrepresented Nations and Peoples Organization, 1 May, p 18

51 J.R. Udofia (1993), Disruption of Work on the 36"Rumueke-Bomu Trunkline: Letter to The Governor of Rivers State, 4 May.

52 E. Nickson (1996), Letter to Paul Brown and Andy Rowell, 6 November.

53 A. Rowell (1996), 'Shell Shock', *Listener Magazine*, 14 December, pp. 26–7; E. Nickson (1996), Letter to P. Brown and A. Rowell, 5 November.

54 MOSOP (1993), Press Release, vol. 11/19, 27 October.

55 E.U. Imomah (1993), Seizure of Fire Fighting Trucks by Korokoro Community Taj / Eleme LGA, Letter to The Governor of Rivers State, 25th October.

56 J.R. Udofia and E.U. Imomoh (1993), Seizure of Fire Fighting Trucks By KoroKoro Community in Taj/Eleme LGA, 26 October.

57 P.B. Watts (1993), Letter to Alhaji Ibrahim Coommassie, Inspector General of Police, 1 December; V.A. Oteri (1994), Acquisition of Ammunition and Upgrade of Weapons, 19 January; V.A. Oteri (1994) Acquisition of Ammunition and Upgrade of Weapons, 17 August.

58 T. Oladipo (1996), 'Ake Wants Shell Probed', *AM News*, 18 January; E. Mainah (1996), 'Nigeria Has Been Privatized, Prof. Ake Alleges', *This Day*, 19 January.

59 A. Rowell (1996), *Green Backlash – Global Subversion of the Environment Movement*, Routledge, pp. 288–319.

60 L. Mitee (2005), Interview with Andy Rowell, 29 June.

61 S. Buerk (2005), Email to Andy Rowell, 11 July.

62 K. Wiwa (2005), Interview with Andy Rowell and Lorne Stockman, 29 June.

63 *Reuters* (2005), Port Harcourt, Nigeria, 17 May.
64 A. Nikiforuk (2005), 'Mythoilogy: Eight Wrong Ways to Think About the Future of Energy', *Canadian Business*, 17–30 January, p. 48; http:www.shell.com/home/Framework?siteId=royal-en&FC2=/royal-en/html/iwgen/who_we_are/a_global_group/zzz_lhn.html&FC3=/royal-en/html/iwgen/who_we_are/a_ global_group /a_global_group.html
65 *US Fed News* (2005), 'Energy Information Administration Issues Country Analysis Brief On Nigeria', 18 April.
66 http://www.heritage.org/Press/Events/ev050803b.cfm
67 http://www.guardian.co.uk/g8/story/0,13365,1518719,00.html
68 http://www.undp.org.ng/abnga1.htm; http://www.guardian.co.uk /g8/story/0,13365,1518719,00.html
69 http://www.undp.org.ng/Docs/NHDR/Executive_Summary.pdf
70 BBC News Online (2005), 'Second Minister Sacked', 4 April; http://news.bbc.co.uk/1/hi/world/africa/4410109.stm
71 D. Blair (2005), '£220 Billion – The Amount Stolen or Misused by Corrupt Nigerian Rules – £220 Billion – The Amount of Aid Donated by the West to Africa in 40 Years', *Daily Telegraph*, 25 June.

Chapter 4: An Intertwined Alliance

1 K. Saro-Wiwa (1992), *Genocide in Nigeria – The Ogoni Tragedy*, Saros International, p. 8.
2 The Shell Petroleum Development Company of Nigeria Limited (2005), *2004 People And The Environment Annual Report*, May.
3 BP (2004), *Energy Focus, BP Statistical Review of World Energy June 2004*, p. 4.
4 J. Bearman (2005), 'Shell Set to Rise Again With Nigerian Gas', *African Energy*, June, p. 8–9.
5 M. Enfield (2005), 'The Oil Industry in the Delta', PFC Energy, Presentation to the Conference on Nigeria's Delta Region, Meridian International Center, 15 February.
6 J. Bearman (2005), 'Shell Set to Rise Again With Nigerian Gas', *African Energy*, June, pp. 8–9; M. Enfield (2005), The Oil Industry in the Delta, PFC Energy, Presentation to the Conference on Nigeria's Delta Region, Meridian International Center, 15 February.
7 S. Buerk (2005), Email to Andy Rowell, 11 July.
8 M. Peel (2005), *Crisis in the Niger Delta: How Failures of Transparency and Accountability are Destroying the Region*, Chatham House, July, p.5.
9 *Ibid.*, p. 4.

10 S. Buerk (2005), Email to Andy Rowell, 11 July.
11 The Shell Petroleum Development Company of Nigeria Limited (2005), *2004 People And The Environment Annual Report*, May.
12 A. Rowell (1996), *Green Backlash – Global Subversion of the Environment Movement*, Routledge, pp. 288–399.
13 http://www.winne.com/nigeria/topinterviews/edmund_daukoru-u.php
14 *Ibid.*
15 P. Adams (1993), 'Nigeria's Burden Of Proof – Arrests Have Been Made But The State Oil Business Has Still To Satisfy The Industry That Its Reforms Are Working', *Financial Times*, 3 November, p. 34; *The Economist* (1993), 'Oiling The Big Wheels', 6 November, p. 107.
16 http://allafrica.com/stories/200507150045.html; http://www.odili.-net/news/source/2005/jul/17/201.html; http://allafrica.com/stories/200507250536.html; *This Day* (2005), 'Oil Exploration: "We Must Take Our Destiny In Our Hands"', 24 July.
17 S. Howarth (1997), *A Century in Oil*, Weidenfeld & Nicholson, p. 259.
18 Shell (2003), *Shell Petroleum Development Company of Nigeria: People and the Environment Annual Report 2002*, p. 52.
19 http://www.shell.com/home/Framework?siteId=nigeria&FC2=/nigeria/html/iwgen/about_shell/what_we_do/zzz_lhn.html&FC3=/nigeria/html/iwgen/shell_for_businesses/exploration_production_shared/dir_spdc_1203_1027.html
20 Shell (2003), *Shell Petroleum Development Company of Nigeria People and the Environment Annual Report 2002*; A. Ling et. al. (2005), *Global Energy 100 Projects To Change The World*, Goldman Sachs Global Investment Research, pp. 255–7.
21 Shell (2003), *Shell Petroleum Development Company of Nigeria People and the Environment Annual Report 2002*.
22 S. Howarth (1997), *A Century in Oil*, Weidenfeld & Nicholson, p. 384.
23 I. Okonta and O. Douglas (2001), *Where Vultures Feast – Shell, Human Rights and Oil in the Niger Delta*, Sierra Club, p. 120.
24 S. Ahmad Khan (1994), *Nigeria, The Political Economy of Oil*, Oxford, p. 50.
25 *Ibid.*, pp. 217–18.
26 Quest Offshore Resources inc (2004), *West Africa 2004 Infra-structure & Quest Offshore's Subsea And Floating Productions Systems Forecast*.
27 S. Ahmad Khan (1994), *Nigeria, The Political Economy of Oil*, Oxford, pp. 217–21; Petroleum Economist Cartographic (2000), *Energy & Power Map of Africa*.

28 S. Ahmad Khan (1994), *Nigeria, The Political Economy of Oil*, Oxford, pp. 217–18.

29 *Ibid.*, p. 50.

30 BP (2005), *Putting Energy in the Spotlight, BP Statistical Review of World Energy*, June http://www.shell.com/home/Framework?siteId=nigeria&FC2=/nigeria/html/iwgen/about_shell/what_we_-do/zzz_lhn.html&FC3=/nigeria/html/iwgen/about_shell/what_-we_do/dir_what_we_do.html

31 http://ue.eu.int/ueDocs/cms_Data/docs/pressData/en/trans/85602.pdf; http://www.euractiv.com/Article?tcmuri=tcm:29–140786–16&type=News

32 http;//www.eia.doe.gov/emeu/ipsr/t410a.xis

33 http://www.nnpc-nigeria.com/index.php?option=com_content&task=view&id=64&Itemid=2

34 *The Vanguard* (2005), 'Why 2005 Oil Bid Round is Delayed', 27 July; http://wm.opec.speedera.net/wm.opec/136Conference/NIGERIANMINISTER.wmv

35 http://www.aei.org/events/filter.all,eventID.786/transcript.asp

36 http://www.winne.com/nigeria/topinterviews/edmund_daukoru.php

37 R. Lawson, W. True, J. Stell (2005), 'Asia-Pacific, Middle East, Europe Lead Construction Plans Transportation Special', *Oil & Gas Journal*, 7 February, p. 57.

38 M. Clark (2005), 'Pipelines: West Africa; All Systems Go', *Petroleum Economist*, 8 February, p. 18.

39 ERA/FoEN (2005), *Pipe Dreams (Conflicts, Participation, Transparency)*, 26 July.

40 M. Watkins (2003), 'Equatorial Money', *Project Finance*, March 2003, p. 54.

41 J. Bearman (2003), 'Perils and Possibilities: Petroleum Opportunities in Africa', Address to Heritage Foundation Conference, 8 May; http://www.heritage.org/Press/Events/ev050803b.cfm

42 *Petroleum Economist* (2004), 'Deep Water: Nigeria; Still A Deep-Water Hotspot', 11 October, p. 9.

Chapter 5: A Shock to the System

1 K. Saro-Wiwa (1995), *A Month and a Day*, Penguin, p. 167.

2 A. Rowell (1995), 'Did Shell Oil Help Execute Ken Saro-Wiwa', *The Village Voice*, 21 November.

3 Shell (2000), *How Do We Stand? People, Planet & Profits – The Shell Report 2000*, p. 7.

4 R. Bhushan (1999), 'Shell International Spruces up its Image', *Business Line*, 21 April, p. 12.

5 A. Jardine (1999), '£20million Drive to Fix Shell Image', *Marketing*, 11 March.

6 *Brand Strategy* (2002), 'Petroleum and Principles', 26 July, p. 16.

7 Shell (1999), 'Triple Vision', *Shell World*, October, p. 10.

8 Shell (1998) *Profits and Principles – Does There Have To Be A Choice? The Shell Report 1998*, p. 6.

9 *Ibid.*, p. 5.

10 *Ibid.*, p. 6.

11 *Brand Strategy* (2002), 'Petroleum and Principles', 26 July, p. 16.

12 Shell (2005), *Summary Annual Report and Accounts 2004*, p. 7.

13 I. Bickerton et. al., (2005), 'Marriage After A Century Of Cohabitation: Shell Prepares For The Next Merger Round', *Financial Times*, 28 June.

14 Shell (2005), *Summary Annual Report and Accounts 2004*, p. 7.

15 D. Adam (2004), 'I'm Really Very Worried For The Planet', *Guardian*, 17 June.

16 Shell (2005), *Summary Annual Report and Accounts 2004*, p. 7; *Annual Report and Accounts 2004*, p. 34.

17 Shell (1998), *Profits and Principles – Does There Have To Be A Choice? The Shell Report 1998*, p. 2.

18 *Brand Strategy* (2002), 'Petroleum and Principles', 26 July, p. 16.

19 Shell (1998) *Profits and Principles – Does There Have To Be A Choice? The Shell Report 1998*, p. 2.

20 *Ibid.*, p. 57.

21 *Ibid.*, p. 46.

22 *Ibid.*, p. 2.

23 *Ibid.*, p. 16.

24 A. Rowell (1996), *Green Backlash – Global Subversion of the Environment Movement*, Routledge.

25 Shell (1998), *Profits and Principles – Does There Have To Be A Choice? The Shell Report 1998*, insert following p. 30.

26 D. Weinberger (2002), 'Dirty laundry on the Web', Contact; www.darwinmag.com; http://www.shell.com/home/royal-en/html/iwgen/tellshell/thread4/thread.htm

27 *Ibid.*

28 E. Shelton (1999), 'Focus – Integrated Marketing', *PR Week*, 17 September.

29 Advertisements regularly placed in *Financial Times* including on 23 March 1999, 25 May 2000, 7 July 2000, 29 July 2000, and 23 October 2000.

30 R. Bhushan (1999), 'Shell International Spruces up its Image', *Business Line*, 21 April, p. 12.

31 *Brand Strategy* (2002), 'Petroleum and Principles', 26 July, p. 16.

32 E. Shelton (1999), 'Focus – Integrated Marketing', *PR Week*, 17 September.

33 *Brand Strategy* (2002), 'Petroleum and Principles', 26 July, p. 16.

34 M. Pawinska (2003), 'Shell Tackles Negative View Of Its Policies – International PR', *PR Week*, 18 July.

35 Advertisements regularly placed in *Financial Times* including on 19 April 2001, 21 November 2001, 12 April 2002.

36 A. Rowell (2002), 'Dialogue: Divide and Rule' in Eveline Lubbers (ed.), *Battling Big Business – Countering Greenwash, Infiltration and other Forms of Corporate Bullying*, Common Courage Press, pp. 36–7.

37 K. Morris (1998), 'The Feel-Good Factor', *Radio National – Australia*, broadcast 16 August.

38 Shell (1996), *Shell Petroleum Development Company of Nigeria People and the Environment Annual Report*, p. 23.

39 Shell (1996), *Shell Petroleum Development Company of Nigeria People and the Environment Annual Report*, p. 24.

40 D. Wheeler, H. Fabig, R. Boele (2002), 'Paradoxes And Dilemmas For Stakeholder Responsive Firms In The Extractive Sector: Lessons From The Case Of Shell And The Ogoni', *Journal of Business Ethics*, pp. 297–318.

41 A. Roddick and G. Roddick (1999), Letter to the Editor, *Guardian*, 18 September.

42 Christian Aid (2004), *Behind The Mask – The Real Face Of Corporate Social Responsibility*, London, April; http://www.christian-aid.org.uk/indepth/0401csr/.

43 *Brand Strategy* (2002), 'Petroleum and Principles', 26 July, p. 16.

44 M. Pawinska (2003), 'Shell Tackles Negative View Of Its Policies – International PR', *PR Week*, 18 July.

45 City insider (2004), Communication with Andy Rowell.

46 Retired Shell Manager (2004), Conversation with James Marriott, November.

47 Gordon Roddick (2003), Conversation with James Marriott, November.

48 Senior Shell Manager (2005), Conversation with James Marriott, June.

49 Ex-Shell Employee (2005), Communication with one of the authors.

50 I. Cummins and J. Beasant (2005) *Shell Shock*, Mainstream Publishing, p. 11.

51 *Ibid.*, p. 12.

52 *Ibid.*
53 *Ibid.*
54 *Ibid.*
55 T. Macalister (2004), 'Shell Chief Contrite but Refuses to Quit', *Guardian*, 6 February.
56 Lex Column (2004), 'Shell Suits', *Financial Times*, 25 August.
57 C. Hoyos; M. Peel, D. White (2004), 'Nigeria Reveals Size of Shell Cuts', *Financial Times*, 2 February, p. 36.
58 Davis, Polk and Wardwell (2004), *Executive Summary to Shell Grup Audit Committee*, 31 March.
59 S. Tucker et al. (2004), 'Shell chief was warned in advance of problems', *Financial Times*, 29 June.
60 I. Cummins and J. Beasant (2005), *Shell Shock*, Mainstream Publishing, p. 12.
61 I. Bickerton et al. (2005), 'Marriage After A Century Of Cohabitation: Shell Prepares For The Next Merger Round', *Financial Times*, 28 June.
62 *Ibid.*
63 I. Cummins and J. Beasant (2005), *Shell Shock*, Mainstream Publishing, p. 26.
64 J. Rossiter (2004), 'Shell Bosses, Auditors Hit By New Us Lawsuits', *Evening Standard*, 25 June.
65 M. Harrison (2004), 'Shell Switch In Strategy Fails To Win Support Of Investors', *Independent*, 23 September.
66 Mudlark (2004), 'Moody-Stuart Talks', *Financial Times*, 15 July.
67 C. Harris (2005), 'Shell Chief Earned £1.8m In "Reserves Cuts" Year', *Financial Times*, 1 April.
68 Shell (2004), *The Shell Report 2003*, p. 2.
69 P. Smith (2005), interview with Andy Rowell, 24 June.
70 *Financial Times* Leader (2004), 'Settling The Bill But Not The Issues', *Financial Times*, 30 July.

Chapter 6: Does Corruption Begin at Home?

1 N. Ribadu (2005), interview with Andy Rowell, 7 July.
2 *Ibid.*
3 http://www.efccnigeria.org/index.php?option=com_content&-task=view&id=353&Itemid=2; http://news.bbc.co.uk/2/hi/africa/4387477.stm
4 *Ibid.*
5 Nigeria House of Representatives Petition Committee (2004), *Interim Report: The Halliburton/TSKJ/LNG Investigation*,

Summary of Facts, September; http://www.halliburtonwatch.
org/news/nigeria_parliament_report.pdf; http://www.halliburton
watch.org/about_hal/nigeria_timeline.html; D. Leigh, R. Evans,
D. Pallister (2004), 'British Lawyer May Have Handled Cash In
Oil Investigation, Serious Fraud Office To Look Into Payments
Of $180m', *Guardian*, 30 October; http://www.guardian.co.
uk/business/story/0,,1339624,00.html; http://financial.washing
tonpost.com/wpost/Quote.asp?Symbol=HAL&Mode=EDGARDIS
PLAY&ReleaseDate=2005–03–31

6 M. Oduniyi (2005), 'Halliburton: Court Orders Access To Sus-
pects' Account', *This Day*, 13 January; T. Catan, S. Fidler, M. Peel,
W. Wallis (2004), 'Halliburton "Backed" Bribes Probe Agent:
Evidence Before A French Judge Raises Fresh Questions Over US
Company's Role In Controversial Nigerian Venture', *Financial
Times*, USA Edition, 17 September, p. 5.

7 M. Peel (2004), 'NLNG Still Faces Challenges: The Nigerian
Liquified Natural Gas Plant Needs To Ensure Adequate Supplies',
Financial Times, USA Edition, 20 September, p. 22.

8 *Africa Confidential* (2004), 'On the Bribe Trail', vol. 45, No. 18,
10 September, p. 2; http://news.bbc.co.uk/nol/shared/bsp/hi/pdfs/
30_11_04_export_credit.pdf; The Corner House (2005), *Memorandum to the Trade and Industry Committee*, inquiry into the
Export Credits Guarantee Department, February.

9 Telephone conversation with author, August 2005.

10 O. Ayorinde (2004), 'Corruption Incorporated', *The News*, 8
November; *Africa Confidential* (2004), 'USA: Gas Probe Widens
After New Allegations', 10 September, vol. 45, No. 18; LNG-
Serviços e Gestão de Projectos Limitada (1995), *Consulting and
Commercial Promotion Services for Nigeria LNG Limited*, 20 March
(signed by Jeffrey Tesler and Richard Northmore 22 March); LNG-
Serviços e Gestão de Projectos Lda (1999), *Consulting and Com-
mercial Promotion Services for the Nigeria LNG Plus Project*, 18 March
(signed by M. D. Kaye and R. A. Parker, 22 March); LNG-Serviços e
Gestão de Projectos Lda (2001), *Consulting and Commercial Pro-
motion Services for the Nigeria LNG Plus Project*, 24 December; R.
Gold and C. Fleming (2004), 'In Halliburton Nigeria Probe, A
Search for Bribes to a Dictator', *Wall Street Journal*, 29 September.

11 M. Oduniyi (2005), 'Halliburton: Court Orders Access To Sus-
pects' Account', *This Day*, 13 January; D. Leigh, R. Evans, D.
Pallister (2004), 'British Lawyer May Have Handled Cash In Oil
Investigation, Serious Fraud Office To Look Into Payments Of
$180m', *Guardian*, 30 October.

12 E. Decouty (2003), 'Nigerian Contract at the Heart of a Corruption Affair', *Le Figaro*, 20 December; http://www.globalpolicy.org/nations/launder/regions/2003/1220heart.htm

13 O. Adeniyi (2004), 'The Unanswered Question', *This Day*, 6 November.

14 R. Gold and C. Fleming (2004), 'In Halliburton Nigeria Probe, A Search for Bribes to a Dictator', *Wall Street Journal*, 29 September.

15 http://news.bbc.co.uk/1/hi/programmes/file_on_4/4066913.stm.

16 http://www.halliburtonwatch.org/about_hal/nigeria_timeline.html

17 T. Catan, S. Fidler, M. Peel, W. Wallis (2004), 'Halliburton "Backed" Bribes Probe Agent: Evidence Before A French Judge Raises Fresh Questions Over US Company's Role In Controversial Nigerian Venture', *Financial Times*, USA Edition, 17 September, p. 5.

18 R. Gold and C. Fleming (2004), 'In Halliburton Nigeria Probe, A Search for Bribes to a Dictator', *Wall Street Journal*, 29 September quoted on http://www.halliburtonwatch.org/about_hal/nigeria_timeline.html

19 *Africa Confidential* (2004), 'USA: Gas Probe Widens After New Allegations', 10 September, vol. 45; No. 18.

20 T. Catan, S. Fidler, M. Peel, W. Wallis (2004), *art. cit.*; *Africa Confidential* (2004), 'USA: Gas Probe Widens After New Allegations', 10 September, vol. 45, No 18.

21 http://www.halliburtonwatch.org/about_hal/nigeria_timeline.html

22 http://www.halliburtonwatch.org/about_hal/nigeria_timeline.html; D. Leigh, R. Evans, D. Pallister (2004), 'British Lawyer May Have Handled Cash In Oil Investigation, Serious Fraud Office To Look Into Payments Of $180m', *Guardian*, 30 October.

23 http://phx.corporate-ir.net/phoenix.zhtml?c=67605&p=irol-sec&control_selectgroup=Quarterly%20Filings

24 M. Peel (2004), 'Nigeria Gas Consortium "Evasive", Says Probe Chief', *Financial Times*, 23 August, p. 8; Nigeria House of Representatives Petition Committee (2004) *Interim Report: The Halliburton/TSKJ/LNG Investigation*, Summary of Facts, September; http://www.halliburtonwatch.org/news/nigeria_parliament_report.pdf; *AFX Europe* (2004), 'Halliburton Names Law Firm with Links to Bush Family to Probe Nigeria Payments', 16 February.

25 C. Offodile (2005), Email communication with Andy Rowell, 9 June

26 M. Peel (2004), 'Halliburton Angers Nigerian MPs in "Bribes"

Hearing', *Financial Times*, 22 October, p.6; http://news.bbc.co.uk/nol/shared/bsp/hi/pdfs/30_11_04_export_credit.pdf

27 http://phx.corporate-ir.net/phoenix.zhtml?c=67605&p=irolsec&control_selectgroup=Quarterly%20Filings

28 http://www.ecgd.gov.uk/ecgdannualreviewandresourceaccounts2003.pdf

29 http://www.gnn.gov.uk/Content/Detail.asp?ReleaseID=33630&-NewsAreaID=2&print=true

30 http://news.bbc.co.uk/nol/shared/bsp/hi/pdfs/30_11_04_export_credit.pdf

31 S. Hawley (2005), interview with Andy Rowell, May.

32 T. Catan and M. Peel (2005), 'UK Agency Failed to Tackle Nigeria Bribes Claim', *Financial Times*, 22 June, p. 9.

33 D. Leigh, R. Evans, D. Pallister (2004), 'British Lawyer May Have Handled Cash In Oil Investigation, Serious Fraud Office To Look Into Payments Of $180m', *Guardian*, 30 October.

34 http://news.bbc.co.uk/nol/shared/bsp/hi/pdfs/30_11_04_export_credit.pdf

35 C. Offodile (2005), Email communication with Andy Rowell, 9 June.

36 P. Smith (2005) interview with Andy Rowell, 24 June.

37 http://www.shell.com/static/media-en/downloads/sgbp.pdf

38 S. Buerk (2005), Email to Andy Rowell, 11 July.

39 http://phx.corporate-ir.net/phoenix.zhtml?c=67605&p=irolsec&control_selectgroup=Quarterly%20Filings

40 http://www.nigeriafirst.org/article_842.shtml

41 http://www.eia.doe.gov/emeu/cabs/nigeria.html

42 N. Ribadu (2005), interview with Andy Rowell, 7 July.

43 http://phx.corporate-ir.net/phoenix.zhtml?c=95816&p=irolnewsArticle&t=Regular&id=667156&

44 O. Amaewhule (2005), 'Willbros Bribery Scandal Linked to Nigerian Operations', *World Markets Analysis*, 25 May; http://phx.corporate-ir.net/phoenix.zhtml?c=95816&p=irol-secToc&TOC=aHR0c-DovL2NjYm4uMTBrd216YXJkLmNvbS94bWwvY29udGVudH-MueG1sP21wYWdlPTM0NzI1NDQmcmVwbz10ZW5r

45 http://phx.corporate-ir.net/phoenix.zhtml?c=95816&p=irol-secToc&TOC=aHR0cDovL2NjYm4uMTBrd2l6YXJkLmNvbS94bWwvY29udGVudHMueG1sP21wYWdlPTM0NzI1NDQmcmVwbz10ZW5r

46 http://www.sbclasslaw.com./case.cfm?id=8806762

47 N. Ribadu (2005), interview with Andy Rowell, 7 July.

48 http://www.cmal.co.uk/

49 *Global News Wire/Asia Africa Intelligence Wire* (2005), 'Nigeria

Picks British Firm To Audit Oil Sector "Plagued By Corruption"', 17 March.

50 http://www2.dfid.gov.uk/news/files/extractiveindustries.asp

51 http://www.neiti.org/

52 http://www.energynet.co.uk/aef/AEF2004/AEF04speakers.htm

53 A. A. Nwanko (1999), *Nigeria: The Stolen Billions*, Enugu: Fourth Dimension Publishing. p. 92; http://www.dawodu.com/aluko72.htm

54 P. Lewis (1999), 'Nigeria's Economy: Opportunity and Challenge', *A Journal of Opinion*. vol. 21, No. 1, p. 51.

55 http://www.bbc.co.uk/1/hi/world/africa/4449587.stm

56 P. Lewis (1999), 'Nigeria's Economy: Opportunity and Challenge', *loc. cit.*

57 A.A. Nwanko (1999), *Nigeria: The Stolen Billions*, Enugu: Fourth Dimension Publishing, p. 124.

58 http://www.bbc.co.uk/1/hi/world/africa/4449587.stm; D. Blair (2005), '£220 Billion – The Amount Stolen or Misused by Corrupt Nigerian Rulers – £220 Billion – The Amount of Aid Donated by the West to Africa in 40 Years', *Daily Telegraph*, 25 June.

59 A.A. Nwanko (1999), *Nigeria: The Stolen Billions*, Enugu: Fourth Dimension Publishing. pp. 76–8; http://www.nigerianmuse.com/nigeriawatch/okigbo/?u=Okigbo_passes_on.htm; http://www.nigerianmuse.com/nigeriawatch/okigbo/

60 http://www.dawodu.com/kalue1.htm

61 http://www.publishwhatyoupay.org/english/index.shtml

62 H. Parman (2005), interview with Lorne Stockman, 21 June.

63 http://www.neiti.org/about.htm

64 http://www.neiti.org/Other%20Minutes-Archive/February%2018th%202004.pdf

65 http://www.neiti.org/Other%20Minutes-Archive/April%201st%202004.pdf

66 http://www.neiti.org/Other%20Minutes-Archive/June%203rd%202004.pdf

67 Shell Petroleum Development Company of Nigeria (2005), *2004 People and the Environment – Annual Report*, May, p.7.

68 http://www.neiti.org/Other%20Minutes-Archive/September%2028th%202004.pdf

69 http://www.goldwyn.org/WhoWeAre.htm#DGoldwyn

70 http://www.neiti.org/NEITI%20NSWG%20Minutes/April%207th%202005.pdf

71 http://www.neiti.org/Hart%20Description%20Mar11%5B1%5D.pdf

72 http://www.tracsint.com/contact_us.htm
73 http://www.neiti.org/Other%20Minutes-Archive/December%2015th%202004.pdf
74 S. Rerri (2005), Email communication with Andy Rowell, 14 July
75 M. Peel (2005), *Crisis in the Niger Delta: How Failures of Transparency and Accountability are Destroying the Region*, Chatham House, July, p. 5.
76 http://www.neiti.org/Hart%20progress%20report%20March.pdf
77 *International Oil Daily*, (2005), 'Nigeria Outlines Plan to Audit Oil Sector', 21 April; J. Pryor (2005), *Funding the Oil Industry*, Chairman and Managing Director, Chevron Nigeria Limited, NEITI Conference held at the Banquet hall, State House, 14–17 February.
78 *International Oil Daily* (2005), 'Nigeria Outlines Plan to Audit Oil Sector', 21 April.
79 C. Nurse (2005), Conversation with Lorne Stockman, 22 June.
80 P. Smith (2005), interview with Andy Rowell, 24 June.
81 http://www.taxjustice.net/e/about/index.php
82 J. Christensen, P. Sikka (2005), interview with Lorne Stockman, 21 June.
83 *Ibid.*
84 S. Rerri (2005), Email communication with Andy Rowell, 14 July.
85 The Shell Petroleum Development Company of Nigeria Limited (2005*), 2004 People and the Environment Annual Report*, May, p. 7.
86 J.G. Frynas (undated) *Is Political Instability Harmful to Business – The Case of Shell in Nigeria*, Presented at the Annual Conference of the Africa Studies Association, 13–16 November, Ohio.
87 http://www.nlng.com/NLNG/BGT/default.htm
88 S. Buerk (2005), Email to Andy Rowell, 14 July.

Chapter 7: The Next Gulf

1 L. Mitee (2005), interview with Andy Rowell, 29 June.
2 http://www.winstonchurchill.org/i4a/pages/index.cfm?pageid=768
3 A. Sampson (1981), *The Seven Sisters – The Great Oil Companies and the World They Shaped*, Coronet, pp. 66–8; D. Yergin (1991), *The Prize – The Epic Quest for Oil, Money and Power*, Simon and Schuster, pp. 11–12; 153–160.
4 http://www.fpif.org/papers/03petropol/politics.html

5 Dr L. Grinter (1983), 'Avoiding the Burden: the Carter Doctrine in perspective', *Air and Space Power Chronicles*, January–February; http://www.airpower.maxwell.af.mil/airchronicles/aureview/1983/jan-feb/grinter.html

6 http://www.whitehouse.gov/vicepresident

7 http://www.chevron.com/news/archive/chevron%5Fpress/2001/2001%2D01%2D16.asp

8 http://rightweb.irc-online.org/ind/rice/rice.php; http://multinationalmonitor.org/mm2001/01june/june01names.html; http://www.sourcewatch.org/index.php?title=Condoleezza_Rice

9 A. Zalik (2003), *Corporate Philanthropy and Social Peace?* Environmental Rights Action, Port Harcourt, Fall; http://www.globalresearch.ca/articles/CAV111A.html

10 http://www.whitehouse.gov/news/releases/2001/05/20010516-7.html

11 http://www.nrdc.org/media/pressReleases/010517.asp

12 http://www.whitehouse.gov/energy/

13 http://www.whitehouse.gov/news/releases/2001/09/20010912-4.html

14 http://www.fpif.org/papers/nigeria2003.html

15 http://www.israeleconomy.org/about.htm

16 http://www.iasps.org/about.htm; http://rightweb.irc-online.org/ind/vancleave/vancleave.php

17 http://rightweb.irc-online.org/org/iasps.php

18 http://www.israeleconomy.org/strat1.htm

19 http://www.israeleconomy.org/strategic/africatranscript.pdf

20 http://rightweb.irc-online.org/ind/kansteiner/kansteiner.php

21 http://www.israeleconomy.org/strategic/africatranscript.pdf

22 http://usembassy.state.gov/nigeria/wwwhp061402b.html

23 http://www.israeleconomy.org/strategic/africawhitepaper.pdf

24 http://www.nopa.net/president_obasanjo/

25 J.L. Anderson (2002), 'Our New Best Friend', *New Yorker*, 7 October, pp. 74–83.

26 US/UK Energy Dialogue, Documents.

27 US/UK Energy Dialogue Commercial Working Group, 16 December.

28 http://www.fpif.org/republicanrule/cabinet_body.html

29 US/UK Energy Dialogue (2003), *Report by Officials to the Prime Minister and the President*, July.

30 M. Rodgers (2003), *Presentation to the Heritage Foundation*, Senior Director, Upstream Group, PFC Energy, 8 May; http://www.heritage.org/Press/Events/ev050803b.cfm

31 http://abuja.usembassy.gov/wwwhp033103a.html

32 http://rightweb.irc-online.org/groupwatch/csis.php; http://www.csis.org/

33 http://www.csis.org/experts/4ebel.htm

34 http://www.csis.org/africa/ANotes/ANotes_016.pdf

35 http://www.csis.org/experts/4morrison.htm

36 http://www.goldwyn.org/WhoWeAre.htm

37 www.csis.org/africa/GoldwynAfricanOilSector.pdf

38 www.csis.org/africa/GoldwynAfricanOilSector.pdf

39 S. Kretzmann and I. Nooruddin (2005), *Drilling Into Debt – An Investigation Into The Relationship Between Debt And Oil*, Oil Change International, IPPR and Jubilee USA, July.

40 http://www.heritage.org/Press/Events/ev050803b.cfm

41 http://www.monbiot.com/archives/2002/06/25/white-lies/

42 http://cbcfinc.org/pdf/cbcfbreakingoilsyndrome2005.pdf

43 O. Douglas (2005), interview with Andy Rowell, 20 June.

44 I. Cummins and J. Beasant (2005), *Shell Shock – The Secrets and Spin of an Oil Giant*, Mainstream, p. 20.

45 http://www.af.mil/bios/bio.asp?bioID=7493

46 http://www.cia.gov/cia/publications/factbook/geos/tp.html; http://www.lonelyplanet.com/destinations/africa/sao_tome _and_príncipe/history.htm

47 *African Energy* (2005), 'Murky End to a Messy Game in Nigeria/ São Tomé JDZ', issue 86, May, pp. 1–3.

48 J.L. Anderson (2002), 'Our New Best Friend', *New Yorker*, 7 October, pp. 74–83.

49 *Energy Compass* (2005), 'São Tomé: Biting the Bullet', 10 June; http:// www.irinnews.org/report.asp?ReportID=47181&SelectRegion=- West_Africa&SelectCountry=SAO_TOME_AND_PRINCIPE

50 http://author.voanews.com/english/São-Tomé-President-Faces- Political-Crisis-Over-Oil-Deals.cfm; *African Energy* (2005), Murky End to a Messy Game in Nigeria/São Tomé JDZ', issue 86, May.

51 http://author.voanews.com/english/2005–06–08-voa28.cfm; http://allafrica.com/stories/200506020133.html; http://www.reu- ters.co.za/locales/c_newsArticle.jsp?type=businessNews&locale- Key=en_ZA&storyID=8660752

52 T. Nwosu (2005), 'When US Indulges in Blackmail', *This Day (Nigeria)*, 9 June.

53 http://www.nigeriasaotomejda.com/PDFs/signing%20of%20PSC.pdf

54 http://www.africanfront.com/2003-b.php; http://news.bbc.co.uk/ 2/hi/business/2210571.stm; http://www.globalpolicy.org/secur- ity/natres/oil/2002/0802mili.htm

55 J. L. Anderson (2002), 'Our New Best Friend', *New Yorker*, 7 October, pp. 74–83; *African Energy* (2005), 'Murky End to a

Messy Game in Nigeria/São Tomé JDZ', issue 86, May, pp. 1–3.
56 http://www.state.gov/p/af/rls/rm/14407.htm
57 E. Schmitt (2003), 'Threats and Responses: Expanding US Presence; Pentagon Seeking New Access Pacts for Africa Bases', *New York Times*, 5 July, p. 1.
58 http://www.globalsecurity.org/military/library/news/2003/09/mil–030904–34e5c6f3.htm; C. Boyd (2004) Africa Trip Report, Business Executives For National Security, September.
59 http://www.globalsecurity.org/military/library/news/2004/05/mil–040506–2c999670.htm
60 http://www.irinnews.org/report.asp?ReportID=42809&SelectRegion=West_Africa&SelectCountry=GABON-SAO_TOME_AND_PRINCIPE; http://www.iss.co.za/AF/current/2004/stomenov04.pdf; http://www.sourcewatch.org/index.php?title=Chuck_Hagel
61 http://www.bens.org/sw_ar100704.html; http://www.energybulletin.net/1071.html
62 http://www.aei.org/about/contentID.20038142214500073/default.asp
63 R. Mokhiber and R. Weissman (2002), 'A Day At The American Enterprise Institute', *Z Net*, November; http://www.zmag.org/content/showarticle.cfm?SectionID=1&ItemID=2580
64 http://www.aei.org/publications/pubID.16197,filter.all/pub_detail.asp
65 http://www.newamericancentury.org/iraqclintonletter.htm
66 http://www.aei.org/scholars/filter.,scholarID.68/scholar.asp; http://www.newamericancentury.org/thomasdonnellybio.htm
67 http://www.aei.org/events/eventID.786,filter.all/event_detail.asp
68 http://www.aei.org/events/eventID.786,filter.all/event_detail.asp
69 http://www.aei.org/events/filter.all,eventID.786/transcript.asp
70 http://api-ec.api.org/filelibrary/BacAprr5.pdf
71 http://www.chevron.com/news/spotlight/12july2003%5Fsummit.asp; http://www.chevron.com/social%5Fresponsibility/community/2002jun20%5Fsullivan%5Fhonors%5Fco.asp
72 J. Bearman (2005), 'Shell Set to Rise Again With Nigerian Gas', *African Energy*, June, pp. 8–9.
73 http://www.chevron.com/news/spotlight/12july2003%5Fsummit.asp; http://www.whitehouse.gov/news/releases/2003/07/20030712.html#
74 http://www.chevron.com/news/spotlight/15oct2003_corpexcellence.asp
75 A. Zalik (2003), *Corporate Philanthropy and Social Peace?* Environmental Rights Action, Port Harcourt, Fall.

76 D. Goldwyn (2005), *Africa's Petroleum Industry*, presented to the Africa Center for Strategic Studies Seminar on Energy and Security in Africa, Abuja, 6–11 March.

77 *US Fed News* (2005), 'Energy Information Administration Issues Country Analysis Brief On Nigeria', 18 April; M. Enfield (2005), *The Oil Industry in the Delta*, PFC Energy, Presentation to the Conference on Nigeria's Delta Region, Meridian International Center, 15 February.

78 D. Althaus (2004), 'High Cost Of Energy: Nigeria; As U.S. Dependence on the Country's Petroleum Exports Grows, the West African Nation's Corrupt Officials get Rich While its Poor Seethe; Niger Delta's Oil Curse', *Houston Chronicle*, 5 December, p. 1.

79 http://www.publicintegrity.org/oil/report.aspx?aid=345&sid=100

80 All available at http://sopr.senate.gov/cgi-win/m_opr_viewer.exe?DoFn=0

81 http://www.csis.org/africa/0507_GulfofGuinea.pdf

82 http://www.aei.org/events/filter.all,eventID.786/transcript.asp.

83 http://www.aei.org/publications/pubID.17936,filter.all/pub_detail.asp

84 http://www.csis.org/africa/0507_GulfofGuinea.pdf

85 Lt Col. P. Mackin (2005), Email communication with Andy Rowell, EUCOM Public Affairs, 24 June.

86 *Ibid.*

87 *Ibid.*

88 M. Peel (2005), *Crisis in the Niger Delta: How Failures of Transparency and Accountability are Destroying the Region*, Chatham House, July, p. 6.

89 http://www.defenselink.mil/news/Mar2005/20050309_125.html;

90 http://www.thecwcgroup.com/conf_detail_agenda.asp?FP=1&-CID=88&DID=138

91 http://www.thecwcgroup.com/conf_detail_agenda.asp?FP=1&-CID=88&DID=128

92 R. Sullivan (2005), 'Chalker To Advise On Oil Exploration', *Financial Times*, 23 June, p. 24.

93 P. Naagbanton (2005), interview with Lorne Stockman, 28 June

94 L. Akande (2005), 'US Admits Fresh Troops' Deployment Near Nigeria', *Nigerian Guardian*, 29 June.

95 http://www.csis.org/africa/0507_GulfofGuinea.pdf

96 D. Goldwyn (2005), Speech to Launch the report *A Strategic U.S. Approach to Governance and Security in the Gulf of Guinea*, 20 July.

Chapter 8: Six Months in the Making of History

1 http://www.nprc-online.org/OBJper cent20Speech.html
2 http://www.nigeriafirst.org/article_3702.shtml
3 O. Douglas (2005), interview with Andy Rowell, 20 June.
4 Anonymous (2005), interview with Andy Rowell, 5 July.
5 http://www.oilwatch.org.ec/english/oilwatch_africa3.htm
6 http://www.eraction.org/index.php?page=modules&name=arti-cles&action=view&artid=32
7 http://www.africacenter.org/Dev2Go.web?Anchor=ACSS_about&rnd=27843
8 http://www.africacenter.org/Dev2Go.web?id=321606&rnd=18651
9 K. Saro-Wiwa (1995), *A Month and a Day*, Penguin, pp. 63–4.
10 K. Saro-Wiwa (1992), *Genocide in Nigeria – The Ogoni Tragedy*, Saros International, pp. 92–103.
11 http://www.ijawcenter.com/kaiama_declaration.html
12 K. Saro-Wiwa (1994), *Ogoni Moment of Truth*, Saros International, pp. 26–7; World Council of Churches (1996), *Ogoni – The Struggle Continues*, December, pp. 10–13.
13 O. Douglas (2005), interview with Andy Rowell, 20 June.
14 O. Douglas (2005), *Minority Report Of The Committee On Environment And Natural Resources Of The National Political Reform Conference*, 9 May.
15 P. Naagbanton (2005), interview with Lorne Stockman, 28 June.
16 International Centre for Reconciliation (2005), *Ogoni Reconciliation Process to Commence In Niger Delta*, Press Release, 31 May.
17 MOSOP (2005), *Response to the Appointment of Facilitators for Dialogue between Ogoni People, Government and Shell*, Press Release, 31 May.
18 O. Douglas (2005), interview with Andy Rowell, 20 June.
19 C. Okocha (2005), 'Shell Out to Destabilize Ogoni, says MOSOP', *This Day*, 23 June; http://allafrica.com/stories/200506230425.html
20 P. Ibe (2005), 'How to Rest Saro-Wiwa's Ghost, By Brother', *This Day*, 21 June; http://allafrica.com/stories/200506210532.html
21 http://www.nprc-online.org/N_117.html
22 http://www.nprc-online.org/share.html;   http://www.nprc-online.org/N_Z130.html
23 L. Mitee (2005), interview with Andy Rowell, 29 June.
24 *Financial Times* (2005), 'Nigerian Militants Kidnap Oil Workers', 16 June.
25 http://www.nprc-online.org/A_B18.html

26 *UN Integrated Regional Information Networks* (2005), 'Nigeria: Row Over Oil Money Delivers Killer Blow to Constitutional Reform Conference', 12 July.

27 http://www.hm-treasury.gov.uk/otherhmtsites/g7/news/conclusions_on_development_110605.cfm

28 http://www.hm-treasury.gov.uk/otherhmtsites/g7/news/conclusions_on_development_110605.cfm

29 L. Elliott and P. Wintour (2005), 'Biggest African Debt Rescue Saves Nigeria £17.3bn', *Guardian*, 1 July; http://www.guardian.co.uk/guardianpolitics/story/0,,1518659,00.html

30 S. Kretzmann and I. Nooruddin (2005), *Drilling Into Debt – An Investigation Into The Relationship Between Debt And Oil*, Oil Change International, IPPR and Jubilee, July.

31 L. Stockman (2005), eyewitness account, 28 June.

32 L. Stockman (2005), eyewitness account, 28 June.

33 C. Newman (2005), 'Rich Nations Must Change To Avoid Climate Disaster', *Financial Times*, 2 July 2005, p. 6.

34 Henderson Global Investors (2005), *The Carbon 100 – Quantifying the Carbon Emissions, Intensities and Exposures of the FTSE 100*, p. 12.

35 *Ibid.*

36 http://www.businessactionforafrica.org/english/documents/G8percent20Businesspercent20Summit.pdf

37 T. Ngwane (2005), speaking at the G8 Alternative Summit in Edinburgh, 3 July.

38 http://www.businessactionforafrica.org/english/documents/21–06–05_pr_business_summit.pdf

39 Environmental Rights Action & Climate Justice Programme (2005), *Gas Flaring in Nigeria: A Human Rights, Environmental and Economic Monstrosity*, June, p. 23.

40 M. Peel (2005), 'Shell Faces Penalties Over Flare Deadline', *Financial Times*, 19 January, p. 23; S. Onwuka (2005), 'Shell Extends Gas Flaring Deadline to 2009', *Daily Champion* (Lagos), 30 May.

41 Environmental Rights Action & Climate Justice Programme (2005), *Gas Flaring in Nigeria: A Human Rights, Environmental and Economic Monstrosity*, June, p. 4.

42 http://www.eraction.org/index.php?page=modules&name=articles&action=view&artid=39; http://www.climatelaw.org/media/gas.flaring.suit/#release

43 Chief Dr H. Dappa-Biriye, Chief R. Briggs, Chief Dr B. Idoniboye-Obu, Professor D. Fubara (1992), *The Endangered Environ-*

ment of the Niger Delta – Constraints and Strategies, an NGO Memorandum of the Rivers Chiefs and Peoples Conference, for the World Conference of Indigenous Peoples on Environment and Development and the United Nations Conference on Environment and Development, Rio de Janeiro, 1992, p. 2.

44 D. Moffat and O. Lindén (1995), 'Perception and Reality: Assessing Priorities for Sustainable Development in the Niger River Delta', *Ambio*, December, vol. 24, No. 7–8, p. 529.

45 http://www.wwf.org.uk/news/n_0000001454.asp; http://www.climateark.org/articles/reader.asp?linkid=38771

46 www.stabilisation2005.com/Tony_Nyong.pdf

47 http://www.stabilisation2005.com/Steering_Commitee_Report.pdf

48 P. Smith (2005), interview with Andy Rowell, 24 June.

49 L. Mitee (2005), interview with Andy Rowell, 29 June.

50 K. Wiwa (2005), interview with Andy Rowell and Lorne Stockman, 29 June.

51 See www.remembersarowiwa.com – the full coalition includes PLATFORM, African Writers Abroad, Amnesty International, Christian Aid, Diversity Art Forum, English PEN, Friends of the Earth, Greenpeace, Human Rights Watch, Index on Censorship, International PEN, Minorities of Europe, South Bank Centre and SpinWatch.

Chapter 9: Voices from the Delta

1 R. Cox (2005), letter to Andy Rowell, FCO, 5 July.

Index